Learning Frameworks
Tyler Junior College

Kay Moran

KENDALL/HUNT PUBLISHING COMPANY
4050 Westmark Drive   Dubuque, Iowa 52002

Cover copyright information:
Background image © Mike Flippo, 2008. Used under license from Shutterstock, Inc.
Image of woman reading © Stephen Coburn, 2008. Used under license from Shutterstock, Inc.
Image of man studying © Dennis Owusu-Ansah, 2008. Used under license from Shutterstock, Inc.
Image of woman smiling © Lee Morris, 2008. Used under license from Shutterstock, Inc.

Copyright © 2008 by Kendall/Hunt Publishing Company

ISBN 978-0-7575-5523-7

All rights reserved. No part of this publication may be reproduced, stored in a retrieval system, or transmitted, in any form or by any means, electronic, mechanical, photocopying, recording, or otherwise, without the prior written permission of the copyright owner.

Printed in the United States of America
10 9 8 7 6 5 4 3 2 1

Contents

SECTION 1: UNDERSTANDING THE COLLEGE COMMUNITY AND CULTURE

CHAPTER 1 Tyler Junior College: Changing Lives   3

CHAPTER 2 Expectations and Challenges   15

CHAPTER 3 Motivate Your Way to Success   23

CHAPTER 4 Creating Time through Effective Time Management   43

CHAPTER 5 Managing the Stresses of Life as a College Student   65

CHAPTER 6 Developing Relationships   83

CHAPTER 7 Connecting Common Threads across a Diverse World   101

SECTION 2: UNDERSTANDING THE LEARNING PROCESS

CHAPTER 8 Learning with Style   117

CHAPTER 9 Critical Thinking: Developing Critical Skills for the 21st Century   139

CHAPTER 10 Becoming a Better Notetaker   157

CHAPTER 11 Studying Effectively   177

CHAPTER 12 The Art of Test Taking   199

SECTION 3: UNDERSTANDING THE FIELD OF EDUCATION

CHAPTER 13 Vocation: More than a Job, More than a Career   221

CHAPTER 14 Understanding Educational Philosophy and Your Professional Beliefs   245

CHAPTER 15 Understanding Learning Theories   279

CHAPTER 16 What Makes a Teacher Effective?   305

Section 1

Understanding the College Community and Culture

Image copyright Ana Blazic, 2008. Used under license from Shutterstock, Inc.

Chapter 1

Tyler Junior College: CHANGING LIVES

Welcome to Tyler Junior College, the finest two-year institution in America. We are pleased that you have selected this college as the place to advance your educational and personal goals. Tyler Junior College was established in 1926 as part of the Tyler public school system. A lot has changed since then. We hope you will take pride in being a part of the "new" TJC as the College continues to grow.

You are part of a growing force in America . . . more than 44 percent of all students enrolled in higher education are attending a junior college. You will quickly see that TJC is committed to providing the best possible learning environment, and you are encouraged to call upon the dedicated faculty and staff who are here to help you.

TJC graduates have been successful both upon transfer to upper-division institutions and direct entry into the work force. Their accomplishments testify to the standards of excellence that is maintained at Tyler Junior College. With the diligent efforts of both you and our faculty and staff, your experience here will be equally rewarding.

WHERE WE HAVE BEEN AND WHERE WE ARE GOING

Established in 1926 as part of the Tyler Public School System, Tyler Junior College (TJC) gave residents of the Tyler area access to higher education, offering limited courses in the traditional liberal arts and pragmatic courses in public school music and home economics.

The college had a small student body during its early years. In the 1930s, as the country struggled through the Depression, only 200 students were enrolled. However, the prosperity of the 1940s signaled major changes. In 1945, Tyler voters overwhelmingly approved a measure to create a junior college district and issued $500,000 in bonds for the College. The expansion of the College included new facilities and new full-time faculty members. Its growth came at an appropriate time for local residents and for many veterans who returned to Tyler to seek new opportunities and realized that those opportunities were linked to higher education. Tyler Junior College has continued to expand since its "rebirth" in the 1940s. The Tyler Junior College District is now composed of six independent school districts: Chapel Hill ISD,* Grand Saline ISD, Lindale ISD, Tyler ISD,* Van ISD,* and Winona ISD.

Today, after 80 years, Tyler Junior College offers more courses in any single major division than were offered in the entire curriculum in 1926. Just as the courses have diversified, so have the students. Although students who reside in the Tyler Junior College District are entitled to priority in enrollment, students from throughout Texas and the United States attend Tyler Junior College. The College now has an enrollment of approximately 10,000 students each Fall semester. In addition, some 15,000 individuals take continuing education courses each year.

CHOOSING A PATHWAY TO A CAREER IN THE FIELD OF EDUCATION

This textbook and its related course, EDUC 1300 Learning Framework, have been specifically designed to assist you with your adjustment to the college environment overall, the uniqueness of the TJC campus experience, and the field of education. EDUC 1300 provides information that will support your overall college academic success, and an introduction to the teaching profession, supplying fundamental knowledge about the learning process that every teacher candidate will need to know.

Teacher Education Career Cluster: Careers related to Early Childhood Paraprofessional, Childcare Provider, Teacher Certification, Teacher Aide, Librarian, Instructional Technology, Learning Support, and School Counselor.

Choose the Correct Educational Pattern: There are two distinctly different ways to pursue your education at TJC. Each pattern has its own particular purpose and its own advantages and disadvantages. Read the descriptions carefully to make an informed choice. You must choose one of the two following patterns:

Do you want the *Academic* Transfer pattern of education?

The Academic Transfer Pattern means that you will be taking General Education Core Curriculum courses and some major prerequisites at the community college. The major courses of the Bachelor's degree will be taken in your junior and senior years at the university after completion of the Associate's degree.

- Is your primary goal to obtain a Bachelor's degree at a university?
- Do you plan on taking the "basics" at TJC so that you can transfer to a university as fast as possible?
- Are you already at a university and wish to take courses at TJC to transfer back to the university?
- If you are answering yes to any of the above, then you will need to follow a Transfer Plan, sometimes called a 2+2 plan. That means you can take the first 2 years of a Bachelor's degree at TJC and then transfer to the university to take the last 2 years of the Bachelor's degree.

Do you want the *Workforce* Career pattern of education? If so, choose *Workforce* Education.

The Workforce Career Pattern means that you will be taking mostly technical, job-focused courses and a few general education courses for the completion of your certificate or associate degree at TJC. Workforce course credit does transfer to some universities and not to others.

- Is your primary goal to obtain the skills to get a job as fast as possible?
- Do you want a short-term, up-to-date, and relevant education using a workplace curriculum?
- Do you want to update your work skills or advance your career?
- Are you thinking about quickly changing careers?
- Do you want your community college education to include both technology competency and human relations skills?
- Do you want to count the tech prep or workforce dual credit courses from high school toward your certificate or degree at the community college?
- Are you thinking about transferring to the university to get a Bachelor's degree but only after you have been working for awhile?
- If you are answering yes to any of the above, then you will need to follow the Workforce Career pattern of education.

CREATING AN ACADEMIC TRANSFER DEGREE PLAN

If you choose the Academic Transfer pattern of education in the Education and Schools (EDSCH) career cluster, you will be taking General Education Core Curriculum courses and some major prerequisites at the community college. The major courses of the

Bachelor's degree will be taken in the junior and senior years at the university after completion of the Associate's degree. This is often called a 2+2 Transfer Plan.

Careers related to Early Childhood Paraprofessional, Childcare Provider, Teacher Certification, Teacher Aide, Librarian, Instructional Technology, Learning Support, and School Counselor are included.

Your educational degree plan will be an Associate in Arts in Teaching or an Associate in Arts.

Associate in Arts in Teaching (leading to initial Texas Teacher Certification)

- **Elementary Track** (Early Childhood–Grade 6, Grades 4–8, or Special Education certifications)
- **Early Childhood Specialization Track** (Early Childhood Degree Specialization or EC–6 Generalist certifications)
- **Secondary Track** (Grades 8–12 or All Level EC–Grade 12 certifications)

AAT EC–6 and 4–8 Certification Components –Total: 60–66 SCHs The curricula components of the three degrees are as follows:

- EC–6 (except Early Childhood Degree Specialization), 4–8, EC-12
  - core curriculum (42–48 SCHs)
  - MATH 1350 and MATH 1351 (6 SCHs)
  - science (6 SCHs)
  - redesigned EDUC 1301 and EDUC 2301 as adopted by the Lower Division Academic Course Guide Manual (ACGM) Advisory Committee August 6, 2004
  - redesigned *TECA 1311 and TECA 1354* as adopted by the ACGM Advisory Committee August 6, 2004
- 8–12, Other EC–12
  - core curriculum (42–48 SCHs)
  - redesigned EDUC 1301 and EDUC 2301 as adopted by the ACGM Advisory Committee August 6, 2004
  - content area teaching fields/academic disciplines (12 SCHs)
- EC–6 Early Childhood Degree Specialization Only
  - core curriculum (42–48 SCHs)
  - MATH 1350 and MATH 1351 or equivalent (6 SCHs)
  - redesigned *TECA 1303, TECA 1311, TECA 1318, and TECA 1354* as adopted by the ACGM Advisory Committee August 6, 2004

NOTE: The Early Childhood "degree specialization" refers only to the degree program offered at a university and not to a particular SBEC certification area. All EC–6 Generalists (except EC–6 Generalist Bilingual and EC–6 Generalist ESL), no matter the university degree's specialization, take the same TExES examination for certification and are certified to teach in any EC–6 classroom.

The AAT degree as defined by the Coordinating Board is fully transferable to all Texas public universities. Because the AAT fulfills the requirements of the field of study curriculum statutes and Coordinating Board rules, all Texas public universities must accept the three AAT curricula if they offer the applicable Baccalaureate degrees leading to initial teacher certification.

However, partnering community/state colleges and universities can enter into articulation agreements that could be considered a "specialized academic associate degree" (see *Section 9.183(c)* of Board rules) but not a Board-recognized AAT.

Students who complete the AAT will be required to meet any and all entrance requirements of the receiving university and the educator preparation program, including grade point average and/or testing requirements.

By Board Policy adopted January 1997, all EC–4 and 4–8 teacher certification degree programs are required to include 6–9 hours of math and 6–9 hours of science beyond the core curriculum requirements. The science component of the EC–4 Early Childhood degree specialization must be fulfilled but may be taken at the receiving university.

Associate in Arts Degree Requirements:

Communication	9 Semester Hours
Mathematics	3 Semester Hours
Natural Sciences	7–8 Semester Hours
Humanities	3 Semester Hours
Visual/Performing Arts	3 Semester Hours
American History	6 Semester Hours
Government	6 Semester Hours
Cross/Multicultural Studies	3 Semester Hours
Additional Major Prerequisites	16–17 Semester Hours

The specific courses in each component area above should be chosen carefully to ensure transferability toward the specific university Bachelor's degree in this Career Cluster. Most universities will transfer a maximum of 60 hours from a community college toward Bachelor's degree requirements. You should see an actual counselor for details.

WORKFORCE CAREER PLAN FOR THE EDUCATION AND SCHOOLS CLUSTER

If you choose the Workforce Career pattern of education in the Education and Schools (EDSCH) career cluster, you will be taking mostly technical, job-focused courses and a few general education courses for the completion of your Marketable Skills Achievement Award (MSA), Certificate of Completion, and/or Associate in Applied Science degree at Tyler Junior College.

Careers related to Early Childhood Paraprofessional, Childcare Provider, Teacher Certification, Teacher Aide, Learning Support, and School Counselor are included in this cluster.

Your educational degree plan will be a Certificate of Completion or an Associate in Applied Science

AAS indicates Associate in Applied Science degree (~2 years full-time or 4 years part-time study) AAS Child Development (60 SCH hours)

Certificate indicates Certificate of Completion (length varies from 1–2 semesters of study)

- Certificate Child Development —Administration (15 SCH hours)
- Certificate Child Development—Preschool Teaching Certificate (15 SCH hours
- Certificate Child Development —Childcare Provider/Assistant (15 SCH hours)
- Certificate Child Development—Certificate of Proficiency CDEC_CERT (33 SCH hours)

LOOKING AT FIELD EXPERIENCE COURSES

All EDUC courses are required to serve as enriched integrated pre-service content experiences; all of the EDUC courses include a state mandated Field Experience requirement. The state mandate states those students who are enrolled in the EDUC courses must complete 15–16 hours of applied, monitored, and supervised field observations in schools with varied and diverse student populations. Students gain practical experience and follow a negotiated and/or directed plan of study established between the student, instructor, and field experience supervisor.

Looking at EDUC 1300 Learning Frameworks

Cognitive psychology and teacher education research has resulted in a greatly improved and greatly increased body of knowledge of how students and teachers learn. At this time, there is a striking gap between the knowledge of learning and the application of that knowledge to teachers' preparation programs. EDUC 1300 enables the student to develop effective academic behaviors for college success and be able to transfer these behaviors into the teaching experience. EDUC 1300 focuses on careers in and related to education and schools.

This course will present learning theories and strategies that will allow each student to determine the learning approaches that work best for them. Students will also determine their individual learning styles. The focus of the course is on (a) research and theory in the psychology of learning, cognition, and motivation; (b) factors that impact learning; and (c) application of learning strategies.

The mission of EDUC 1300 is to enable TJC students to develop and model effective learning skills and strategies in a way that:

- Offers maximal opportunities for students to transfer and apply these skills and strategies across their academic programs;
- Targets those students who can most benefit from the course by a coordinated system of referrals from each undergraduate school and publicizes the course to all potential students;

- Facilitates professional development, research, and collaboration among the faculty teaching this course.
- This means students can achieve their academic goals and the program supports the TJC mission of academic excellence and student retention.

At the end of the semester the student will:

- Understand learning strengths and weaknesses
- Have healthy view of themselves
- Set realistic and appropriate goals
- Manage their behavior
- Use effective strategies
- Adapt those strategies
- Use appropriate resources

ADDITIONAL TOPICS

Constructivism—Familiarize students with this significant learning theory—help them see its numerous applications to learning, motivation, instruction, and self-regulation.

Instruction and cognition—Increase understanding of this area of learning theory—help students recognize and appreciate the interdependence of teaching and learning.

Development and learning—Give prospective teachers a more complete picture of developmental influences—reflects expanding research on the role of these factors in human learning.

Integration of instruction and self-regulation—Facilitate comparison among theories—explain how each theory affects these objectives and identifies which works best in which situations and with what type of learners.

A thoroughly updated bibliography—Ensure students access to the latest research and the most recent publications.

Detailed examples of learning theories applied in actual educational settings—Reinforce the rationale for specific implementation strategies—help future teachers learn to recognize when and with whom to apply particular theories.

Motivation—Delineate different perspectives on motivation—assists future teachers to understand how motivation affects learning and which learning principles best affect motivation.

Content-area learning—Help students understand how general learning principles apply to specific content areas and why certain specific principles are particularly relevant to individual subject matter.

Course Requirements

Instructors are responsible for providing and explaining written information regarding course requirements to all students enrolled in a course. **Students are responsible** for understanding the stated requirements of a course in which they are enrolled. Both students and instructors are responsible for complying with the written requirements of a course.

Disability Services

Tyler Junior College welcomes students with disabilities who have the potential for academic success in the post-secondary educational environment.

TJC is committed to providing qualified students with disabilities equal access to its facilities, activities, and programs. Section 504 of the Federal Rehabilitation Act of 1973, as amended, and the Americans with Disabilities Act of 1990 (ADA) require that public colleges and universities provide reasonable and appropriate accommodations for otherwise qualified students with disabilities.

Accommodations may include permission to tape record lectures, relocation of classes or programs to accessible locations, arranging special testing locations, the use of a sign language interpreter, etc.

At TJC accommodations are provided on an individual basis following presentation (by the student) and assessment (by the College) of documentation that confirms the presence of a disability that causes a substantial limitation as defined under Section 504 and the ADA.

A *Disability Review Committee* has been established at the College in order to process the student request in an efficient and timely manner.

Course Attendance, Requirements and Withdrawal Policy

TJC enters into a *partnership for success* with each of its students and willingly assumes the responsibility of offering the quality of instruction, facilities, and services necessary to provide its partners with opportunities to achieve their individual academic goals. The following policies are designed to facilitate this process.

Administrative Drop Policy for Non-Payment of Tuition and Fees

Tyler Junior College reserves the right to administratively drop a student for non-payment of tuition and fees by any published due date. Non-payment includes but is not limited to: insufficient fund checks as well as non-payment of bridge loans and installment plans.

Attendance

Regular attendance at classes is strongly associated with academic success. **Students are responsible for regular attendance in credit classes in which they are enrolled. There is an attendance policy in all college preparatory classes, however.**

Instructors will maintain student attendance records throughout the semester. Students who will be absent from class for the observance of a religious holiday are responsible for informing their instructors **prior** to the holiday. (Section 52.911, Texas Education Code.)

Students who will be absent from class due to their participation in a TJC sponsored or approved activity are responsible for informing their instructors **prior** to their absence in the form of a **written** notification prepared and signed by an instructional dean.

Students are responsible for arranging to make up any course work missed due to absences for any reason. A student who is absent due to an official religious observance or a TJC sponsored or approved activity, and who has appropriately informed the instructor prior to the event, is entitled to make up missed course work. In other cases, the instructor will determine whether a student will be allowed to complete makeup work and the time and nature of the makeup work.

Withdrawing from Courses

Students are responsible for withdrawing from courses. A student may initiate a withdrawal from a course or the College for any reason. An instructor may initiate an administrative withdrawal for any student who has missed so many classes that he/she cannot achieve a passing grade for the class. The student will receive a grade of "W" for a course if a withdrawal form, signed by an advisor, is submitted to the Registrar's office by 5 p.m. the last day of the 14th week of classes during a 16-week semester, the 7th week of an 8-week session, or on the 15th day of any summer session. Students should consult the Registrar's office for withdrawal dates during special sessions. Students will receive a failing grade (F) if they have not met minimum course requirements for a passing grade and have not submitted a withdrawal form or been withdrawn from a course by the above deadlines. An instructor seeking to withdraw a student from a course for disciplinary reasons should comply with the "Student Discipline Policy" guidelines written in the current *TJC Policies and Procedures Manual*. A grade of "I" (incomplete) can be assigned for **emergency situations only** and requires the approval of the appropriate department chair. Students must complete work for the course within 30 days after the start of the next regular semester or the "I" will convert to a grade of "F."

A student who has been withdrawn from a course may be reinstated only with the approval of the instructor and the college prep department chair. The student must initiate the reinstatement by contacting the instructor within 2 weeks in a 16-week semester, 1 week in an 8-week session, or the second day of a summer session from the official date of the withdrawal. Students should consult the Registrar's office for reinstatement dates during special sessions.

Classroom Etiquette

Tyler Junior College is committed to promoting a level of classroom etiquette conducive to maximum teaching and learning. It is with this context that the following statements on expected level of classroom etiquette are prepared.

Thus, you are expected to:

- Attend class each time the class meets.
- Be on time for class and remain for the entire period. You are inconsiderate of your classmates if you arrive late and leave early.
- Refrain from talking while the instructor is lecturing. Idle chattering and giggling are disruptive to the class and disrespectful to your instructor and your classmates.

- Refrain from using cell-phones, beepers, walkmans with headphones, or any electronic device in class without prior approval from your instructor.
- Be attentive and participate in class.
- Use designated smoking areas only.

Academic Integrity

Definition and expectations: Academic integrity is the pursuit of scholarly activity in an open, honest, and responsible manner. Academic integrity is a basic guiding principle for all academic activity at Tyler Junior College, and all members of the College community are expected to act in accordance with this principle. Consistent with this expectation, the College states that all students should act with personal integrity; respect other students' dignity, rights, and property; and help establish and maintain an environment in which all can succeed. Academic dishonesty will not be tolerated in the Tyler Junior College Testing Center.

Examples of academic dishonesty include but are not limited to:

- Plagiarism.
- Copying or any unauthorized assistance in taking quizzes, tests, or examinations.
- Dependence upon the aid of sources beyond those authorized by the instructor when writing papers, preparing reports, solving problems, or carrying out other assignments.
- The acquisition, without permission, of tests or other academic material belonging to a faculty member, staff member, or student of the College.
- Using a cheat sheet during a quiz or exam.
- Looking at someone else's answers.
- Talking during an exam.
- Any other act designed to give a student an unfair advantage.

APACHE ACCESS

Apache Access is a secure Web site designed to provide students, faculty, and staff with Intranet and Internet services and applications. Apache Access provides a collection of tools for your academic and work success at Tyler Junior College. The site is where faculty, staff, and students learn about upcoming events, access announcements, join interest groups, and store Internet links and bookmarks. It is also where students check e-mail, register for courses, access financial aid and scholarship information, and check grades. Your secure log-in grants you access to a highly customizable view of TJC tools within Apache Access. An Apache ID number is required for authentication. Each student of Tyler Junior College is assigned a unique ID number referred to as your A-Number. In order to receive your A-Number or reset your password, you may contact one of the following offices:

- TJC Helpdesk, 903-510-3269
- Applied Studies, 903-510-2507
- Allied Health and Nursing, 903-510-2662

- University Studies, 903-510-2548
- Financial Aid Office, 903-510-2385
- Residential Life, 903-510-2345
- Student Affairs, 903-510-2261

Apache Alerts

Apache Alerts is a method of learning about campus emergencies and school activities via text messages received on equipped cellular telephones. Apache Alerts is a voluntary, opt-in cellular service that requires registration. The service provides text messages about school closings, schedule delays, and other emergency notifications, as well as sports and campus event reminders. Depending upon their level of interest, students may subscribe to emergency notifications only—or they may select athletic activities and other campus events. Apache Alert text messages are presented to TJC students and employees on a limited basis by authorized College offices. Students and employees of TJC may subscribe to Apache Alerts through Apache Access, the TJC Intranet portal, http://apacheaccess.tjc.edu.

TJC Student Handbook

The Tyler Junior College *Student Handbook* is a source of important information, including student responsibilities, obligations, and privileges. Students are expected to retain their handbook as a reference tool. Because the programs, policies, and statements included in this document are subject to continuous review and evaluation, TJC reserves the right to make changes as they become necessary.

For information on academic policies, please consult the current *College Catalog*. Students are strongly encouraged to enhance their achievements at TJC by participating in proper extracurricular activities, as described on pages 27–33. Many extracurricular events and academic deadlines and reminders are also listed on the separate Campus Planner/Calendar available in August at registration.

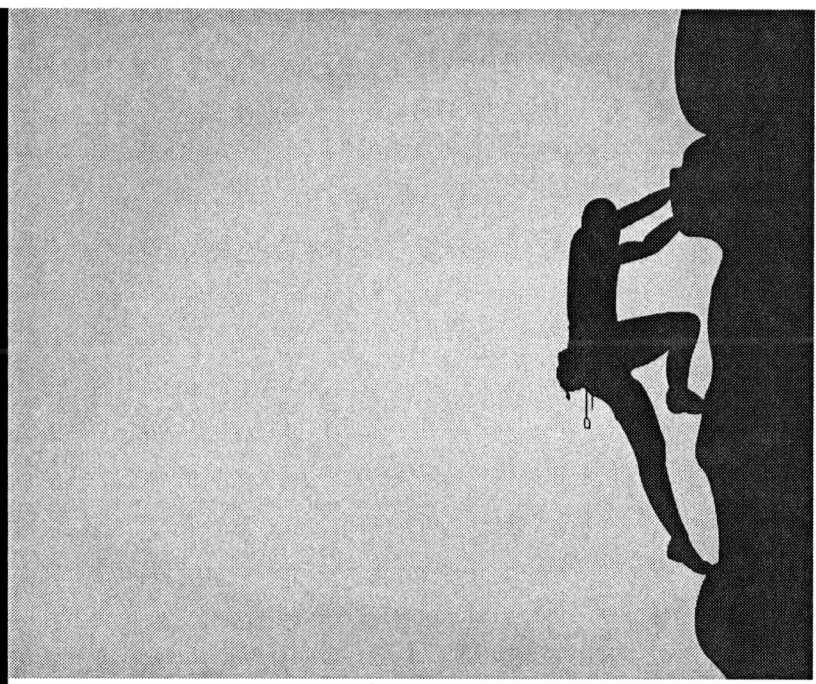
Image copyright Pavel Richter, 2008. Used under license from Shutterstock, Inc.

Chapter 2

Expectations and Challenges

Surely there is a mine for silver, and a place for gold which they refine . . .
But where shall wisdom be found?
—THE BOOK OF JOB

WHAT DOES IT MEAN TO HAVE A COLLEGE EDUCATION?

When asked what college means to them, students say such things as it's:

- " . . . a means to a better job."
- " . . . something to do instead of working."
- " . . . my parents' dream for me."
- " . . . something that comes after high school."
- " . . . a place to learn."
- " . . . a place to be irresponsible and have fun."

From Your Utah State Experience: Strategies for Success *Ninth Edition by Noelle Call and Lavell Saunders. Copyright © 2004 by Noelle Call and Lavell Saunders. Used with permission.*

While a college experience may be any or all of the above for a student, a college education is not a product nor a "thing" one gets; it is a process one participates in. A college education:

- Is an exposure to a life and a way of looking at the world through many new and different lenses.
- Can provide a better understanding of the world in which we live and increase our ability for meaningful interactions within our environments.
- Expands and deepens an increasing awareness of our creativity.
- Provides an opportunity to grow in compassion and understanding of other people, to gain a new appreciation of differences, and to obtain a new sense of responsibility for our life.
- Helps develop effective problem solving skills and strategies that equip us for various employment, cultural, and interpersonal opportunities.

The comedian Woody Allen is reported to have said that 80% of success in life simply comes from "showing up." Unfortunately "showing up" is not enough to guarantee success in college. It's what a student chooses "to do" after "showing up" that makes the difference. College furnishes the environment and the opportunities for success. The task for every student is to decide whether or not to take advantage of those opportunities. Attending class, completing assignments, interacting with professors, passing tests, and being involved in extracurricular activities are important parts of your years in college. Equally important are the decisions made, the goals set, and the relationships formed. In sum, what a college experience means depends on what one chooses to do now that they have shown up.

Now, here, you see, it takes all the running you can do to keep in the same place. If you want to get somewhere else, you must run twice as fast as that.
—LEWIS CARROLL
THROUGH THE LOOKING-GLASS

Realizing that the freshman year is a challenging time, your college provides a wealth of resources to help its new students with the transition. This text details a number of transition issues and changes you will encounter. Read carefully and think about the transition and what it means to you. There are clubs and organizations covering special interest groups, service clubs, religious groups, recreational clubs, and scholastic organizations.

New students are encouraged to join clubs and participate in campus activities. Campus involvement is one way of making a connection with the larger student body. A word of caution: balance in life is an important ingredient of success. A careful examination of personal goals and use of time gives one a fairly good idea of how to balance the time between studies, work, and extracurricular activities.

WHAT IS EXPECTED OF NEW STUDENTS?

If the extent of personal freedom in college is an eye-opening experience for new students, an equally important element of the transition equation is the personal responsibility that accompanies the new freedom. It is important to maintain personal and academic freedom and maximize individual responsibility.

Chapter 2 | Expectations and Challenges

The freedom from work, from restraint, from accountability, wondrous in its inception, became banal and counterfeit. Without rules there was no way to say no, and worse, no way to say yes.
—Thomas Farber

As a new student, you become a part of an exciting new community on campus. As a member of the community, you are expected to be treated and treat other members of this community with honesty, courtesy, tolerance, and respect. It has been said that a well-educated person can disagree without being disagreeable. A valuable part of your experience will be getting to know people with very different values and backgrounds from your own; your ability to treat them with respect and to engage in meaningful discourse will enhance your life and theirs.

In all of your communications, whether they are in person, in writing, or electronic, avoid vulgarity, profanity, and other offensive content. Any remarks or acts that may be interpreted as sexist, racist, or discriminatory against certain groups are prohibited.

New students are expected to assume responsibility for their education and behavior. Among those expectations are the following:

Classroom conduct. Appropriate classroom conduct is expected of all students. Students should arrive at class on time and be prepared with the necessary books, notes, paper, and writing supplies. Coming prepared to class also means having completed assigned readings, reviewed notes, and prepared questions.

Working on homework from another course, carrying on side conversations, and chatter during a lecture are not appropriate.

Cultivating relationships with faculty is important. Develop the interpersonal skills that promote interaction with professors and instructors. The first step is to find out what they expect of students and what students can expect from them. This information is usually found in the course syllabus and/or is discussed on the first day of class. Generally speaking, most professors expect students to:

- *Attend class regularly.* You lose when you skip a class. If you must miss a class, arrange for another student to keep notes for you (don't expect the professors to give you theirs). Make sure you get any assignments that were announced.
- *Accept responsibility.* Don't make excuses; accept responsibility for your own learning.
- *Submit high-quality work in both content and form.* Do the best you can in quality and neatness. Some instructors accept only typed papers, and students without personal computers should take advantage of the campus computer labs.
- *Turn assignments in on time.* Late assignments suggest a lack of enthusiasm and commitment. Habitually handing assignments in late is a bad habit that employers are less forgiving of.
- *Arrive on time and be attentive in class.* Late arrivals are a distraction to the entire class. If you must be late, find the nearest convenient seat and quickly and quietly sit down.
- *Participate in class discussions.* Participation in class is valued by some professors and not encouraged by others. Follow the preferences for each professor.

- *Meet with professors outside of class.* A good way to get to know your professor is to prepare some questions based on previous classes, readings, and your own reflections that you can ask the professor before or after class, or in his/her office.

Academic honesty. Faculty and staff expect students and faculty alike to maintain the highest standards of academic honesty. Academic dishonesty includes but is not limited to:

- Stealing a copy of the exam ahead of time
- Copying from someone else's paper
- Sending or receiving signals during an exam
- Using unauthorized notes during an exam
- Taking an exam for another student
- Letting another student take an exam for you
- Handing in a paper that you have not written

Plagiarism is a specific form of cheating in which a student fails to give proper credit for written work that belongs to someone else. It is trying to pass off the work of others as one's own. Students falsely assume that they will not be caught; however, professors are very adept at identifying work that has been incorrectly documented or "borrowed" from another source without proper citation. Also, new technology has been developed to compare a student's papers with other students' work and papers collected from sources like the Internet, journals, books or other publications. Knowingly representing the words or ideas of another as your own in any academic exercise or activity carries with it serious consequences.

DEVELOPMENTAL CHANGES

When we plant a rose seed in the earth, we notice that it is small, but we do not criticize it as "rootless and stemless." We treat it as a seed, giving it the water and nourishment required of a seed. When it first shoots up out of the earth, we don't condemn it as immature and underdeveloped; nor do we criticize the buds for not being open when they appear. We stand in wonder at the process taking place and give the plant the care it needs at each stage of its development. The rose is a rose from the time it is a seed to the time it dies. Within it, at all times, it contains its whole potential. It seems to be constantly in the process of change; yet at each stage, at each moment, it is perfectly all right as it is.

—W. Timothy Gallwey
The Inner Game of Tennis

You can expect to go through a great number of changes during your college years. Most of these changes will not be noticeable to the naked eye because they take place inside of you. How you cope with these changes will be determined mainly by your personality, your past experience, and your current life situation. Many students glide right through this time of transition with little awareness that anything new has occurred. Others come through thrashing and kicking. Regardless, the one thing you can count on is that you will grow and change during the next few years.

As you begin to explore your personal values and set goals for your future, you will be creating a world view that is unique to you. This is good, and this is healthy. It is important to realize that there are some very normal developmental tasks which you will be completing during the next few years.

One of the most challenging tasks is redefining relationships with your family. The important thing to remember is that these next years will be a period of adjustment for you and your family. Your first trip home may start out as a hero's welcome and end in tears and disagreement. Be patient! Don't try to flex all of your new freedom at once. Give your family a chance to get used to the new you. And remember, your family hasn't been standing still while you have been gone. They may have changed and grown as well. Finding your new place within the family may take patience and time.

There is no way to predict how you will move through these next four years. To be sure, at times you will find yourself struggling and feeling out of sorts. At other times, life will seem wonderful, and you will be on top of the world. The important thing to remember is that normal developmental changes will take place. The college years are a time of change and, while you may not always be at ease as those changes unfold, you are OKAY!

ELEMENTS OF SUCCESS

Success in all of its forms and varieties is a goal of every student. However, wanting to succeed and doing what is necessary to succeed are two very different things. This section details suggestions and ideas about how to bridge the gap between desiring and actually achieving success. We encourage you to read and make use of the ideas presented, because they are only as helpful as you make them. There are no quick fixes, no easy answers.

The first step in succeeding at something is realizing that wanting to succeed is just the starting place. Additional factors in any successful college experience include: (1) attitude about school and life; (2) prior academic experience and ability; (3) ability to effectively manage time and to discipline one's self; (4) ability to relate to and get along with others; and (5) the learning environment.

*Two roads diverged in a wood and I took the one less traveled by,
and that has made all the difference.*
—ROBERT FROST
THE ROAD NOT TAKEN

Attitude. Attitude is a combination of thoughts and feelings. Much of a student's attitude about college is determined by how and why he/she chose to be here and how he/she feels about that choice. Some students find themselves in college, but are not aware how they arrived at the decision to attend. Do you want to be here? Are you in school because someone said you had to come? Enrolling in college because someone else said you should, may motivate you to enroll, but won't necessarily enable you to succeed. In order to succeed, you need to have your own reasons for attending; you need to "own" the decision to come to school.

There are many different (but no right) reasons for attending college. Some students pursue a degree in order to get a good job or to advance into a higher position in their current job. Others come to school for social reasons—high school was fun, so college will be even more fun! Some would rather go to school than work full-time. Others find it an easy way to move away from home and have their parents or others pay for it! Some students decide on a college education because they love learning and see college as an opportunity to pursue that love.

The reasons for choosing to go to college are as limitless as the persons attending. Reasons for attending also change over time as events and circumstances unfold. Be reflective; visit with yourself from time to time about why you are in college. Are those reasons being fulfilled? What are you doing to fulfill them?

The thing to remember is that, when the days are long and the nights are short, your attitude about school will determine how hard you are willing to work to make it work!

Experience and ability. Prior academic experience and ability play an important role in your success. Students who arrive at college with a strong academic background have an advantage. New ideas are more quickly assimilated when they can be associated with prior knowledge. Don't rest on your laurels however; professors expect a lot.

This is not to say that a lack of prior strong academic experience prohibits success, but it will take greater commitment and hard work to catch on in some of your classes. It is also a fairly common experience for "average" high school students to "catch fire" in the stimulating environment of college.

Prior academic experience includes a knowledge of basic learning and life skills. Do you know how to study, how to manage time, how to set goals, and how to communicate effectively? Many students come to college unaware of the need for these skills. They register for classes, buy their books, attend the first day of class, and begin to "study." They are quickly disillusioned with college and their own abilities, as the old habits that worked in high school don't seem to be working now, as the work piles higher and higher, and as the probability of success sinks lower and lower.

Success is not a matter of studying more or studying harder, it is a matter of studying smarter. An average student in high school will probably need to work harder and smarter to be an average student in college. College is definitely more difficult than high school, and success in high school does not necessarily ensure success in college. Taking the time to learn some study strategies that are applicable in all of your classes is time well spent.

We challenge you to examine and reflect on your values and your goals and the strategies you need to develop as school begins. Principles and strategies that are helpful in learning how to successfully juggle the demands of college, work, family, friends, and extracurricular activities are described herein. Discover how learning takes place and how you can best structure your own learning experiences to promote success.

Experiences are dynamic. Periodically take the time to stop and reflect on yours. What's going right? Wrong? What can you do to sustain or alter the experiences you are having at college?

Self-discipline. Self-discipline and effective time management are vital keys to success. Students who are self-disciplined are better able to handle the increased freedom that comes with college. One of the first things that is discovered about college life is that in many classes attendance is not required. Unfortunately, some students interpret this to mean that attendance is not important. Nothing can be farther from the truth. Skipping class is a poor strategy for achieving success. Having decided to enroll in college, and after having paid the tuition, deciding not to attend class is counter-productive and costly!

Interpersonal skills. Another very important part of success at any college is the ability to relate to and get along with other people. This includes roommates, friends, other students, faculty, and family. Although satisfactory progress towards a degree is measured in grades, the sense of well-being and accomplishment may well be measured by the ability to make friends, relate to classmates, and interact with faculty.

Having significant people who support you in your decision to attend college is a big help in your success. These are the people who remind you of your commitment and encourage you to continue on with your plans when you are tired and discouraged. They are the same people who share in your accomplishments and your success. These people comprise an important part of your support network. Although they cannot make you succeed, they can remind you of your goals and even help lighten some of the burden you carry. Recognize their support. "Good strokes for good folks" goes a long way to ensuring their continued support.

Environment. Finally, success in college is determined by the learning environment, which includes defining and setting up an area for studying. By following a few basic suggestions, a supportive study environment can be created. Study in the same place at the same time and use a signal to tell roommates and yourself that you are studying.

This book is a practical aid to understanding and developing the strategies necessary to make satisfactory progress as a college student. The rate of progress (time it takes) and the qualitative measurement of that progress (grades received) are determined by individual circumstances. Understanding the factors that impact on that success—attitude, prior academic experience, self-discipline, relations with others, and the working/studying environment—helps to bridge the gap between wanting success and achieving success.

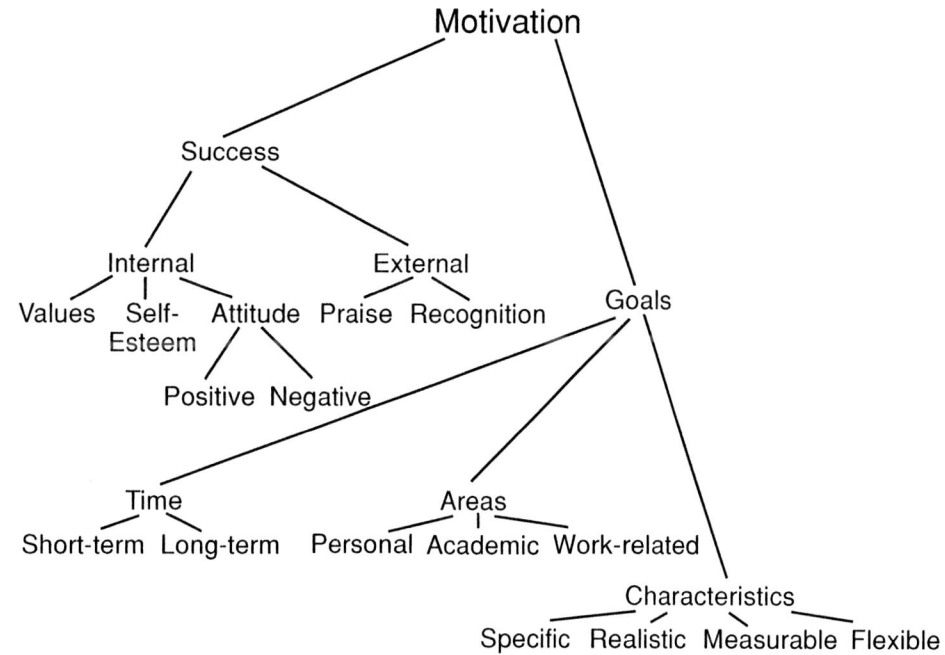

Chapter 3

Motivate Your Way to Success

WELCOME TO COLLEGE!

You have a lot of neat experiences ahead of you, some frustrating, and hopefully many rewarding. Are you excited about this new learning venture? Think back to your first day of elementary school. Do you remember how excited you were? Do you have that same enthusiasm today?

Unfortunately, many students associate learning with "school" and they don't have a lot of positive feelings toward school. Learning performance tends to drop as we go along in our academic pursuits. School is associated with "drudgery," and before we know it our attitude starts to be indifferent.

Let's try and start fresh with a good attitude like we had in first grade!

WHY ARE YOU HERE?

This is an important question for you to answer. There are several reasons why students attend college. Fill out Exercise 1 titled: Why Are You Here?

From Practical Approaches for Building Study Skills and Vocabulary, Second Edition *by Gary D. Funk, Jan Bradley, JoBelle Hopper, Myrna Hite-Walker, and Michele M. Jerde. Copyright © 1996 by Kendall/Hunt Publishing Company. Used with permission.*

You need to stop and think about why you are in college. Are your reasons for being here due to others? Will these people be responsible for your success in life? Will they be attending class for you? Taking your tests? Receiving your diploma?

A recent study at a midwestern university revealed the top three reasons chosen for attending college were:

1. To increase the chances for a higher paying career
2. To expand knowledge
3. To help ensure success in life

This is a good time to examine your values and decide what you feel is important. Fill out the worksheet on clarifying your values. These values affect the choices you make in life.

The Coat of Arms Exercise will help you think about your personal feelings. Fill in this worksheet and think about the priorities in your life.

The student who is "educated" is the one who has learned how to learn. It is important to be aware of your values and goals because that will help motivate you to do your best. You need to recognize what is important to you, and strive to reach your potential. A college education can help you develop a flexible and open mind, sharpen your ability, and enrich your life.

WHAT IS A SUCCESSFUL COLLEGE STUDENT?

We all want to be successful. There is not one college student that attends college to be unsuccessful. How can we be successful? There have been numerous studies done in this area. Most of these studies show that successful students tend to possess the following characteristics:

1. *They have a definite reason for attending college.*

    You must decide what you want out of college. After completing the Exercise, Why Are You Here, you have had the opportunity to think about what is important to you.

2. *They have selected a vocation and are pursuing this course.*

    Don't panic if you don't have a career chosen. But, be aware that it provides motivation to have a career goal. Spend this first year trying out several courses in varying fields. Maybe one will ring a bell! When you have chosen your career, you will be motivated by a clearer sense of direction.

3. *They realize the need for understanding the material in each class and envision the value of it.*

    A successful student does not study just to pass a test. They usually have a three-pronged approach to the material.

    a. They master the basic facts. Without doing this, there is nothing on which to build.

    b. They take these basic facts and draw supporting details in for a total picture.

c. They learn to "think" with the subject. Once you are able to explain a concept in your own words—it's yours!

This approach allows them to "learn" the subject matter, not just memorize it.

4. *They have a desire for success.*

The more success you experience, the more you will want.

"Success Breeds Success"

"Success Creates Interest"

What a wonderful feeling accomplishment can bring! Have you ever failed a class that you really liked? Probably not. Success can create interest, which further ensures success. One way we have of achieving success is the attainment of goals. Much more about that later!

5. *They have the will to succeed.*

Abraham Lincoln loved to read. It was told that he walked 20 miles to borrow a book. Would you exert that much effort? If we can't park close to the library, we probably will not bother to check out a book!

How can we develop this kind of will to succeed?

GOALS → SUCCESS → STRENGTHENS WILL → MORE SUCCESS

We can develop this will to succeed by the attainment of short-term goals. Small successes strengthen our will, and the strengthened will provides us with additional power to work even harder.

6. *They have developed good study skills.*

The definition of study skills is the efficient use of our mind and our time. The key word is "efficient." There are other phases of our life that need attention, and we need to develop study skills so we can accomplish the maximum in the minimum amount of time. Study skills are not instinctive, but something that we need to learn. The goal of study skills is independent learning. As long as you look to someone else for interpretation, you are not a free person intellectually.

7. *They know they must set priorities. "This is the time to learn."*

Rank your needs at this time. It is not necessary for school to be number one, but it must be extremely high on the list.

Consider this scenario:

Greg was studying for a physics test. Doug and Jeff were on their way for pizza and a movie. They stopped by Greg's room and invited him along. Greg's decision could be crucial toward a high grade on his test the next day. What would you do?

WHAT IS MOTIVATION?

Webster's Dictionary defines motivation as the condition of being motivated; an incentive or drive. How do we apply this to ourselves? Let's think for a moment about ourselves.

How many brain cells do you have?

Hint: A lot more than you think!

You have 13 billion brain cells. Do you feel smarter already? One thing you should be thinking about right now is how to use these 13 billion cells to their fullest potential. In this book you will be able to find several effective ways to learn; ways that are the best for *you*.

Let's imagine that we have an assembled computer sitting in front of us. This computer contains one million parts.

What is the first thing we would need to do in order to use it?

Hint: Think electricity.

O.K., we should plug it in to the electrical outlet. What do we need to make our 13 billion part computer work? Our electric current is called *motivation*. Motivation is what makes learning come alive!

What Is Your Source of Motivation?

Our source of motivation is human needs. The psychologist Abraham Maslow believed that all human beings have a need to grow, to develop abilities, to be recognized, and to achieve. He viewed human needs in hierarchical order. Some needs take precedence over others. We need to satisfy the lower needs in order to achieve the higher ones (see Figure 1). If we don't take care of our fundamental needs which are our basic physiological needs

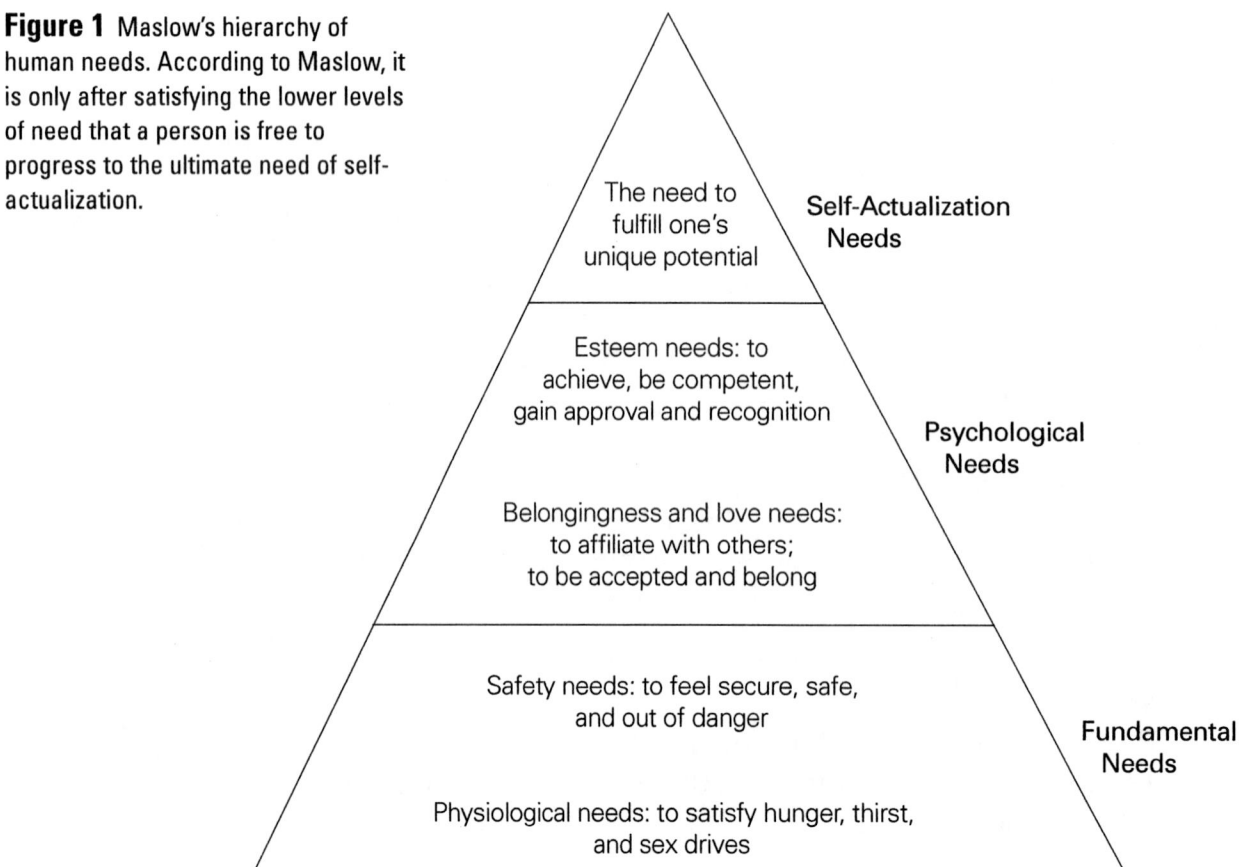

Figure 1 Maslow's hierarchy of human needs. According to Maslow, it is only after satisfying the lower levels of need that a person is free to progress to the ultimate need of self-actualization.

(hunger, thirst, sex) and our need to feel safe, then we have difficulty proceeding to the next level which involves our psychological needs. These in turn need to be fulfilled in order to reach the top which is our self-actualization needs. For self-actualized persons, problems become a means for growth. Wouldn't it be nice to view problems in this manner?

What Is the Difference between External and Internal Motivation?

1. *Internal Motivation*—These are motivational elements that are within ourselves. We have feelings of pleasure or disgust as we meet or fail to meet our own standards. This is the reinforcement level we should all strive to meet. We should try to find value in our work, enjoy success, develop an appropriate value system, and thereby reinforce ourselves for our efforts. People differ in what they think provides reinforcement.

2. *External Motivation*—These are motivational elements that come from outside stimuli. Rewards in the form of material things, privileges, recognition, trophies, praise, or friendship. These are a "public" way of saying a job is well done.

CRITICAL THINKING

Todd felt he had prepared for his first major exam in geology. Science was difficult for him. He had attended all lectures, revised his notes, and read the chapters. He made an appointment with his professor to clarify some points that he didn't understand. He felt he was ready for the exam. When Dr. Jones returned the test, Todd had scored 94%. The reward of the high score was a real high! He felt successful, and knew he could continue to do well in this course. He called his parents that night and they were elated. Their praise echoed their feelings. Todd had received internal and external praise. Do you believe the external or the internal motivation that he received from the test score was the best motivator?

As you progress through school, internal motivators should become stronger. We should not always feel the need for external motivation. This doesn't mean we don't want external rewards, but its value should begin to lessen.

WHAT ARE YOUR GOALS?

Motivation is the first step in all goals. A goal should be something that you desire and that you will be motivated enough to try and reach.

Goals can be divided into three categories:

1. *Personal*—These will be determined by your value system. You have already filled out the Value exercise. This should give you an idea of what you feel is important to you. Personal goals can also include personal fitness, developing a positive attitude, and overcoming a bad habit.

2. *Academic*—You can be successful if you set your goals on what you want to get out of college. The exercise on reasons to attend college should also include some academic goals.
3. *Work Related*—What do you want from your chosen field of work? Improving your performance? Changing jobs? Learning new skills?

Why Do You Need Short-Term and Long-Term Goals?

It is necessary to have short-term and long-term goals. It is easy to lose motivation with only long-term goals. Short-term goals are necessary to act as our motivational elements. The accomplishment of these goals give us the will to succeed. Long-term goals clarify our direction.

What Are Some Important Characteristics of Goals?

There are four characteristics of goals that we will discuss. While you are reading about these characteristics, think about how you can apply these points to your life.

1. *Goals should be realistic*—A realistic goal is one you can reasonably expect to achieve given your abilities. If your goal is too high and you don't reach it, it can certainly affect your self-concept. If your goal is too low, when you attain this goal there is no real feeling of success.

   Amy attained a 3.0 (out of a 4.0) in high school. Her college goal was to attain a 3.0 average. Is this a realistic goal? Is Amy setting herself up for failure, or is this a possible goal?

   Bill was valedictorian of his graduating class. His goal in college was to maintain a C average. His goal was not high enough to give him the sense of accomplishment that he would need to make him feel successful.

2. *Goals should be measurable*—A measurable goal establishes a time frame and it also has a foreseeable outcome. You should have daily and weekly goals. Attaining these short-term goals will give you the successful feeling that you need to experience to keep you going. Semester, yearly, and other long-term goals (college degree, marriage, family) are also vital because they clarify your direction.

3. *Goals should be flexible*—Decide what you want to do and be willing to change your plans if necessary. Rarely do we set goals and follow through to completion without any problems. You might change your major, withdraw from a class, or experience any number of setbacks. Reassess your plan for reaching your goal. You might need to revise it or make a new plan. It's alright to change your goals if you make a mistake or decide to change your plans.

4. *Goals should be specific*—The purpose of goals is to make us "act." In order for a goal to activate us, we must have specific objectives in mind. If we are too vague, we never receive the satisfaction of success that we should feel when we attain the goal.

   Nancy's goal this semester is to attain a 3.0 grade point average. Peggy's goal this semester is to "do well" in her classes. Who will receive the greater satisfaction if they attain their goal? Who will know if their goal is met?

CRITICAL THINKING

Your long-term goal is to be a lawyer. Is that enough to motivate you to attend and be excited about the basic psychology class that you have at 8:00 a.m. on Monday, Wednesday, and Friday? Maybe at first, but as the semester rolls along there will be mornings that being a lawyer doesn't quite have the zip that it once did. The short-term goal of making a B in psychology that will complete three hours of general education requirements just might! (Hopefully your short-term goal will be to learn as much as you can about human behavior so you can effectively deal with people in your law practice.) It will help you to have a goal that you can accomplish in a short period of time to serve as an inspiration. An even better short-term goal would be to make a B on the first exam. Once this is accomplished, hopefully the adrenaline will flow!

Goals do not have to be major events. Your goal for today may include:

Pick up cleaning

Read Chapter 3 in sociology

Do math problems 2.1 through 2.6

Clean the bathroom

These are specific goals. You will know at the end of the day if you have attained them. These are much more motivating than:

Run errands

Study

Catch up on housework

IS THERE A RELATIONSHIP BETWEEN SETTING GOALS AND ACADEMIC SUCCESS?

After what we have learned to recognize about goals, this is an easy question to answer—Yes—Yes—Yes. Goals are activators, they provide a successful background that enables you to continue to strive. They are like gas to a car, food to our bodies, and rain to the grass.

The attainment of goals is also related to a positive attitude and high self-esteem. When we attain goals, we feel successful!

HOW CAN YOU DEVELOP A POSITIVE ATTITUDE?

Visualize yourself being successful. Jeni Burnett, a Pittsburgh State University basketball player, relates her success technique at the free throw line:

> *First of all, I block out the crowd noise. I dribble a couple of times and feel the ball. During this time I visualize my entire body. I think about my legs bent properly, my arms' and hands' position, my release, the ball being "up," the correct spin, the right arch, my follow-through. I see the ball "swish" the net.*

It is amazing how powerful positive thinking can be! It is also very contagious. Of course, negative thinking is also contagious. It is unbelievable how a "down" person can pull others "down" with them. We all know some people that constantly dwell on the negative side of life. They sometimes do not even realize it—it has become a way of life.

Fred woke up with a headache. He had worked a double shift the previous day. His roommate, Jim, was on his way out the door to class. Jim had actually read his history chapter and he hoped it would help him take better notes. Fred noticed it was raining; he had worked a double shift the previous day. He rolled over and muttered that he wasn't going to fight the rain to listen to Dr. Smith's boring biology lecture. It was annoying enough that he had a headache. He could have gotten the notes from Sue, but he recalled after his remark about her sweater that she probably wouldn't share her notes. He told Jim that he couldn't understand why teachers always seem to enjoy frustrating students. There had to be more to life. Jim walked out the door to go to class. He was beginning to wonder why he got out of bed today.

WHAT ABOUT THAT NEGATIVE VOICE?

Should we look at the negative side of a situation? We don't like to because being a "positive" person is crucial to our success. We also need to be realistic (unfortunately or fortunately—life is "real"). What are you going to do if you fail the first test in one of your classes? That is a possibility (distant, of course). What will your plan be? Inside we have two voices that are always screaming to get out of us. One is a positive voice, the other is the dreaded negative voice. Unfortunately, the voice seems to have more volume at the most inopportune times.

Jane came to college from a large high school. She took college prep classes and maintained a B average. She was active in a lot of social activities in her high school. Studying was a concern, but certainly not a major one. She kept up in her classes with very little effort. Jane came to college and since she had experienced success in high school with very little effort, why should this change? The social scene was important to her in college (that's o.k.) and she knew everything would just fall in place. In sociology and biology her first exams fell on the same day. (Don't teachers ever get together and try to avoid this?) The night before the tests (as in high school), Jane sat down and started digging. "Surely, I won't need to know all of this, so I'll concentrate on my notes," she rationalized. "The notes are obviously what the teachers will think is important. After all, that is what they talked about!" A lot of the information didn't seem that vital, so Jane picked out what she thought would be on the tests. About midnight, after telling at least twelve of her friends how hard she was studying, she was ready to call it a night. After all, her biology test was at 11:00 and her sociology was at 1:00. There was a mild panic at 9:30 the next morning when she realized she had slept through her alarm. But, not to worry, she had plenty of time to shower and review once more. Food could wait until lunch.

The biology test was given to the class. How could it be that many pages? Where did he come up with these questions? She found a lot of questions that she thought she knew, but the wording was ridiculous! What a relief when that was finished! On for a quick lunch and the sociology test.

She thought, "These teachers must get together and decide to ask weird questions." She wondered if there was an upper level education class for teachers that taught them to ask sneaky questions. "Why don't they ask questions that come directly from the book? After all, they wanted us to read it."—were two thoughts that Jane had. Jane definitely needed a nap after these two tests. She wasn't very concerned until the tests were handed back. There must be a mistake! She had never made a D in her life! How could she have made a D on both exams? She quickly folded back the corner of the tests so no one could see. What voices were screaming to be heard?

This could and might very well happen to you. It's not important that it happened, but it's how you are going to react that is important. You can turn this experience into a productive event. Before you throw this book in the trash, let's analyze the situation. Which voices will be dominant?

"I'm not smart enough to be here!"

"The teacher is a jerk—he didn't cover this!"

"He tried to trick us!"

"I hate this class!"

"At least I did better than Sally."

"I didn't really understand, I just memorized."

"I could have used the book to help me understand the notes."

"Now I know the type of questions that he asks."

High school students are usually concerned with the "literal" meaning of their textbooks. This means they are interested in the exact meaning—the words that are obviously stated. In college it is important to have an understanding of the material so you can *apply* the information. Concepts or ideas should be the result of studying your text. Maybe this means one of our *goals* should be the understanding of what the author is trying to say along with your teacher's interpretation. What do you think?

SUMMARY

It is important to think about *why* you are attending college. You should recognize your values and goals because they clarify your direction. Your motivation is directly related to achieving your goals. Success in our endeavors strengthens our will to succeed.

A good positive attitude is vital in achieving success in college as well as in life!

NAME: _____ DATE: _____

EXERCISE 1. WHY ARE YOU HERE?

What are your reasons for attending college? Listed below are some reasons why some students attend college. Check those which are closest to the reasons why you are here.

1. I want to earn a degree.
2. My friends are in college and I want to be with them.
3. I want to please my parents.
4. I want to meet new people.
5. I want to prepare myself for a career.
6. College graduates make more money.
7. I want to broaden my knowledge.
8. College graduates have more status.
9. I don't want to work full time.
10. I want to improve my skills so I can get a better job.
11. My parents gave me no other choice.
12. I have a strong desire to achieve.
13. I want to become more independent.
14. I wanted to get away from home.
15. I want to participate in campus social life.
16. I have an athletic scholarship, veteran's benefits, etc.
17. College graduates have better jobs.
18. I couldn't go when I was younger.
19. I can advance to a higher level position at work.
20. To help ensure success in life.
21. I want to please my family.
22. I want to provide a good role model for my children.
23. I am being retrained because I lost my job.

List 5 of your reasons in order of priority (1 = highest priority).

1. _____

2. _____

3. _____

4. _____

5. _____

NAME: _____ DATE: _____

EXERCISE 2. VALUES

In the first column check 10 of the values that are most important to you. In the second column, rank from 1–10 the order of priority of these 10 values.

A world without prejudice

A satisfying and fulfilling marriage

Lifetime financial security

A really good love relationship

Unlimited travel opportunities

A complete library for your use

A lovely home in a beautiful setting

A happy family relationship

Good self-esteem

Freedom to do what you want

An understanding of the meaning of life

Success in your chosen profession

A peaceful world

Recognition as the most attractive person in the world

A satisfying religious faith

Freedom within your work setting

Tickets and travel to any cultural or athletic event as often as you wish

The love and admiration of friends

A chance to direct the destinies of a nation

International fame and popularity

The ability to eliminate sickness and poverty

A month's vacation with nothing to do but enjoy yourself

Write a brief paragraph describing what goals you are setting for yourself that reflects your top value choices.

_____

_____

_____

_____

_____

_____

_____

_____

NAME: _____ DATE: _____

EXERCISE 3. THE COAT OF ARMS

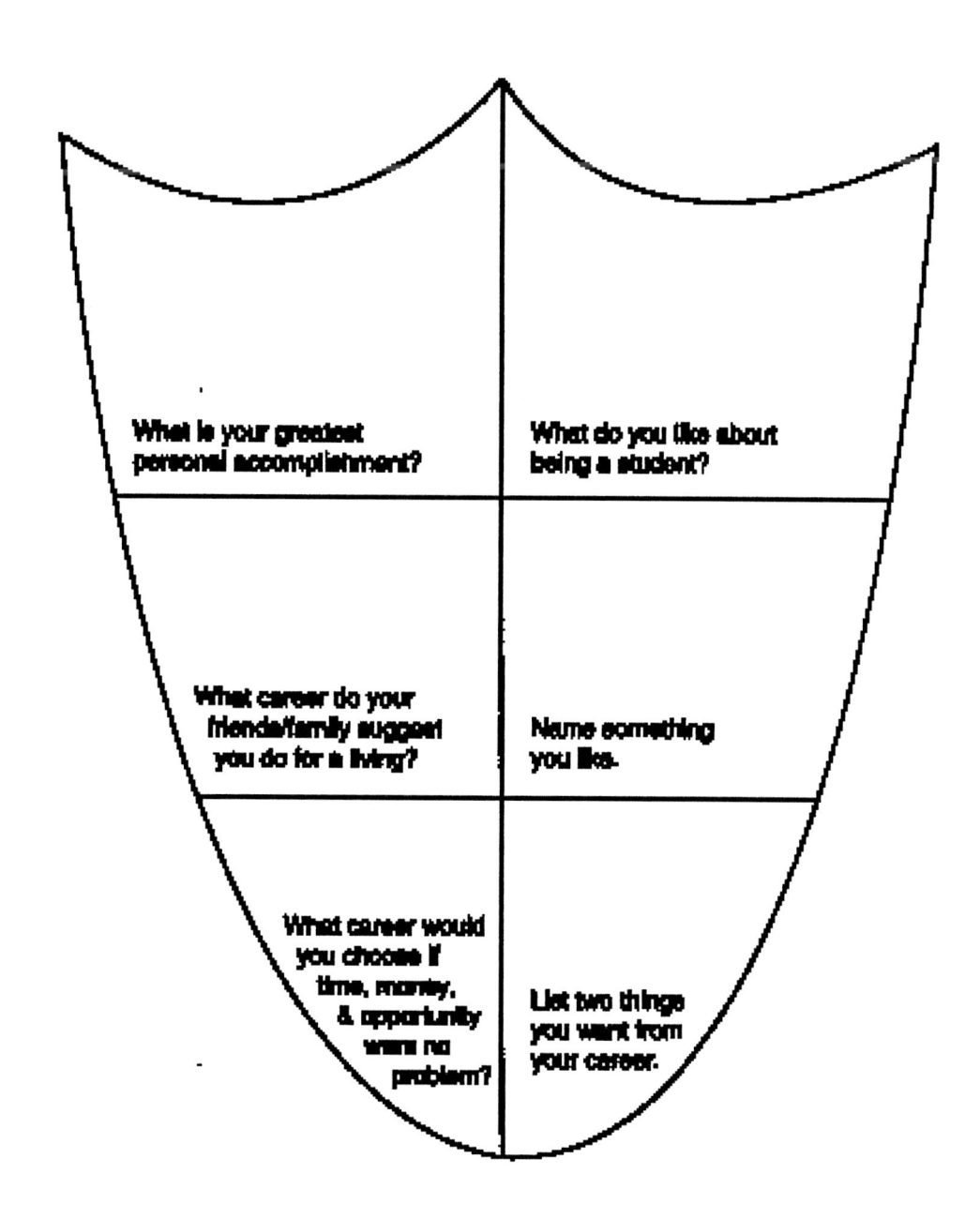

What is your greatest personal accomplishment?	What do you like about being a student?
What career do your friends/family suggest you do for a living?	Name something you like.
What career would you choose if time, money, & opportunity were no problem?	List two things you want from your career.

NAME: _____ DATE: _____

EXERCISE 4. PERSONAL GOALS

Your responses must meet the established criteria for goals!

Semester/quarter goals: _____
_____
_____
_____

Mid-term goals: _____
_____
_____
_____

One-year goals: _____
_____
_____
_____

Monthly goals: _____
_____
_____
_____

NAME: _____   DATE: _____

EXERCISE 5. EXTERNAL OR INTERNAL MOTIVATION?

Considering your experience in classes that you have taken, what has motivated you to learn, to work, to achieve?

In the first column, put a check mark if the experience has been used to motivate you. In the second column, decide whether the motivation was *E* (external motivation) or *I* (internal motivation).

1. Teacher paying attention to me
2. Not wanting to disappoint the teacher
3. Getting on the honor roll
4. Getting a job in the future
5. Wanting to learn and understand
6. Parents caring about me
7. Teacher caring about me
8. My satisfaction from receiving a high grade on an exam
9. Not wanting to disappoint parents
10. Being praised by classmates
11. Finally figuring out the correct answer
12. Putting words together that became concepts that made sense
13. Helping other students
14. Pleasing my family

List below the latest internal motivator that you have experienced.

_____

List below the latest external motivator that you have experienced.

_____

Write a brief paragraph describing how you feel you became motivated. Do internal or external motivation factors seem to be the most important? Do you feel motivated at this time of your life? Why?

_____

_____

_____

_____

_____

_____

_____

_____

_____

_____

Chapter 4

Creating Time through Effective Time Management

Frequently, a student's reason for not succeeding at a college is attributed to such things as not being able to devote sufficient time to studying, overloading himself or herself with too many tasks, putting things off to the last minute, or having difficulty utilizing time that has been set aside to complete academic tasks. In the last instance, the problem may be one of concentration, an often cited complaint that may result from anxiety, sleep deprivation, stress, personal problems, or any number of interfering factors. All these reasons for not doing well are related to time management or, more accurately, time mismanagement. The major areas of discussion in this chapter are time management strategies tied to one's personal values, getting organized via a schedule, utilizing a to do list, and effectively carrying out what you have planned.

SEEING THE BIG PICTURE IN RELATION TO TIME MANAGEMENT: ACHIEVING VALUES-CONGRUENCE

To accomplish major tasks (the "big picture") in one's personal, academic, social, and professional life requires consideration of one's values. When goals are in line with our values, they have **values-congruence**. Achieving a values-congruent perspective will help you maximize your academic performance and your overall potential. Another outcome is likely to be greater general happiness.

Steps necessary to achieve values-congruence are the following:

1. Identify the most significant values in your life (e.g., financial security, working with others, utilizing creative ability, supervising others, influencing others, working with computers).
2. Identify how your academic preparation and choice of a major ties to your values.
3. Identify all the steps, activities, and academic opportunities involved in accomplishing lifelong educational and career objectives.

Now, identify, apply, evaluate, and modify your time-management plan for academic and career success. Simply stated, you should develop your own personal model of time management to accomplish what is of true value to you. The basic ingredients of this model are fourfold.

- **T**ie your plans to specific objectives (e.g., "I think I will take a survey course to decide what area of a particular career I want to enter.").
- **I**nvest the necessary time to establish how you will implement, evaluate, and effectively modify, if necessary, your personal model (e.g., "I will take the survey course in the spring, visit a career counselor after completing the course, and discuss the major I am interested in to determine if this is the correct career path for me.").
- **M**anage your time in a way to reach your goals, but do this in a flexible manner without losing your focus on key objectives—objectives that are based on your personal values (e.g., values such as wanting to have a career in an area where you will be allowed to creatively express your ideas as well as being able to work with others, so you can apply your people skills).
- **E**nd each day (or some other specifically designated period of time such as once a week) by achieving at least one positive step to meet your objectives. The positive step can be a major step or a minor step, the most important thing is to be moving in a direction that results from values-congruence.

THREE KEYS FOR CREATING AND UTILIZING AN EFFECTIVE TIME MANAGEMENT MODEL

Keys for putting this model in effect involve the following areas: getting organized, the to do list, and the carry-through.

Getting Organized

The following are points to consider when scheduling or structuring your time.

- Be reasonable. Construct a schedule you will actually live by. Do not try to change everything in your life to "finally get organized, once and for all." Keep this jingle in mind: "Inch by inch, it's a cinch. Yard by yard, it's too hard."

Chapter 4 | *Creating Time through Effective Time Management* 45

- Time-management is really self-management. There are 24 hours in a day, 168 hours in a week and 2,520 hours in a semester (i.e., 15 weeks). Use it or lose it.
- Maintain flexibility when scheduling. Allow for mishaps. Schedules that are too tight with no buffers for the unexpected can create stress once the person is off track because of the interruption.
- Establish time limits for tasks being scheduled. Move on to the next task when the established time limit is up. (If you are not allowing enough time for tasks, learn from the experience and in the future allow yourself more time.)
- At the end of your efforts (usually at the end of the day), reward yourself for accomplishing a step toward reaching a big goal. Visit downtown and walk around, purchase that DVD you've been wanting, eat at your favorite restaurant. Just take a break and enjoy your accomplishment.
- When getting organized and setting your schedule, think in terms of prioritizing. Periodically ask yourself, Is this the best use of my time now?
- Use a planner or appointment book with a daily, weekly, and monthly calendar. We advise purchasing the type of planner sold at the college bookstore because these note important academic calendar dates, such as when the residence halls open, new student orientation is scheduled, classes begin, the midpoint of the academic session falls, classes end, the reading day is assigned, final exams are given, commencement ceremonies are scheduled, holidays fall, and special exams are given.
- Always allow time for breaks. Breaks of at least 10 minutes after studying for an hour will rejuvenate you and help to maintain a higher level of efficiency of learning.
- When working on a task, concentrate on the task. Do not allow yourself to be distracted. (We will discuss handling distraction in much more detail later.)
- When setting up your schedule, be sure to break tasks into manageable units. Spending 1 hour or 2 hours per evening studying a topic is much more efficient than trying to cram in 10 straight hours of studying. Avoid marathon study sessions.
- Plan in terms of specific and realistic goals.
- Schedule time to relax. This is an extended period (e.g., an hour) when you set aside time for yourself. Allow time for creative incubation to occur; sometimes serious students are studying so hard they forget to take time to just think.
- Complete a task. Finish each task before moving on (unless you misjudged the time required). Finishing a task creates a sense of accomplishment and psychological closure. Researchers have found that unfinished tasks tend to linger in our minds, contributing to a sense of frustration and possibly stress.
- Know what resources are available and use them as part of your time-management efforts. For example, if you are taking a difficult course, schedule time to take advantage of any free tutoring offered through your college's academic assistance services.
- Organize your schedule to allow yourself to review difficult curricular material soon after being exposed to it (e.g., stop and look over the notes taken in the psychology class where the professor lectures in a rapid manner; aim to achieve an overview and fill in gaps left in the notes while the lecture is still fresh in your mind). Even in cases where there is a delay (you have classes scheduled back to back and have to wait to review the material), aim to review the material within 24 hours of first being exposed

to it, even if for no longer than 10–15 minutes. Failure to review in this manner might result in a significant portion of the information (understanding) being lost. Keep in mind that the sooner the review takes place, the better the result.

- Know when to stop. Some individuals work past the time scheduled or needed. The result, if this becomes an established pattern, is decreasing return for the effort and possibly even stress because the work never seems to end. Find ways to stop yourself if you have to (use a kitchen timer to remind yourself to stop).
- Before going to sleep at night, use five minutes to visualize your future and see yourself as moving toward the goals you are striving to reach. Such visualizations can serve as motivation boosters.
- Some individuals find it helpful to make an oral (or written) contract with another person (e.g., significant other, study partner) concerning an important task. Knowing this other person is "watching" can foster and maintain motivation. Sometimes even writing a contract to ourselves can provide added initiative to meet a goal.
- Write reminders and post them if need be. Jotting down one's most important time-management goals on a note and sticking the note on your computer, bathroom mirror, or textbook can help you stay on task.
- Periodically review your goals (from small intermediate goals to large end goals you are working toward), reassess the steps you are taking, and make appropriate changes when necessary.
- Schedule the things you like to study last. The importance of this is illustrated by the typical behavior of math-anxious students. Math-anxious students frequently study for the math course they are enrolled in at the end of their study time. By this time they are getting tired, so they become easily frustrated and thus do not devote the needed time to a subject they are having trouble with.
- Plan to carry your schedule with you. In questioning students over the years, we have found that some good organizers forget important tasks simply because they have forgotten to carry their schedules with them.

To-Do List

This is not to be confused with a schedule that is set up in a planner. The to-do list can stand alone or be incorporated into the planner. Many individuals have found a to-do list to be an indispensable time-management technique. In its simplest form, a to-do list is a list of things that must be accomplished that have been prioritized. Some people mistake a simple list of things to do for a to-do list; the two are not the same. A genuine to-do list keeps a person on track. A random, unprioritized listing of tasks can keep us off track.

If you simply list items to do (e.g., go to library to read a reserved book, study two hours for next week's history test, buy a new pair of shoes at the mall, drop off CD at friend's house), you may wind up spending too much time on items that could have been put off (you go to the mall and decide to also see a movie, or you spend three hours at the friend's house because of a spontaneous invitation to stay for some barbecue being cooked) and not devoting enough or any time to important tasks and then rationalizing your mismanagement of time ("I can study the night before the test."). Thus, to have a genuine to-do list, you should list and prioritize the items. Mark the most important task with a star, an asterisk, the letter A, or the number 1.

Another tip is to have a variety of things to accomplish that are not all top priorities (some items should be things you will get to if you can, but if you do not, it is not really a problem). Follow the 20/80 rule. In a list of 10 items, aim to have 2 (maybe 3) that are top-priority items. Think of it this way: we never read everything in a newspaper, only certain sections (20%) and leave much of it unread (80%); office workers refer to a few filing drawers in an office (20%) and not the others (80%) except on rare occasions; and we walk mostly on a small amount of floor space where we live each day (20%) but do not walk on the rest (80%). While there is not always a clear 20/80 breakdown, the point is that when we list things to accomplish, the top priority items should be fewer in number.

Adding the use of a to-do list to your repertoire of time-management skills can increase your efficient use of time dramatically. The effectiveness of a to-do list is reflected in the world of business where whole-day workshops on time management are often sponsored by major companies to get employees to be more effective users of time, which, of course, adds to earnings. It is unlikely that large corporations would invest in such workshops if there were not a monetary return. For people in the business world, time-management techniques can become almost second nature. To-do lists are constructed for important tasks automatically. Review the two examples of to-do lists in Figure 1. Which example represents a poorly constructed to-do list? Why is this an example of a poor to-do list?

The Carry-Through

A vital part of being an effective time manager is to be able to carry through on what you have planned. Your scheduling skills and to-do lists may be impeccable, but the perfect schedule and perfect to-do list will do nothing for you if you cannot achieve what you have planned. Here are some points to consider.

- Think of the place you study as a **study territory** to be defended. The notion that all that is needed to establish a place to study is a neat desk with a cup to hold sharpened pencils is antiquated. In many ways a place to study is more of a frame of mind that fits your needs and unique personality. But regardless of the place, it should be one you can claim as your property. If you mark this place as yours, others are less likely to intrude on your study time. Interestingly, this sort of response to another territory cuts across many life forms.

  Dogs protect their territory (e.g., a student's apartment) from strangers and other dogs. The protector in this case is likely to win in a battle with an even stronger dog because fighting in one's territory provides a competitive edge. This is even true in some wars between countries where stronger countries have attempted to invade and take over weaker countries only to lose the war to the weaker country defending its home territory.

  Having areas that we claim as ours is more common than most people realize. For example, early in the academic term, part of settling into a classroom is finding a chair. Students frequently mentally mark a chair as theirs. Think of those times when you entered a classroom where you have sat in the same chair since the first day for several weeks only to find another student seated in "your" chair. You felt irritated because you had come to view that particular chair as your territory.

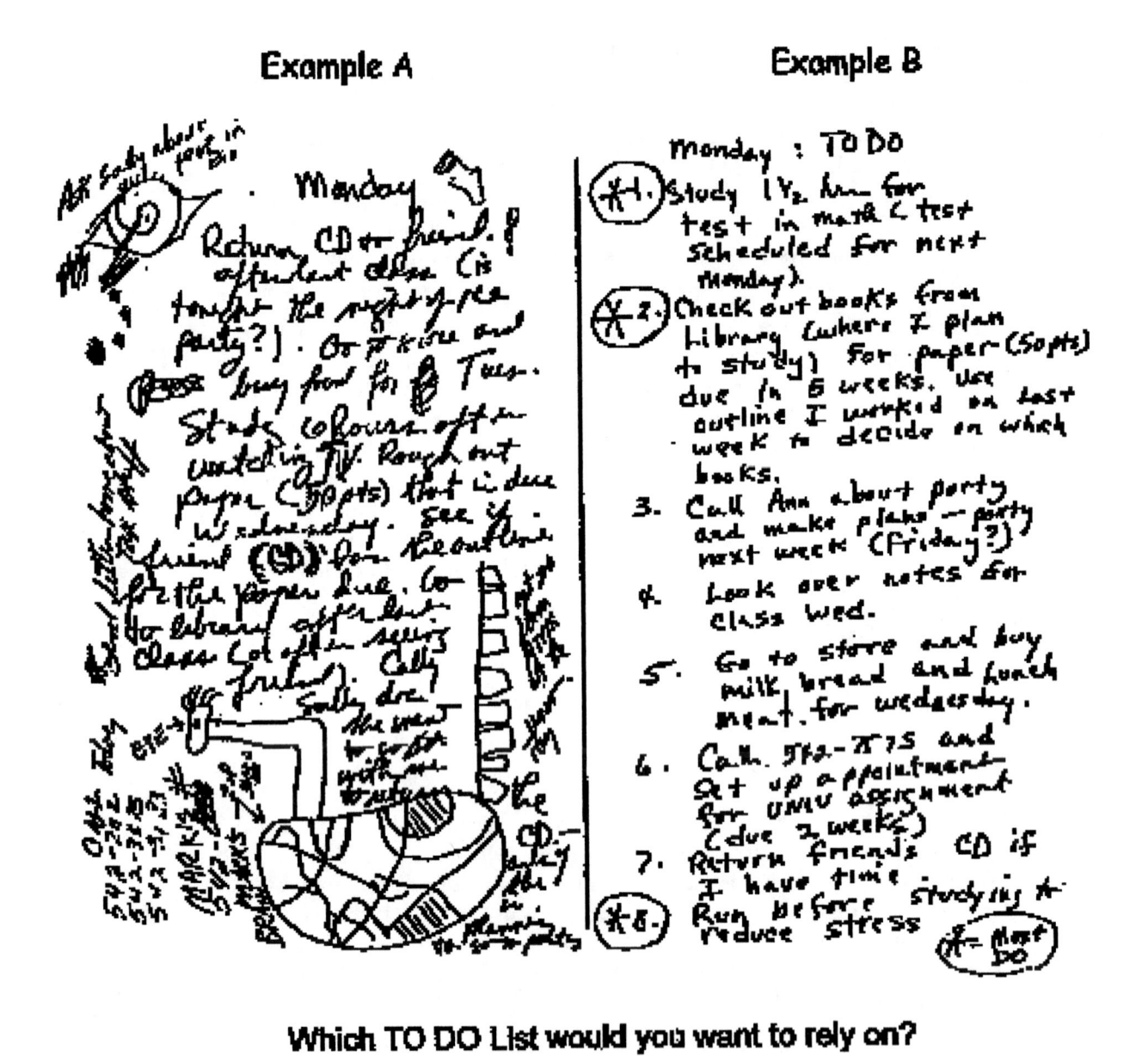

Figure 1 Two Examples of To-Do Lists

Interestingly, we even have portable territories that we carry around with us. It is as if we all move about with an invisible bubble that shields us from others. This invisible bubble extends out to differing distances depending on the environment and on who is approaching. On a dark street at night it extends out so far that seeing a stranger walk toward us might cause us to cross the street. And even though during the day the bubble's boundary is much smaller (extending only a few feet from our bodies), think of those times when another student whom you did not know crossed this invisible boundary by standing too close. During such "invasions," we maneuver to reestablish the boundary. We step back or look away (similar to what occurs on crowded elevators where eveyone looks at the door). Such intrusions, coming within a few inches of our face or body, are rare because most people understand innately that territories (stationary and portable ones) are not to be violated.

The point is to have a place to study that is yours. For example, if a person knocks on your door to visit at a time when you must study for an important test, you should stand at the door (the boundary) and tell the person you are studying and will see or call him or her later. Use assertiveness skills if necessary (see Chapter 10). Learn to say no to requests that involve invasion of your scheduled time. Mark the territory with a sign on the door such as "Do not disturb" or "Back in three hours." The reader of the latter sign does not need to know you are behind the door and really mean that you will be back from studying in three hours.

- Cut down or eliminate possible distractions. If you live in a noisy dorm or apartment, schedule time to go to one of the college's libraries. If phone calls keep occurring, unplug the phone. Anticipate possible distractions, and take steps to block the interference before it occurs.

- Sometimes the distraction is from within. In such cases the persistent thought (e.g., about meeting friends later or the upcoming football game) can sometimes be put aside by using an old Zen Buddhist trick. Welcome the intrusive thought, and honor its presence by writing the thought down on a scrap of paper (e.g., write "Prepare for trip to Gainesville, Florida, in two hours") and put the slip aside saying to yourself, I'll get back to you after I study for two hours.

- Another possible contributor to distractibility from within is a low energy level. Are you a morning person, afternoon person, night person? When does your energy peak? If at all possible, and in many cases it is (at least more than we sometimes realize), we should schedule difficult, or mentally taxing, tasks at peak times and simple tasks that require little mental effort (e.g., shopping for groceries) at those times of low mental energy. When we mismatch a task with our energy level, we are going to be either over taxed or under taxed. Neither condition is an efficient use of our energy or time.

- Sometimes the internal distraction is of such a nature that we give it a label—procrastination. We put off doing something that we perceive to be unpleasant until a future date. (In extreme cases of procrastination the future date never arrives.)

Procrastination deserves special attention because it is often the identifying problem presented by students who are having difficulty managing their time. Rita Emmett (2000) suggests that two "laws" should be considered in relation to complaints about procrastination. Careful consideration of these laws can help you discover ways to address habitual procrastination.

EMMETT'S TWO LAWS GOVERNING PROCRASTINATION

First Law: The dread of doing a task uses up more time and energy than doing the task itself.

Second Law: Obsession with perfection is the downfall of procrastinators.

In her second law Emmett uses the words "obsession with perfection" to refer to various fears that block us from starting on a project, task, or assignment. A number of fears are listed next which Emmett believes can cause procrastination.

Fear of . . .
Low proficiency

Unknown

Judgment (What will others think or say?)

Making mistakes

Success

Having to live up to a high standard

Change

Too much responsibility

Feelings (e.g., not doing something because you fear the reaction of another person)

Finishing (e.g., "Once I finish this project, I have to start that other project—the project I am dreading.")

Being rejected

Making the wrong decision

Emmett believes the best way to manage procrastination is to identify your fear and then face your fear. "Once you identify your fear and face it, once you magnify that fear and decide you'll survive it and perhaps even learn from it, you can start moving and do whatever it is you've been putting off—and start taking control of your life" (Emmett, 2000, p. 94).

Procrastination is not an unusual event. Everyone procrastinates from time to time (e.g., scheduling a doctor's appointment may be consistently put off), but procrastination can become a vicious cycle. This vicious cycle can become a mental and behavioral prison. Individuals caught in such a cycle reveal its strength when they say things such as, "There's no point in getting started—I can't get anything done," "I feel overwhelmed and stressed out and don't know where to start." Such self-defeating thoughts and behaviors tend to intensify the problem and frequently contribute to lower self-esteem. For example, a student puts off doing math homework because he does not like math. Because less time is being devoted to math, the student starts to do poorly in math. This drop in performance leads to longer delays and increased avoidance of the topic, which results in another drop in grade average. The student now repeatedly states self-defeating messages about math whenever confronted with the topic. Sometimes these statements are made to others, but most of the time they are simply repeated silently, as if a taped message were playing over and over inside this person's head. According to David Burns (1980), a **mind set** has been established.

According to Burns, mind sets interfere with motivation and can be fueled by many different things. A syndrome is created, in which a group of signs are found together. The procrastination mind set is characterized by a feeling of hopelessness, a sense of being helpless, magnification of events leading to feeling overwhelmed, a tendency to jump to conclusions, negative self-labeling ("I am a loser"), undervaluing rewards due to perceiving outcomes as not worth the effort, self-coercion in the form of shoulds and oughts (e.g., "I should do X; otherwise I am a rotten person"), low tolerance of frustration, and a general sense of guilt and self-blame.

According to Burns, procrastination can be effectively dealt with. He suggests taking actions such as these.

1. **Use a schedule.** Prioritize tasks and do so using a weekly/monthly/annual planner.
2. **Keep a record of dysfunctional thoughts.** Record the self-defeating language you are feeding yourself and use cognitive restructuring techniques to break this pattern. This involves changing the negative scripts in your head and creating and using self-affirming scripts. ("I am a capable person, so I can find ways to learn math!")
3. **Endorse one's self.** If you find yourself operating from a perspective of "what I do doesn't count," you should argue with yourself. Turn the old perspective around. ("I have always thought others were more deserving, but there is no reason to not place myself in the deserving group of people. The people I have been placing on a pedestal also have strengths and weaknesses. I am just as deserving as they are!")
4. **Avoid the oughts and shoulds that are governing your behavior.** Albert Ellis has referred to the destructive impact on one's quality of life because of absolutes ("I must always be the A student. Less than an A means I am a failure") by saying we are performing "*must*erbation."
5. **Use disarming techniques.** If something or someone is contributing to a negative mind set, disarm it or the person by taking its or the person's power away. In cases involving others, you can call upon assertiveness skills to change the situation.
6. **Think about little steps.** Seeing too far into the future sometimes leads to procrastination. If you have to write a 25-page term paper for an early American history class, you might see the finished product in your mind and become overwhelmed, wondering "How can I ever write that 25-page paper?" When this takes place, stop and think about the task a step at a time. Break up what you see as the end product into manageable smaller stages.
7. **Visualize success.** Envision yourself completing the task. See yourself as succeeding when you start to experience self-doubt.
8. **Test your can'ts.** When you say you cannot do something, stop and do a specific assessment of what is involved in completing something. Often when we carefully assess what is required, we start to understand exactly what steps are needed to succeed, and the feeling of "I can't" loses its power.

CLOSING REMARKS

This chapter covers many tips and concepts that deserve careful consideration. Above all, you should leave this chapter knowing you possess valuable tools for gaining control over your time. Keep in mind the information and skills discussed are to be used when needed. Using time-management tactics should not gobble up a lot of your time. If you are spending hours each week getting organized, that in itself is a time-management problem. Start using those things suggested in this chapter that seem to fit your time-management needs best, and add other tactics when appropriate.

SOURCES

Burns, D. D. (1980). *Feeling good: The new mood therapy.* New York: Morrow.
Emmett, R. (2000). *The procrastinator's handbook: Mastering the art of doing it now.* New York: Walker.
Lakein, A. (1973). *How to get control of your time and your life.* New York: New American Library.
Schmitt, D. E. (1992). *The winning edge: Maximizing success in college.* New York: HarperCollins.
Taylor, H. L. (1981). *Making time work for you.* New York: Dell.

NAME: _____   DATE: _____

EXERCISE 1. WHERE DOES MY TIME GO?

Estimate the amount of time you typically devote to each activity listed below in a full week. After entering your estimates, record the exact amount of time spent on each activity during one week. Then answer the questions posed at the end.

	Estimated Hours/Minutes	Actual Amount of Time
Attending classes	_____	_____
Working at job	_____	_____
Sleeping (include naps)	_____	_____
Showering/bathing	_____	_____
Traveling to and from work	_____	_____
Eating (include snacks)	_____	_____
Studying for test(s)	_____	_____
Completing homework	_____	_____
Socializing (include time just talking to friends)	_____	_____
Organizational activities (band practice, fraternities/sororities, clubs, special groups, etc.)	_____	_____
Time devoted to physical fitness	_____	_____
Shopping (clothing, groceries, other)	_____	_____
Religious/spiritual activities	_____	_____
Time with family	_____	_____
Other (list)	_____	_____

a. _____

b. _____

c. _____

d. _____

Totals _____ _____

How accurate was your estimated total compared to the actual total?

Look over the list. Which three activities are of greatest importance to you? Does the actual amount of time you are devoting to each seem to be enough?

How might you change the manner in which you manage time to boost your time-management skills to a higher level? Provide five ways to do this.

1. _____
   _____
2. _____
   _____
3. _____
   _____
4. _____
   _____
5. _____
   _____

NAME: _____ DATE: _____

EXERCISE 2. CONSTRUCTING A TO-DO LIST

List 10 items that need to be done by this date: _____. Use A, B, and C to indicate each task's importance (A = top priority).

Importance	Check if completed on time	List tasks here
_____	_____	1. _____
_____	_____	2. _____
_____	_____	3. _____
_____	_____	4. _____
_____	_____	5. _____
_____	_____	6. _____
_____	_____	7. _____
_____	_____	8. _____
_____	_____	9. _____
_____	_____	10. _____

Were any of the items you listed not completed by the specified date? Explain why for each item. Briefly discuss any feelings of accomplishment or frustration you experienced in completing or not completing the tasks listed. Suggest at least one change you would make in the future when you use a to-do list.

NAME: _____ DATE: _____

EXERCISE 3. EFFECTIVE PLANNING FOR THE WEEK

Select Option A or B.

Option A. Create a plan for the week starting next Monday. Use the blank calendar that follows. At the end of the week, evaluate what you planned. Were you able to follow the plan? The evaluation section appears on the last page of this exercise. What did you learn about your strengths and areas needing improvement?

Option B. Create a plan for a typical week using the blank calendar that follows. Then, evaluate your time-management skills by completing the evaluation section at the end of this exercise. What did you learn about your strengths and areas needing improvement?

Note: You may use an arrow to indicate when an activity carries over into another box at a different time or when an activity is repeated at the same time on another day. Do not leave any of the boxes empty. Account for all of the 168 hours that make up your week.

Example

	Mon	Tue	Wed	Thu	Fri	Sat	Sun
11	Work on project for FINA	→	Prep for class	Study for STAT Exam	→	Speak with Mom/Dad about Sust.	Call Fred G. about tickets
12pm	Attend Class (STAT)	Meet with Fred G. about project	Attend Class (STAT)	↓	Attend Class (STAT)	Lunch with family	→
1	Go to Lunch	Attend Class (FINA)	Go to Lunch	Attend Class (FINA)	Go to STAT LAB (tutor)	↓	Start packing to go back

Plan

Option Selected: _____

	Mon	Tue	Wed	Thu	Fri	Sat	Sun
5 a.m.							
6							
7							
8							
9							
10							
11							
12 (noon)							
1 p.m.							

NAME: _____ DATE: _____

EXERCISE 3 (continued)

	Mon	Tue	Wed	Thu	Fri	Sat	Sun
2 p.m.							
3							
4							
5							
6							
7							
8							
9							

	Mon	Tue	Wed	Thu	Fri	Sat	Sun
10							
11							
12 a.m.							
1							
2							
3							
4 a.m.							

Evaluation

1. Discuss the strengths of your time-management approach based on the plan you completed.

2. Discuss ways you may plan each week differently in the future to increase your effective use of the 168 hours in a week.

NAME: _____ DATE: _____

EXERCISE 4. UNDERSTANDING PROCRASTINATION

1. List three situations in which you typically find yourself procrastinating, or, putting off what you need to do.

   a. _____

   b. _____

   c. _____

2. How do you feel about putting off what needs to be done in these situations (e.g., guilty, angry, depressed)? What thoughts come to mind when you think about these situations (e.g., "I tell myself I'll get started, but I never do")?

3. What steps should you consider using to overcome procrastination (e.g., "I need to divide the work up into amounts I can handle")?

4. You know what to do, based on question 3, so what obstacle prevents you from doing what needs to be done (e.g., "I feel like a failure in math, so I delay doing homework")? What specific action will you take to overcome the obstacle that prevents you from doing what you need to do?

   The obstacle is

   The specific action I will take is

   The date I will initiate this specific action is _____.

NAME: _____ DATE: _____

EXERCISE 5. PLOT YOUR ENERGY LEVEL

Review the example below. Then plot your typical pattern of mental energy for a day.

Changes in Mental Energy Level during a Typical Day (example)

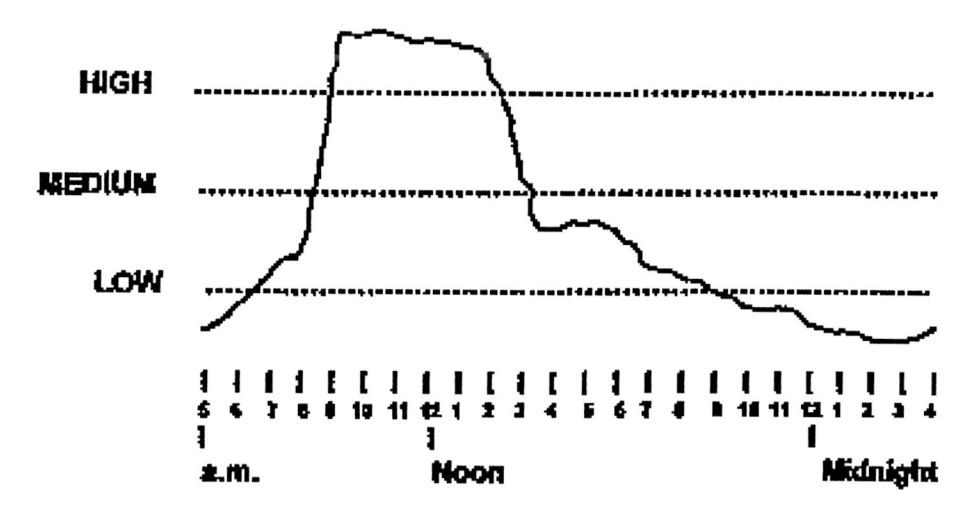

How might you use the information and understanding you obtained from plotting your changing energy level? Specifically, how could you schedule some activities differently to take full advantage of your periods of peak mental energy?

Chapter 5

Managing the Stresses of Life as a College Student

CASE STUDY

Nadir

Nadir and his wife have three boys between the ages of 6 and 12. Although he works full time, Nadir didn't think returning to college to get a degree would be too much for him. He signed up for two classes in the fall semester and plans to take three in the spring. However, it's near the end of the first semester, and he's already feeling the stress. He's highly motivated to succeed in college because he currently has a construction job and knows that he won't be able to do such a physically demanding job forever. His goal is to get into management or become a building inspector.

His job is somewhat seasonal, which gives him more time during the winter months to take classes, but the semester is not over when spring construction really picks up. Then the workload becomes intense. In addition, Nadir commutes to various job sites, which can add considerable time to his day. He would like to take more online or teleclasses, but most courses in his major are not offered in that format.

From The Community College: A New Beginning Fourth Edition *by Linda S. Aguilar, Sandra J. Hopper, and Therese M. Kuzlik. Copyright © 2005 by Kendall/Hunt Publishing Company. Used with permission.*

At home things are not all that stress-free either. Nadir's wife, Jennifer, and his recently widowed mother do not get along well. Some of their problems stem from cultural misunderstandings. He is an only son and feels a strong responsibility to take care of his mother. He knows that is what his father would have wanted him to do. His mother doesn't make it easy for him, though, as she expects Nadir to be at her beck-and-call every time she needs the least little thing done. She would never consider hiring strange workmen to come to her house. No; a good son should do whatever is needed.

All of the running around for his job and his mother doesn't leave Nadir much time for recreation, exercise, or to take care of the chores at his own house. He realizes he needs to spend quality time with Jennifer in order to keep their marriage strong. He would also like to spend more time with his boys. They need a father's influence and guidance, especially the preteen son.

The biggest stress of all is the approaching holiday season. Jennifer comes from a large family that has always made family gatherings the focal point of the holidays. A few years ago her parents divorced, and now her father is remarried. Celebrating with both of her parents adds to the already overcrowded schedule. At the same time, Nadir's mother expects them to spend the holidays with her, especially now that she is alone.

Nadir finds it difficult to concentrate on his studies and is struggling with his one-day-a-week algebra course. Not only is the class long, but the instructor covers several chapters at each session. Nadir is feeling quite anxious about the final exam. He needs to do well in order to build strong skills, pass the course with a "C" or better, and move on to the next math level.

Reflections

- What are some ways Nadir can spend time with his family while also taking care of his own needs?
- How might Nadir and Jennifer lessen the stress of the holiday season?
- What, if anything, can be done to help improve the relationship between Nadir's wife and mother?
- How can Nadir adjust his college schedule to accommodate all of the demands on his time?

INTRODUCTION

You probably didn't expect college to be easy, but many students are unprepared for how stressful going to college can be. As a college student, you are likely to have more roles than the average person. Most students work at least part time, but many are full-time employees. If you live at home, you probably have additional responsibilities. If you are married and/or a parent, you are aware of the time and energy involved in building strong relationships and running a household. If you're just starting to live on your own, you have the pressure of paying bills, grocery shopping, doing laundry, etc.—things that your parents used to do for you.

Many of you are also involved in activities either on campus or in the community. Now you've added the hours of homework and studying that it takes to maintain good grades.

In addition, if you were not a strong student in high school, or if it has been a few years since you were in school, you might be feeling anxious about taking tests, working math problems, or writing papers. College courses move very quickly, and the pace frequently accelerates after midterm.

This chapter will help you *identify the things in your life that cause you stress*. In addition to college stressors, many people these days are trying to *deal with unreasonable feelings of anger*. Similar coping strategies are used in both anger and stress management. The *stress-reduction and relaxation techniques* introduced in this chapter may help you achieve balance in your life. *Math and test anxiety* are such common student stressors that a special section is devoted to ways of reducing them. So, if you're feeling a little stressed-out these days, read on; this chapter is for you.

Pretest

Identify the major changes that are happening in your life right now. Check as many as apply to you *within this past year*.

Family changes:

- Death of spouse, parent, sibling
- Death of grandparent or other close relative
- Divorce or marital separation (you or your parents)
- Marriage
- Pregnancy
- Gaining a new family member/s (birth, adoption, stepfamily, elder moving in, etc.)
- Major changes in health or behavior of a close family member

Health changes:

- Serious personal injury or illness
- Major change in sleeping habits
- Major change in eating habits
- Quitting, starting, or major increase in smoking, drinking, or other drug use
- Major change in amount of exercise or activities

Financial changes:

- Sudden loss of income
- Major change in financial status (a lot better or a lot worse-off than usual)
- Taking on a mortgage
- Foreclosure on a mortgage or loan
- Taking on a loan

Employment changes:

- Being fired
- Retiring
- Major change in work responsibilities (promotion, demotion, transfer)
- Changing careers
- Major change in working hours or conditions
- Major conflict with your boss/supervisor, or co-workers

Personal changes:

- Detention in jail or other institution
- Death of a close friend
- "Breaking-up" with girlfriend/boyfriend
- Conflict with spouse, in-laws, parents, or a close friend
- Beginning or ending formal education
- Moving to different residence/Major change in living conditions
- Outstanding personal achievement
- Revision of personal habits (dress, manners, associations, etc.)

Social changes:

- Changing to a new college
- Major change in usual type or amount of recreation
- Major change in church and/or social activities
- Vacation
- Major changes in holiday celebrations and/or number of family get-togethers

What does it mean? Change frequently causes stress. The more check marks—the more changes you have going on in your life—the higher your risk for a stress-related illness. If you have major changes taking place in all areas of your life (check marks in each category), that can also signal the potential for trouble.

WHAT IS STRESS?

Stress is the body's reaction to an occurrence or an event. You're driving to class and suddenly notice flashing lights and hear the siren of a police car behind you. Your body instinctively reacts. You look down at your speedometer; it shows 10 miles over the speed limit. Tension mounts. You prepare for what may follow. You don't really have time to stop and certainly can't afford a ticket. Your heart starts beating faster, and your mind is racing as you try to think of what to say. Even if the police car continues down the road, you may still feel a little shaken. Your adrenaline is high; you're stressed. A police car driving with its lights and siren turned on is not in itself a stressful event. If you were stopped at a red light on a side street or driving in the opposite direction, you would have a much different reaction to that event. The event is neutral, but your reaction to it can be positive or negative.

How we react in any situation is largely determined by our past experiences and our expectations of certain consequences or results. Our perceptions, beliefs, habits, level of self-confidence, and physical, mental, and emotional health also influence our reactions. No two people react exactly alike. What may be a challenge for one person may be distressful for another.

We usually think of stress as always being from negative or bad events, but stress also may occur from happy occasions. Starting college, planning a wedding, the birth of a child, celebrating the holidays with family, getting a new job, moving to a new house, or remodeling your current one are usually considered positive events. Yet, all of these can produce stress. *Change of any kind may produce stress.* That's why the pretest asked you to identify how many major changes are going on in your life right now. A little stress may be just what you need to motivate you. However, if you get too much stress in a very short time period, your body may become overloaded. When that happens, your natural immune system may be unable to defend itself against all of the germs, bacteria, and viruses that surround us. Your resistance is lowered, and you succumb to whatever illness is "going around." Being overloaded for a long period of time can be very damaging to your health. That's why it is important for you to use common sense and practice good health habits as your first line of defense.

Stress is unavoidable and affects everyone. Relationships with our families, friends, and others, as well as money, health, work, and college issues may all produce stress. Anger is a normal emotion that, if left unchecked, can result in serious problems. Major life events, everyday irritations, conflicts, and frustrations frequently result in feelings of anger that also boost our heart rate, adrenaline, and blood pressure levels. A specific event, such as a traffic delay that causes you to be late for class or work, or a specific person, e.g., a co-worker who is frequently late thus causing you to work overtime, both result in angry feelings that you need to resolve to eliminate further stress.

Sometimes we "set ourselves up" by developing unrealistic goals or setting our standards too high. When we expect too much of ourselves by overrating our abilities, we may fail to make satisfactory progress toward or not achieve our goals. Failure can produce a state of depression that prevents us from functioning effectively. The opposite is also true. We may set our standards too low or not try to achieve. Then, we're stressed by the consequences of our laziness and irresponsibility.

Another cause of stress is a conflict in our values. When we are in situations where we act contrary to our core beliefs and values, we feel the pressure of being phony. Time constraints or the feeling of always being overloaded is yet another huge stressor. When we lack the proper support and/or resources or feel that college or job demands interfere with our personal activities, we may exhaust our abilities to reduce or resist stress.

HOW TO REDUCE STRESS AND MANAGE YOUR ANGER

We cannot control all of life's stressors, but we can control our reactions to the people and events that cause us to become angry or stressed. Identify what is causing your stress, and then implement your own personal stress-reduction program. If you alter your beliefs and your way of thinking, you can reduce anxiety levels and their negative effects on your body. Stress is manageable, providing it does not approach a life-threatening level.

Step One: Look for Stress Symptoms—Be aware of the symptoms of anger and stress. Awareness always precedes action. Recognize the symptoms and don't deny that you have them. Be especially aware of times when you may "lose control" by using loud/abusive language, criticizing others, withdrawing socially, or inappropriately confronting others. You can start to solve the problem once you know it exists.

Step Two: Identify Stressful Times, Situations, and People—Identify the times and places when stress strikes you. Did you respond strongly to any of the pretest items? Think of the current causes of stress or anger "triggers" in your life right now. If it helps, keep a diary to pinpoint problem issues. Record what happened and your reaction. Think of other possible ways you could have reacted. List the kinds of things that were helpful in relieving the stress or reducing your anger level.

Step Three: Eliminate Unnecessary Stress—Whenever possible, eliminate the causes of unnecessary stress. From your diary you might have noticed a pattern of things or people that always stress you. When you come to that situation/person again, try to change your response. Don't jump to conclusions, and refuse to let anger and frustrations take over. Then, avoid those stressful situations. "That's easier said than done," you say, but remember that you control your own actions and reactions.

Changing your physical environment or your timing may also help you reduce your stress.

- Plan a different route if traffic jams cause you to become tense or you tend to develop "road rage."
- Shop at "off-peak" hours if you hate waiting in line at the grocery or mall.
- Try to schedule discussions on important issues with family members, friends, or co-workers when you feel alert and refreshed rather than just reacting without thought.
- If possible, take ten minutes for "personal down-time" to be alone when you arrive home from work, and let the stress of the day fade away.
- Be sure to take a few minutes for yourself during your workday.

You cannot change someone else, but you can change yourself and your attitudes. Don't let conflict with your significant others become your way of life. It's too exhausting and frustrating. Learn new skills such as assertive communication to improve and soften all your relationships.

Step Four: Reduce the Effects of Unavoidable Stress—For the stress in your life that you can't eliminate, try to control and reduce its effects. Remember to keep your perspective. Think about how important this event really is. Will you even remember it next week? Next month? If not, why get upset about it? Keep your stress at a minimum, and don't overreact.

It may not be possible to reduce all of life's irritations. Keep in mind that reacting with anger is ultimately a choice. Angry responses such as yelling, hitting, or confronting others can be outright aggressive. They may also be passive-aggressive—for example, backstabbing, gossiping, or manipulating others.

People have successfully dealt with the stress in their lives by using some of the techniques listed in Table 1.

Table 1 — COMMON STRESS REDUCERS

ESTABLISH SUPPORT SYSTEMS	MANAGE YOUR TIME
• Keep the positive, supportive relationships you have and build new ones. • Ask for help when you need it. • Use available campus and community resources.	• Develop a schedule using "Time Management" techniques. • Simplify your life. • Learn to say "No" to requests that are not priorities. • Delegate when necessary. • Use mini "downtime" breaks.
PRACTICE EMOTIONAL CONTROL	**MAINTAIN A HEALTHY LIFESTYLE**
• Use assertive communication techniques to prevent anger/frustration from causing undue stress. • Eliminate self-defeating behaviors and keep things in perspective. • Practice forgiveness. • Use cooperation rather than confrontation to reach your goals. • Be willing to compromise and seek alternative solutions to problems. • Use humor and laughter to lighten your emotional load. • Seek professional counseling if necessary.	• Eat nutritionally-balanced meals. • Get plenty of sleep. • Exercise regularly. • Avoid using drugs, including alcohol and tobacco. • If sexually active, protect yourself and your partner from sexually transmitted diseases or from unwanted pregnancy. • Take time for yourself—do whatever you enjoy to help promote balance in your life. • Try massage therapy or other relaxation techniques.
UNDERSTAND YOURSELF	**ACCEPT CHANGE AND LEARN NEW SKILLS**
• Think through what you really believe and why you believe it. • Be open to new experiences and ideas. • Practice critical thinking when faced with decisions. • Use your faith for motivation and to guide you through difficult situations.	• Learn something new to energize and revitalize your spirit and to increase your productivity. • Accept change with a positive attitude and as an opportunity to grow.

Relaxation and Anger Management Techniques

It is difficult to eliminate all the stress in your life, but you can learn to reduce your anger and control your frustrations or anxiety by practicing relaxation exercises. Some are more involved, but others are simple enough to do anywhere—even in the classroom. Try one or more of the following exercises whenever you feel yourself becoming angry, tense, or overly tired, or if you feel that others may be taking advantage of you.

Deep Breathing

Anger and stress result in shallow, rapid breathing. Deep, slow breathing can reduce stress and help you relax. Oxygen is the body's natural stress-reducer, and increasing your body's oxygen intake helps relieve tension. Begin by closing your eyes. Exhale slowly, and clear the air from your lungs. Then inhale deeply through your nose and hold your breath for a count of five. When taking a deep breath, your stomach (actually, your diaphragm) should be expanded. Slowly exhale, using your lips to control the rate of air that you move out of your lungs. Begin the cycle again. Repeat several times until you feel calmer. You can do this anywhere and any time you feel stressed, whether you are taking an exam or confronting a family member or co-worker.

Deep Muscle Relaxation

One of the most common reactions to anger and stress is muscle tension. Think of a time when you've been very angry or frustrated, and remember the tenseness in your jaw, neck, shoulders, arms, and hands. Deep and progressive muscle relaxation will help you relax your entire body from head to toe by first tensing and then relaxing the various muscle groups. The whole process can take anywhere from one to twenty minutes.

Find a comfortable position either sitting or lying down. If you are alone, you may want to loosen any tight clothing. Close your eyes. Begin with your head and facial muscles—scalp, brow, eyes, lips, jaw, etc. Tighten your muscles and hold tense for ten seconds, then relax. Continue contracting and relaxing your muscles by moving through your neck, shoulder, back, and chest areas. Keep doing this through every major muscle group. Concentrate on your breathing (slow, deep breaths) while you work your way down to your hips, legs, and feet.

When you have completed all the muscle groups, you will feel refreshed, calm, and relaxed. This type of relaxation may also help you sleep better. You can do a shortened version of this exercise in class or almost anywhere. Close your eyes; tense up all of your muscles for a couple of seconds; then release them slowly, one body part at a time.

Meditation

An ancient relaxation technique—meditation—can help you clear stressful thoughts from your mind, but it may take time to learn how to do it effectively. Find a location where you are comfortable and won't be disturbed. Close your eyes and focus on a peaceful word or image. Your goal is to find a quiet, peaceful state of mind. Concentrate on something calming, and do not let any other thoughts enter your mind. Learning to abandon all other thoughts is the hard part. Return to the one image or word you have selected, clearing your mind of any stress and worry. Breathe deeply. At the end of your meditation session, you will feel calm and relaxed.

Imagery

Imagery is another type of mental exercise. It is like taking a mini, mental vacation or daydreaming with a purpose. You can achieve the same feeling of tranquility that you do with meditation, but the technique is different. Rather than concentrating on a single thought, you create an entirely relaxing, though imaginary, place of your own to which you can escape. Once again, close your eyes and visualize the perfect place to relax. It might be in the woods by a brook, on a warm, sandy beach, in the mountains, floating on a cloud—wherever seems right to you. See yourself there, calm and satisfied with life. You can go to this special place in your mind whenever you need a few seconds of escape-time. You can also use this technique to build confidence. While in your perfect place, visualize yourself accomplishing one of your goals.

Pampering Yourself

There are a variety of products currently on the market to help you relax. Everything from bubble bath to scented candles can be used to create a soothing environment. Relaxing music, pleasant aromas, multimedia that captures the sights and sounds of ocean waves, raindrops, a crackling fire, or any number of other auditory and visual images can produce a tranquil state of mind. Massage therapy is now readily available in a variety of forms—chair massages for the neck and shoulders, pulse or wave massages, and full-body massages.

STUDENT STRESSORS

Adjusting to new and unfamiliar situations is a cause of stress for most people, and students are no exception. A new college, new course, or new instructor may create a great deal of anxiety. How much depends on his/her personality and past experiences. For a student, quizzes, tests, and final examinations can induce stress. A more extreme form is called test anxiety. Another high stressor for students is their fear of math. Both of these kinds of anxiety could be caused by a history of not doing well in school or on tests, having poor study skills, fear of failure, and outside pressures.

Test Anxiety

It is not abnormal to be anxious about a test. Almost everyone feels some apprehension, fear, uneasiness, or worry about taking a test. A little pressure can be beneficial if it is moderate and controlled, and some students view an exam as an opportunity to show what they can do. Their attitude is similar to that of an athlete who enjoys competition because it enhances his/her own performance. If moderate anxiety keeps you alert and provides you with a burst of energy, it can help you do your best.

Test anxiety may result in noticeable physical symptoms such as headaches, nausea, sweating, or dizziness. It can reduce your ability to concentrate and make you feel overwhelmed and unable to perform. The anxiety is self-induced, but outside pressures to maintain good grades may be contributing factors. If you suffer from anxiety because you think you have to be perfect, you need to let go of some of your unrealistic expectations. When stress and anxiety become so extreme that they affect your performance or become detrimental and threatening to your well-being, however, you may need the help of a professional to get your anxiety under control. If your anxiety is less extreme, you may be able to use the following strategies to handle it yourself.

Test Anxiety Reduction

- **Attitude Adjustment**—Be realistic about the importance of any single test or exam. What is the worst that could happen? You could get a lower grade than you wished; you could be embarrassed about your performance; you could fail the test; or a poor test grade could cause you to fail a course in which you are struggling. You might even lose an opportunity for a scholarship or have to pay back some of your financial aid. Yes; these are all terrible consequences, but none of them will determine the outcome of the rest of your life. A test is just a test—usually part of your total grade for one course in any one semester. Recognize that your value as a person is not dependent on what you do on any one test or in any one course.
- **Effective Study Techniques**—Previous chapters have introduced you to strategies and techniques designed to increase your ability to perform successfully in the classroom. Faithfully practicing the note-taking, time management, and test-taking strategies outlined in this book will give you the confidence you need to go into the test with a winning attitude. Be sure to use tutoring and other academic support services as needed.
- **Positive Self-Talk**—Negative thinking increases your anxiety levels. Recognize any self-defeating thoughts you might have and replace them with positive thoughts designed to increase your confidence levels. Believe that you have the ability to control what happens and visualize yourself doing your absolute best. Practice using positive statements to boost your confidence and self-esteem. In your mind, tell yourself, "I am well prepared; I am confident; I will do my best."

Math Anxiety

The physical and psychological reactions to math that affects performance in class and keeps you from remembering what you learned when taking a math test is termed math anxiety. It is usually the result of negative past experiences. Most students with math anxiety can trace its roots to a school experience that convinced them they could not be successful in mathematics. Sometimes the pressure to do well, or conversely, the excuse to do poorly, came from parents and/or other family members.

If you suffer from math anxiety, think about your first negative experience with math. Was it failing to learn the multiplication tables right away? Was it being made to stand at the board in front of the class until you could work out a difficult problem? Was it the result of someone telling you, "You'll never be good in math"? To combat the causes of math anxiety, you need to recognize their sources, reject the untrue things you've been programmed to believe, and adopt a new approach—a willingness to go at it with a fresh start. If math anxiety can be learned (and it is), then it can be unlearned.

Math Anxiety Reduction

Effectively reducing math anxiety requires most students to combat negative self-images about their ability to be successful in math by taking positive steps to change their attitudes.

First, they must develop and practice strong math study skills. Each small success in math performance will build confidence levels.

How can you change a negative attitude about math? Start by examining the math myths listed in Table 2, and become aware that these common assumptions are, indeed, myths.

Table 2 — FALSE ASSUMPTIONS ABOUT MATH

- Math is linear and logical; therefore, creative people cannot be good in math.
- There is only one right way to solve a math problem.
- Women are not good in math. It's genetic. Variation: No one in my family is good in math; therefore, I can't/won't be good in math.
- Math has no value in the real world.
- I haven't been good at math in the past, and it's too late for me to learn math now.
- Math is hard and boring.
- It doesn't help to ask questions because I won't understand the explanation anyway.
- I've always been good in English, so I can't expect to be good in math.
- Math isn't logical.

Now that you've recognized these math myths, take a look at the following **math facts**:

- Math is sequential, building upon itself, so it is important to study every day. Studying once a week will not produce the same results as keeping up daily, especially if you have a class that meets three or more times per week.
- The key to solving math problems is practice. Keep up with your homework and work the problems whether or not the instructor collects or grades homework.
- It is more important to understand the concepts, principles, and relationships than it is to memorize the formulas and work the problems.
- Choosing math courses that meet as many times a week as possible is to your advantage. Classes that meet only once or twice a week tend to produce stress, especially for students who do not excel at math. If you don't understand the material, you may have to wait a whole week to ask your questions. In a five-day-per-week course, fewer concepts can be presented per day, which gives you time to practice before moving to the next topic.
- Avoid taking math during accelerated summer sessions because these sessions are even more intense and move *much more rapidly* than the traditional fall/spring semester courses.
- Missing a math class can cause a real gap in your knowledge and understanding. Remember, math is sequential. Missing any material can cause confusion and lack of understanding.
- Math anxiety is learned, and it can be unlearned.

We've reviewed some common myths and some truths about math. If you have difficulties with math and/or math anxiety, how can you counteract any negative attitudes you may have developed? First, you need to examine your past math experiences. Can you remember the first time you felt unhappy with your math performance? If you can uncover the source of your negative attitude, you can work on changing it to a positive one. If your problems with math stem from knowledge gaps or not understanding some fundamental concepts, then you can correct them by working in a computerized learning center or taking a basic math course to learn what you don't know.

Take a look at your current attitude. Do you truly believe that you will never be successful at math, or are you willing to change your attitude? The following tips for improving math performance will help you build a stronger, more positive attitude.

- Confront any math myths you've held in the past and recognize that they are myths.
- Use the relaxation techniques and positive self-talk approaches discussed earlier in the chapter to help you develop a positive attitude about your math ability.
- Attend every math class, take good notes, and record all steps in the examples covered in class so you will remember them later.
- Ask questions in class and seek tutorial assistance as soon as you do not understand any material. *Don't get behind!* Remember that sequential process.
- Review as soon as possible after class.
- Before registering for your next math class, talk to other students and try to identify instructors who are receptive to questions, use cooperative learning techniques, review material prior to tests, and teach in a style that matches your learning style.

Do all of your assignments and the sample problems provided. Practice makes perfect.

Practice the following steps to help you solve math problems:

- Make sure you understand basic definitions, symbols, and other math terminology.
- Know and understand the formula being used.
- Read the problem aloud.
- Draw a picture to help you see relationships within the problem.
- Examine the problem. Ask,
  ▫ What information is given?
  ▫ Specifically, what do I need to find?
  ▫ What do I need to do?
- Estimate the end result.
- Ask yourself if your answer makes common sense.
- Check your answer.
- Practice until you understand how to do that kind of problem perfectly and completely.

SUMMARY

We all live complicated lives and are faced with stress on a daily basis. Moderate amounts of stress are normal and sometimes can motivate us to do our best. Too much stress, however, can cause serious physical, emotional, and behavioral problems.

Math and test anxieties are common problems experienced by many students. Both are learned responses that can be unlearned. Practicing good study habits, having a realistic attitude about the importance of tests in our lives, practicing positive self-talk, using relaxation techniques, and dispelling the math myths we have been taught will help us create success experiences.

We need to acquire the skills necessary to control or eliminate excessive stress in our lives. A number of strategies to help you develop your own stress management program were covered in this chapter. Maintaining a healthy lifestyle, using support systems, and practicing relaxation techniques are especially effective. If you have very high stress levels that have lasted for long periods of time, seek professional help. Remember that you can reduce many of your life stressors by identifying the people and events that cause you stress. Change the things in your life over which you have control, and release the rest. Don't worry; be happy!

NAME: _____ DATE: _____

JOURNAL QUESTIONS

In the case study, Nadir faced many stressors. Which of the suggestions in this chapter would help him deal more effectively with them?

Now think about your own life and continue your essay by writing a response to one or both of the topics below.

1. Do you have test or math anxiety (or both)? To what do you attribute your fear of taking tests and/or your problems with math? What do you need to do to overcome these fears? List several strategies you will use.

2. Identify the major causes of stress in your life. Describe how you can eliminate some of them and what strategies you will use to reduce the effects of stress that can't be eliminated.

NAME: _____ DATE: _____

EXERCISE 1. ACADEMIC ANXIETY

When taking math or other difficult courses, how much effort do you make to ensure that you can be successful?

Check your responses to the following:

	Usually do	Sometimes do	Never thought about it
Course Selection I schedule my difficult classes at a time when I am most alert. I choose instructors that match my learning style. I schedule the next course in a sequence as soon as I complete the prerequisite course.			
Preparing for and Taking Tests I keep up-to-date so I don't have to cram the night before the test. I look over the entire test before I begin. If necessary, I take the full amount of time allotted. I carefully review and check my answers before I turn in the test. When my tests are returned, I keep track of the kinds of mistakes I've made. If I don't understand what I did wrong, I meet with the instructor after class or during her/his office hours to make certain I will be able to work a similar problem correctly (e.g., on the final exam).			
General Anxiety Issues I believe that I can be academically successful. I recognize that preparedness will help lessen any anxiety. I know and am willing to practice simple relaxation techniques.			

Look at your responses in the "sometimes do" or "never thought about it" column. Outline the steps you can take so your responses will be "usually do" for your next test or when you next register for classes.

_____
_____
_____
_____
_____

Chapter 6

Developing Relationships

Never doubt that a small group of committed individuals can change the world; indeed, that is the only thing that ever has.

—MARGARET MEAD

DEVELOPING RELATIONSHIPS

Going to college is perhaps the most difficult step that you have ever taken. It is difficult because of the many changes which will occur simultaneously in your life. Relationships will change too. You will change and others close to you will change.

There are reasons why change comes at this time in your life. First, there is a big difference between "going to school" and "attending college." It may immediately appear that there are no differences because you may be doing things in the same ways you did in high school: getting up, driving to school, going to classes, driving home, studying, and doing homework.

You will quickly discover, however, that university classes are probably larger than those you attended in high school. Some lecture sections may have as many as 200 students in class; this means the professor may not provide the same time and attention to you as a student. Some may not even know your name. You may know some people in your class or you may see no familiar faces. Further, no one but you will monitor what you do in and out

From The First Year: Making the Most of College Fourth Edition *by Glenda A. Belote and Larry W. Lunsford. Copyright © 2003 by Kendall/Hunt Publishing Company. Used with permission.*

of class. **You** will decide whether to attend or not. **You** will decide whether or not to buy your textbooks. **You** will decide whether or not to complete assignments and turn them in on time.

This new independence is difficult for some students who find the added responsibilities too challenging. In high school, others watched out for you; in the university, you watch out for yourself. As you begin to explore your new freedoms and choices, you are likely to make some good decisions and some poor decisions. Important relationships in your life will begin to change as you learn to handle each situation.

You will meet people who do not view the world in the same ways you and your family do. Some of these people will be students and some will be professors. You will make choices about your openness to new experiences and new people. If college is about learning, it includes what we learn from others about ourselves, our values, and our beliefs.

In this chapter, we will explore some of the ways in which your relationships with others will change during your time in college. We will also consider questions of difference and openness to change.

LIVING WITH PARENTS

New college students who continue to live at home almost immediately find a change in various long-standing relationships in their lives. As students begin to assert a new-found independence, many find that relationships with parents become strained. For students, the freshman year is a time for meeting new people, developing new ways of managing day-to-day decisions, and becoming more independent in the choices made. It is a rite into adulthood. For parents, this first year of college is a time to let go and establish new relationships with you as a young adult.

The problem is, however, that some parents have difficulty letting go. The problem is magnified when you continue to live at home. Parents often assume that you will keep the same hours as you maintained in high school, be available for family-related activities, and continue to perform certain household chores or manage family responsibilities. They may not realize that students really do study in the library past midnight, attend events on campus that don't begin until 10:00 p.m., and have classes that begin or end at unusual times.

You probably want your parents to be there to listen, but not tell you what to do. Your parents may say they want you to be independent but then don't seem to trust your judgment when you make your own decisions. What is needed is compromise on both sides. Be patient and allow your parents to adapt to the changes you are making and the new demands placed on your time. They are not being difficult; they are just accustomed to the way things have been at home for many years.

How are your relationships at home right now? Over the years, most students have developed a level of trust with their parents. As you have grown and matured, the trust and corollary freedoms given to you have increased. Open and honest discussion with your parents before you encounter problems is a good way to begin exploring what changes may be needed now that you are in college. Anger and confrontation create hostilities on both sides and rarely lead to any productive changes for either of you.

Remember that your adjustment to college and its demands, if you continue to live at home, is almost as difficult for your parents as it is for you. They are beginning to realize that you are finally a "grown-up" and that you have begun the process of leaving home for good. Subconsciously, they know that in just a few years, you will graduate, join the professional working world, and be on your own with your own family and responsibilities!

LIVING ON CAMPUS

Most college campuses provide some type of on-campus residence halls or apartments for students who either live too far away to commute from home or who want the experience of living away from home. Living on campus provides more freedom and independence but also carries more responsibility; for some students, it proves to be more difficult than living at home. Every year, there are students who move into college residence halls and do not make it through the first night without calling home or, in some cases, returning home without ever attending a class!

Living on campus can be an exciting, challenging experience which provides many opportunities to learn about living on your own within a supportive environment. Roommates, resident assistants, other students, and professional staff can provide assistance and encouragement as you make the transition to college. There are people with whom you can talk about what you're experiencing. Better still, there are other students who share some of the same experiences and feelings.

For many students the biggest change from home to campus living is learning to live with others. At home, relationships were established over many years of living together. Once you move into a residence hall, you have to start developing a new set of relationships, often with people who are total strangers. Living with another person presents wonderful opportunities and, sometimes, presents serious problems.

Don't wait for little problems to reach crisis proportions! As soon as possible, sit and talk with your roommate about each other's idiosyncrasies. In a living situation, compromise is essential. If you are a night owl and your roommate likes to go to sleep right after the 11 o'clock news, you need to discuss how the two of you can compromise so that you don't argue every night about one another's habits.

There are many possible points of conflict that you can anticipate and discuss up front such as cleanliness, sharing cleaning duties, taking phone messages, having overnight guests, and adhering to university and housing rules and regulations. You will find that if you discuss differences, you can head off many potential problems. You can also find ways to compromise so that each of you feels "at home" and can maintain your preferred personal and academic routines. Keep in mind that early discussions are more likely to resolve issues than waiting until there is a problem and you or your roommate is angry.

Should you find that all your efforts fail and that you just can't get along with your roommate, don't allow the situation to have a negative effect on your academics. Make an appointment with a housing staff member to discuss the problem and what attempts have been made to alleviate the situation. You will receive advice as to what to do next, including a possible move to another room. Leaving college or moving back home should be a last resort! Learning to cope with others different from you is part of your education and will be invaluable in your future endeavors.

Living on campus can be a rewarding experience and will allow you to continue your growth and maturation to independent adulthood. While it is not always easy to live in a college residence hall, students who have this experience often form friendships that last for the rest of their lives.

HAVING A BOYFRIEND/GIRLFRIEND

Just when you think everything is going well—you made an "A" on your first college examination, you got a raise at work, and you won a pair of free tickets to a sold-out concert—you get a phone call from your boyfriend or girlfriend telling you that he/she wants to break up with you. Your world suddenly comes crashing down.

There is never a good time for a break-up, but during college, broken relationships often have a negative impact on academics. A relationship takes time, energy, and commitment, all of which are also required to be a successful student. Losing an important relationship can send you into a downspin that, if you are not careful, may cause you to hit bottom. Grades may drop and you may feel overwhelmed by all of the pressures.

The same recommendations suggested for dealing with roommates are useful in relationship problems. You should discuss the possible effects that college attendance may have on your relationship even if you have been dating for a long time and feel you know one another very well. If attending the same university, or living in the same town, share your class schedules and the amount of time you each may need for studying. Add time for extra-curricular activities, work, and other time commitments that may not involve time together. Your relationship doesn't have to suffer if you plan ahead and are clear with regard to your expectations.

The situation changes if your boyfriend/girlfriend lives elsewhere. The relationship may become strained simply because of distance. You will each meet new people and develop lives apart from one another. Be prepared for this potential problem and openly discuss your expectations. Is it okay to go out with other people? How often will you try to see one another? Talk on the telephone? Send e-mail or write letters?

Regardless of what your personal situation is, a sour romance can really put you down in the dumps. Believe it or not, it will pass! As the old song says, "breaking up is hard to do," but you will get over it. College is one of the best places to meet new people if you are interested. You can strike up a conversation with someone in class, in the library, or in the cafeteria; you can join a club or play intramural sports. From there, you are on your own!

If things are not going well, don't hurt in silence. Talk to a friend or relative; make an appointment with the university counseling center to speak with a staff member. It is perfectly normal to discuss your problems with another person, whether it is a friend or a staff member who is professionally educated to work with students. If you do decide to talk with a counseling center staff member, all conversations are confidential.

During the coming years, you will form a number of relationships and friendships. Some will be more serious than others; some will develop into life-long friendships, while others will fade away. One of these relationships may even develop into the "love" of your life! You will face challenges, particularly in your first year of college when you are feeling most alone and are, perhaps, separated from your family and friends. Learn from the challenges; use the campus resources available to assist you as you gain new experiences.

DIFFERENCES ARE VALUABLE

A college or university campus is one of the few places where every facet of society can be found, and every conflicting voice has a right to be heard. There may be times when you will be offended by what you see or hear on campus; realize that these occasions, too, are a part of your education! While you may not agree with or condone what others do or say, it is an opportunity for you to understand others better. On campus, open dialogue and discussion of issues is important to the academic process known as "academic freedom."

In the classroom, faculty members have the right to present materials and differing points of view and to delve into controversial areas openly and honestly. You will sometimes find a class uncomfortable because the views presented are different from your own; you may even feel that the professor has crossed the boundary of good taste or is talking about matters not appropriate to a college classroom. When you find yourself in this situation, ask yourself what is happening. Are your beliefs being challenged? Is the topic one that is never discussed at home?

In fact, if your education is to be genuinely valuable to you, you should encounter differing views; you should feel a little uncomfortable. More important, you should be open to hearing what professors and other students have to say! Be open to learning from others and you will learn a lot. You may not change your values or beliefs but you will have consciously chosen them from among a range of options.

NON-TRADITIONAL STUDENTS

Most of the students in this class are recent high school graduates who are considered "traditional" college students. In fact, many students are older when they begin college. Some have worked or served in the military; others have been raising children or have retired from their job; some are single parents; some are in school "just for the fun of it!" Many are attending college part-time while they hold full-time jobs or balance home and family responsibilities; some attend classes only at night or on the weekends. These are considered "non-traditional" students. They make up a growing segment of every university campus today.

As you sit in your classes, look around and see if there are any non-traditional students. Older students often have knowledge and expertise that can be valuable in and outside the classroom; yet, traditional students are often reluctant to approach them. It is difficult to return to college or begin college after a long absence from a classroom; don't be afraid to introduce yourself to a non-traditional student. Invite him or her to participate in a study group or to join you for coffee after class.

STUDENTS WITH DISABILITIES

Another growing population on college campuses is students with disabilities. While some are visible, many more are invisible because of the nature of the disability. Many students come to campus with little knowledge of the various disabilities and little experience in dealing with a person who is disabled in some way.

The most visible of the disabilities are those which are physical: the student in a wheelchair; the student using a guide dog or a cane; the student wearing a hearing aid. Many other students, however, have some form of learning disability that may not be apparent to the casual observer. On the first day of class, for example, a professor may ask for volunteer note takers to assist one or more students whose disability makes note taking difficult. You could volunteer and, as a result, become acquainted with a student who requires some accommodation in order to meet course requirements. This will broaden your experience and provide assistance to another student.

Most campuses have offices that provide assistance to students with disabilities to assure that the campus and all of its programs and services are accessible, regardless of the accommodation required. Under requirements of the Americans with Disabilities Act, any student should be able to participate in any activity or academic program offered to all students. Over the years, campuses have modified their buildings to include ramps, elevators, visual as well as audio fire alarms, and wheelchair seating in athletic arenas and theaters. Access on campus has made it possible for more students with disabilities to attend their college of choice and to successfully complete their degree of choice.

RACE AND ETHNICITY

Race and ethnic background are among the most common differences on a college campus. For many students, college is the first place they will meet people who are different from themselves in ways that are very apparent to the casual observer. Race is one of these differences and ethnic or cultural background is another.

You will probably meet people from other countries who have come to the campus to study; you will also meet people from other parts of this country whose backgrounds are different from your own. Each person you meet who is culturally or racially different from you presents an opportunity to learn about another culture or their race. In addition, the campus offers many opportunities to learn about other cultures through clubs and organizations, through programs and social activities, and through formal classes for which you might register.

SEXUAL ORIENTATION

Another visible population on many campuses are gay, lesbian, and bisexual students. College is a place where many students openly explore and question their sexual identity or orientation. It is generally accepted that approximately 10 percent of the general population is gay or lesbian, so it is likely you already know someone who is gay. Consider this as another opportunity to expand your appreciation for differences.

For many students, college is the place where they discover they are sexually attracted to someone of the same sex. Some students have been aware of such feelings for years but have never acted on them. These feelings may be unsettling because they are often in direct conflict with family beliefs, religious teachings, and attitudes of friends. To admit one might be gay or lesbian may mean being rejected by family or friends. Worse yet, it might mean being subjected to verbal harassment or physical attack.

Other students who are not gay may learn for the first time that a good friend or family member is lesbian or gay. This, too, can be unsettling and challenge one's beliefs. What does it mean if my friend is gay? How will others perceive me? How will I feel about that? What if a parent or sibling "comes out?" What will this mean to the family's relationships? These are difficult questions for which there are no simple answers.

There are many resources available to assist students who are dealing with questions of sexual orientation, whether it is their own or someone close to them. Gay and lesbian student organizations exist on many campuses; counseling centers have trained staff to provide assistance. Some campuses offer gay/lesbian studies or gender studies courses that provide an academic perspective on sexual orientation. Students who are harassed may use services available under the campus sexual harassment policy or other non-discrimination policies.

The biggest question for you is knowing who you are, understanding and accepting your feelings, and being open to others who may hold different views. You don't have to agree with someone's personal choices to be caring and supportive as a friend.

UNDERSTANDING DIVERSITY

Most students do not consider diversity on a day-to-day basis. Some simply are unaware; others have limited contact with certain groups, have no friends who are different from them, and see no reason to make changes in friendship patterns or relationships. Let's consider a context in which the importance of awareness and broadening one's knowledge of others might become more important.

According to information published by the United Nations in an **Information Bulletin** (December 1997), there are approximately 5.8 billion people in the world. Think about this population as it might be represented on a campus of 100 students. The campus population would include (based on world demographics) the following mix of students:

57 Asians
20 Europeans
7 North Americans
7 South Americans
9 Africans

Seventy percent of our group would be non-white and 30 percent white; 65 percent would be non-Christian and 35 percent would be Christian; 70 percent would not be able to read; 50 percent would suffer from malnutrition; 80 percent would live in substandard housing. The odds are only one would complete a university degree! Students in this university would know that half of the entire wealth in the world is controlled by six people, three from the United States, two from Japan, and one from Germany.

Is there a reason to become more aware of the diversity which exists around you? Keep this mythical university in mind because it represents the world in which you live and will work.

Let's go back for a moment and ask how all of this diversity is affecting **YOU**. To create new visions and missions, isn't it necessary for everyone to consider the impact of diversity at the individual and personal levels? If we are to become change agents and allies, don't we first have to become aware of our own inherent beliefs about others? And in the process, don't we also have to become aware of how these beliefs affect the day-to-day choices we make about our behavior?

Valuing diversity begins with understanding yourself. It means taking a closer look at your own experiences, background, and culture. What are the messages from your background that you embrace? That you feel might be hindering you in some way? How do you view others? Are you aware of your own stereotypes and biases? How do you view others who are different from you?

Once you have faced the first challenge, AWARENESS, you are ready to continue exploring some additional concepts regarding diversity.

STEREOTYPES

John Glenn, the first man to orbit the earth (1962), participated in another space flight when he was 77 years old. Reactions were positive, for the most part, but gave rise to many questions. Should a 77-year-old man participate in a space flight even for scientific purposes? Is he crazy or just trying to recapture his youth? Could he manage the grueling physical, psychological, and emotional stress? Is this good for a person of his age? Are the skills and abilities required for this mission found in an older person?

Think about your reactions for a moment and be honest with yourself! What are the assumptions we often make about "older" people? Are they viewed as less productive? Less physically able? Slower? Not as able to learn new things? What John Glenn did by participating in a space flight at age 77, violates our **stereotypes** about older people.

Stereotypes are views and attitudes based on our assumptions about certain groups of people. These assumptions may or may not accurately represent the group but may guide our actions toward that group or our beliefs about that group. Let's consider another situation and look at how stereotypes might influence thinking.

You are at the library and see a pregnant woman checking out a number of books on parenting. What are your assumptions? You might make the assumption that she is pregnant for the first time and wants to learn all about parenting. Your brain has interpreted some limited information by using your past experiences and beliefs about what you have observed to make a decision about this woman. Your assumptions might even be correct.

What you do not know, however, is that the woman you observed has a younger brother who recently adopted a young child and became a single parent. She is checking out the books for him because she thinks he will find them useful. She found them useful when her first child was born.

Missing information changes your view of the situation, doesn't it? Now you might ask yourself about your stereotypes regarding single men who adopt children!

Some common forms of stereotyping include the following:

Abelism: A system of exclusion and discrimination that oppresses people who have mental, emotional, or physical disabilities.

Anti-Semitism: Systematic discrimination against, condemnation, or oppression of Jews, Judaism, and the cultural, intellectual, and religious heritage of the Jewish people.

Classism: Individual, institutional, and societal beliefs and practices that assign differential value to people according to their socio-economic class.

Heterosexism: Individual, institutional, and societal beliefs based on the assumption that heterosexuality is the only normal and acceptable sexual orientation.

Sexism: Individual, institutional, and societal beliefs and practices that privilege men, subordinate women, and denigrate values and practices associated with women.

Racism: The systematic subordination of members of targeted racial groups who have relatively little social power in this country. This subordination is supported by individual, institutional, and societal beliefs and practices.

What are your stereotypes? What views based on limited information have you formed about others? How did you acquire these views and attitudes? Have you encountered exceptions, that is individuals who do not fit the stereotype?

PREJUDICE AND DISCRIMINATION

There are two more concepts which are important if you are to fully understand and begin to value differences. These are **prejudice** and **discrimination**.

Prejudice refers to a negative attitude toward members of some distinct group based solely on their membership in that group. Prejudice has behavioral, cognitive, and affective components. In other words, prejudice affects our choices, the way we see the world, the way we interpret information, and the way we feel. All of these components can cause one to take actions that may discriminate against others.

We learn prejudice just like we learn everything else: by hearing the views expressed by our parents, teachers, friends, and the media. In some cases, children are rewarded for adopting the views of their elders and punished in some way if they do not.

To begin combating prejudice, your own and that of others, the following steps are useful:

1. Become aware of your own prejudices and their origins.
2. Educate yourself about the customs and beliefs of other cultures and peoples.
3. Challenge others' prejudicial statements, ideas, and beliefs.
4. Increase contacts with individuals and groups you might otherwise avoid or with whom you might not interact on a regular basis.

Discrimination involves negative actions toward another person. Actions may be mild or severe. Avoidance, for example, is a mild form of discrimination. Not inviting someone of a different race, age, or with a disability to join a study group could be considered a form of discrimination. This form of discrimination is subtle and often denied by those who engage in it.

The most severe forms of discrimination include outward aggression and violence. Consider the pictures you've seen of the civil wars in Bosnia or in the Middle East that, in part, are linked to religious and ethnic differences among people in those regions. Consider the Civil Rights movement in this country during the 1960s or, more recently, the reports of attacks on people who are gay or lesbian. These, too, are examples of violence directed at one group by another group.

In order to combat stereotypes and discrimination, it is important to be open-minded, ask questions, and become a good listener. You need to confront your own feelings and attitudes, become better informed about people different from yourself, and challenge others who use stereotypes or discriminate in some way. Finally, become aware of media images and the possible biases presented, both positive and negative. A good way to begin is with your own campus environment.

SUMMARY

The next time you come to class, look at the classmate sitting to your right and to your left. Look at the person seated in front and behind you. These classmates are experiencing similar problems in adjusting to college. They are questioning their old habits, beliefs, and attitudes. They, too, are meeting new people different from themselves and are learning more about themselves in relation to others.

How many of your classmates have you met? Have you elected to sit with someone you already know, perhaps a friend from high school? Have you introduced yourself to anyone who appears to be different from you in some way? Someone who is older? Of a different race? With a disability? New relationships and friendships are an important part of this exciting time in your life; welcome them as learning experiences that will expand your horizons, make you a better student, and better prepare you for the world of work. The first step is the most difficult; why not start with those four people seated near you?

NAME: _____ DATE: _____

EXERCISE 1. PARENT RELATIONSHIPS: AN ASSESSMENT

Relationships with parents or other individuals who have been involved in raising you can become difficult as you approach and enter college. This is a time during which both you and they are undergoing some major life changes. Let's take a few minutes to assess what has been happening and what you would like to see happen in the next few months.

Part I. My Current Situation

1. Right now, I am living:
   - _____ at home with my parents and siblings.
   - _____ at home with one parent and siblings.
   - _____ on campus in a residence hall.
   - _____ in my own apartment or home.

2. There are other family members living in our house: _____ yes _____ no _____ sometimes

3. I share a room with:
   - _____ a brother or sister.
   - _____ another family member or spouse.
   - _____ a roommate in the residence hall.
   - _____ no one. I have my own room.

4. With regard to transportation to school:
   - _____ I have my own car.
   - _____ I drive a car my parents own.
   - _____ I share a car with a sibling.
   - _____ I use public transportation.
   - _____ I live on campus and have no car.

5. Most of my school expenses are paid by:
   - _____ me.
   - _____ my parents.
   - _____ financial aid.
   - _____ a combination.

6. For spending money, I:
   - _____ have a part-time job.
   - _____ have a full-time job.
   - _____ use savings.
   - _____ get money from parents or relatives.

7. In my living situation: _____ I decide when I come and go.

   _____ There are some rules I have to follow.

   _____ We discuss what I can and can't do.

   _____ Rules are very restrictive for me.

8. I am the: _____ oldest child _____ middle child _____ youngest child

9. I am the first child in my family to go to college. _____ yes _____ no

Summary Statement: In my living situation, I feel . . .

Part II. Thinking about My Relationship with Parents

As you think about your living situation and your family, what thoughts do you have about yourself and your relationships with parents and siblings or other family members?

1. As I thought about my living situation, I became aware that . . .

2. My parents sometimes surprise me when they . . .

3. I wish my parents understood about . . .

4. If I could say anything to my parents right now it would be . . .

Summary Statement: I see my relationships at home as . . .

NAME: _____ DATE: _____

EXERCISE 2. CULTURAL PURSUIT

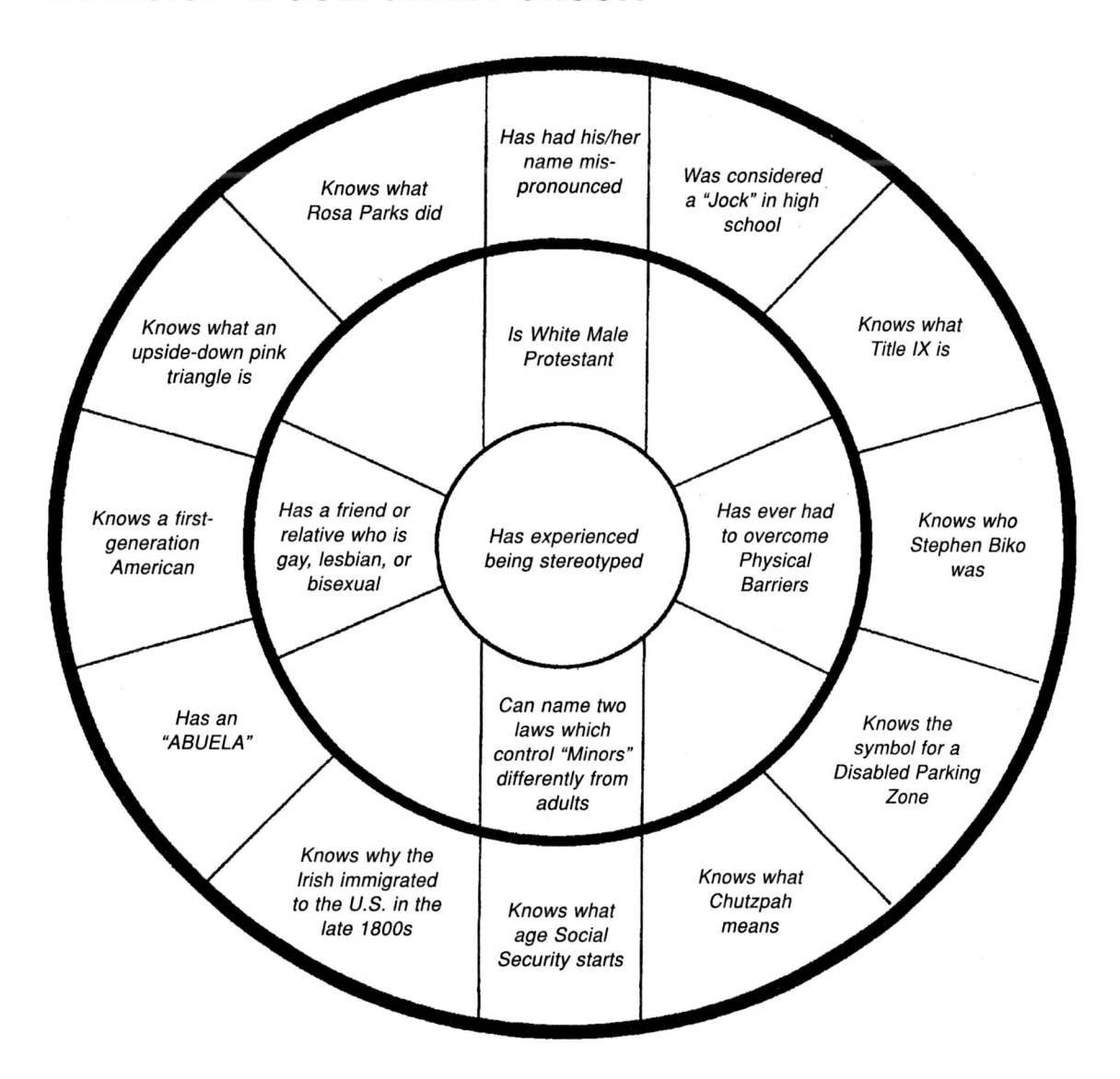

Outer ring:
- Knows what Rosa Parks did
- Has had his/her name mispronounced
- Was considered a "Jock" in high school
- Knows what Title IX is
- Knows who Stephen Biko was
- Knows the symbol for a Disabled Parking Zone
- Knows what Chutzpah means
- Knows what age Social Security starts
- Knows why the Irish immigrated to the U.S. in the late 1800s
- Has an "ABUELA"
- Knows a first-generation American
- Knows what an upside-down pink triangle is

Middle ring:
- Has a friend or relative who is gay, lesbian, or bisexual
- Is White Male Protestant
- Has ever had to overcome Physical Barriers
- Can name two laws which control "Minors" differently from adults

Center:
- Has experienced being stereotyped

Directions: Locate an individual in the class who knows the answer to a question on the circle. Write that person's name in the block. Use each person only once.

95

NAME: _____ DATE: _____

EXERCISE 3. WHAT DO YOU KNOW ABOUT MINORITY GROUPS?

1. A dulcimer is:

    a. An Appalachian folk instrument

    b. One who is low in spirits

    c. An Italian term of endearment

    d. A Native American weapon

2. The meaning of "Wounded Knee" is that:

    a. Native Americans in the 19th century viewed this as the last battle and a significant break in relationships with whites

    b. It was a rallying point for Native American militancy in the 1960s and 1970s

    c. None of the above

    d. Both a and b

3. A barrio is a:

    a. Political organization

    b. A small donkey

    c. Spanish speaking community

    d. None of the above

4. The letters "AME" are an abbreviation for:

    a. Anti-migration Effort

    b. American Muslim Enterprises

    c. African Methodist Episcopal

    d. Association of Moderate Encounters

5. Puerto Rico is an independent territory of the United States with self-governing powers.

    a. True

    b. False

6. A noted Chicano labor organizer and leader was:

    a. Pancho Villa

    b. Manuel Cortez

    c. Cesar Chavez

    d. Simon Bolivar

97

7. Name three prominent African-American writers:

8. According to most studies, what portion of the population in the United States is gay or lesbian?
   a. 1 in 50
   b. 1 in 10
   c. 1 in 100
   d. 1 in 5

9. Major league baseball did not allow any Black players until:
   a. 1925
   b. 1961
   c. 1947
   d. 1938

10. Match the following names with their achievements:

    _____ Arthur Ashe   a. wrote *Frankenstein*
    _____ Jim Thorpe   b. Gay author and activist
    _____ Jackie Robinson   c. Pilot who set speed records
    _____ Thurgood Marshall   d. First Black man to win US Open
    _____ Mary Shelley   e. First Black to win Academy Award
    _____ Frances Perkins   f. Native American Olympic athlete
    _____ Hattie McDaniel   g. First woman to hold Cabinet office
    _____ Randy Shilts   h. First Black Supreme Court justice
    _____ Henry Cisneros   i. First Hispanic mayor of major city
    _____ Jackie Cochran   j. First Black major league baseball player

NAME: _____ DATE: _____

EXERCISE 4. WHO ARE WE?

The questions below are intended to help you think and talk about your background and experiences, and learn about the experiences of other students in your class.

Instructions:

1. Form a **random** group of three students.
2. Each student should take a few minutes to complete the chart below.
3. When everyone in the group completes the chart, have each person read his/her responses to the members of the group (members should feel free to ask questions, share experiences).
4. Each student will share with the remainder of the class something interesting learned about another student's background.

Who are we?

My full name:	
The name I prefer to be called:	
The cultural meaning of my name:	
My ethnic identity:	
Place(s) my grandparents and parents were born:	
The language(s) I speak:	
My family's educational achievements:	
A person I admire:	
An attribute I like about myself or am proud of:	
A characteristic I like about my culture:	
A challenge I would like to conquer this semester:	
A challenge I would like to achieve in my lifetime:	

Adapted from materials created by The National Conference's "Actions Speak Louder: A Skills-Based Curriculum for Building Inclusion," 1995.

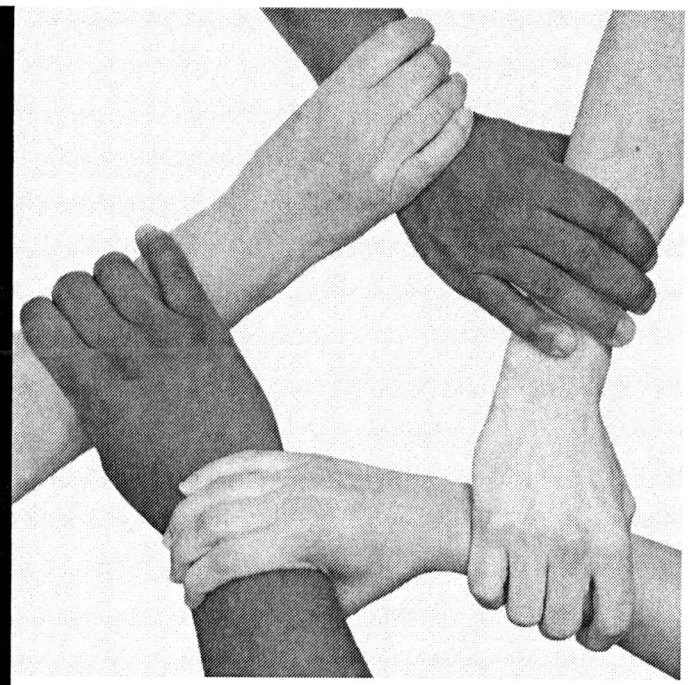

Chapter 7

Connecting Common Threads across a Diverse World

We live in an increasingly complex world that requires us to be adept in many life-skills (interpersonal communication/human relations, problem solving/decision making, physical fitness/health maintenance, and identity development/purpose-in-life). In a pluralistic society differences exist among and between various groups of people (e.g., ethnic, racial, religious, gender, sexual orientation, physical, and other groupings). While living in a pluralistic society can create tension as various groups attempt to sustain and develop their traditional culture or special interests within the confines of a common society, the experience can also create a rich source of energy that can fuel the creative potential of a society and advance it culturally and democratically. To fully develop as a person requires one to be aware of both the common threads that hold people together as a community, a nation, and a world and the unique threads of various hues and textures that complete the tapestry called humanity. It takes a multitude of skills to negotiate a diverse world.

From Life Skills for College: A Curriculum for Life *by Earl J. Ginter and Ann Shanks Glauser. Copyright © 2005 by Earl J. Ginter and Ann Shanks Glauser. Used with permission.*

MULTICULTURALISM

If we are to achieve a richer culture, rich in contrasting values, we must recognize the whole gamut of human potentialities, and so weave a less arbitrary social fabric, one in which each diverse human gift will find a fitting place.

—Margaret Mead

Multiculturalism is a philosophical belief based on ideals of social justice and equity that recognizes not only that diversity does exist but that it is a valuable resource in a community. Proponents of multiculturalism believe that it is to each and every person's advantage to acquire a set of skills, knowledge, and beliefs about diversity. These life-skills are needed individually to help us achieve success in a multicultural world and collectively to move our society beyond a toleration of differences among people to a respect for cultural pluralism.

Multiculturalism challenges us to recognize multiple perspectives, and in doing so, we enhance our problem-solving and critical-thinking skills. While adopting a multicultural perspective can prepare us to live in a multicultural world, it can also create discomfort, fear, denial, guilt, and anger during the process. People often believe that their own standards are the right standards; this view is known as *ethnocentricity*. When you have different groups of people living close to one another, and each group is functioning quite well by its own set of standards, conflict can arise as groups try to figure out what set of standards is right for the society as a whole.

College administrators understand that change is inevitable and recognize the value of a multicultural education in helping students to develop multicultural competencies. College campuses are a part of this multicultural world, and many colleges require students to take a multicultural class and, in addition, offer multidisciplinary programs (e.g., women's studies and African studies). As pointed out earlier, activities that challenge your mind expand the number and strength of neural connections that learning is based on. Engaging in activities that are unfamiliar or different (e.g., talking with people from cultures different from your own and engaging in diverse cultural experiences) helps to create a more complex system of thoughts, perceptions, assumptions, attitudes, feelings, and skills that can lead to a greater learning potential.

Manning Marable (2000) informs us that the racial composition of the United States is based on immigration, and that about a third of the total growth rate in the U.S. labor force is supplied by legal and illegal immigration. Pragmatically, students as well as others need to learn how to deal with diversity because the world in which we live is becoming more diverse. It is inevitable that among your neighbors, teachers, fellow students, coworkers, friends, and teammates will be individuals with backgrounds quite different from your own. You will need effective interpersonal skills to interact with these people. As a college student, you are in a unique learning situation that offers numerous opportunities to increase your diversity skills. If you have not formed relationships with people who have dissimilar backgrounds from you, now is your chance. People who ignore or resist opportunities may find themselves both vocationally and personally deficient in a global, multicultural society.

DEMOGRAPHIC CHANGES

The U.S. Bureau of the Census reported that in 2000 there were an estimated 281,421,906 million people living in the United States, an increase of 32.7 million people since the 1990 census. About 75.1 identified themselves as white only (down from 83% in 1990), 12.3% were black or African American only (down from 13% in 1990), 3.6% were Asian and Pacific American only, .9% were American Indian and Alaskan native only, and .1% were native Hawaiian and other Pacific Islander only. In addition, 5.5% identified themselves as some other race only, and about 2.4% selected more than one category. In response to a separate question on the census about ethnicity, 13% identified themselves as Hispanic or Latino, who may be of any race (up from 11% in 1990). The Hispanic or Latino population rose about 69% since 1990 (from 22.4 million to 35.3 million). Projections for the year 2050 are that the percentage of white people living in the United States will continue to decline and the percentage of current minorities will increase. The Hispanic or Latino population will show the largest increase (24%) followed by African Americans (15%). Today, most immigrants in this country come from Latin America, followed by Asia, and most immigrants settle in the western and southern parts of our nation. Some cities like Miami, where more than 59% of the population is foreign born, are more diverse than other cities.

Along with racial and ethnic demographic shifts there have been dramatic changes related to gender and age. Females (143,368,000) outnumbered males (138,054,000) in the United States in 2000, and women and minorities were identified as the largest groups of people to enter the work force. The *World Almanac* (2002) refers to the United States as an "aging nation" with a median age of 35.3, the highest ever reported. In 2000, it was estimated that there were about 4.2 million (1.5% of the total population) Americans 85 years or older and about 50,454 centenarians (people aged 100 and older) living in the United States. Centenarians have increased 35% in numbers since 1990. The 2000 census identified South Dakota, Iowa, and the District of Columbia as the states having the largest percentage of centenarians among their populations. What do you think accounts for such longevity? Researchers are looking for the answers as you read this.

Unfortunately, with the rise in diversity has also come a rise in the number of incidents related to prejudice and discrimination. According to the National Institute Against Prejudice and Violence (NIAPV), more than 250 of the nation's 3,300 colleges and universities have reported acts of violence against people due to their ethnicity since mid-1986.

LIVING IN A PLURALISTIC SOCIETY

Two primary goals of a college education are to help you develop life-long skills for continuous personal growth and to be a responsible community member. Today's college students do not believe that there are any quick fixes for our nation's social problems. One of the biggest social problems facing college students today on college campuses throughout the United States is racism. Racism is a form of discrimination based on biased assumptions about what people are and are not. It is a powerful force throughout the nation, weaving in and out of cultures, institutions, and individuals. Racism, ableism, sexism, heterosexism, ageism, and classism are all powerful discriminatory forces. These isms have the power to include, exclude, legitimize, and marginalize groups of people. Assumptions about what people are and are not enable prejudices and discrimination to flourish.

Throughout the world, countries are becoming more pluralistic. Diversity encompasses differences in educational level, gender, ethnicity, race, age, sexual orientation, religion, socioeconomic level, and physical ability. In the last 25 years there has been a dramatic shift in population trends in the United States, and the demographics of this country will continue to shift. The pluralities and complexities that exist between and among groups of people will also continue to change as differences in language, politics, regional differences, social class, religion and nationality further subdivide groups. Marable (2000) calls for a new and critical study of race and ethnicity to understand the changes that are taking place around us. He believes that one of the reasons that discussions about race and social diversity are so difficult is the complicated relationship between ethnicity and race.

TERMINOLOGY

The terminology associated with multiculturalism is continually changing to more accurately reflect changing attitudes about diversity. Currently you will read about "people of color" rather than nonwhites; gays, lesbians, and bisexuals rather than homosexuals; and people with disabilities rather than disabled or handicapped. Even though many people, through a process like stereotyping, choose to define you rather narrowly, most people choose to define themselves in broad, diverse categories. What comes to mind when you think of a nontraditional student? A fraternity member? A gay student? A Hispanic or Latino student? An Asian student? A student with disabilities? Culture refers to a way of being, the way we define ourselves. If someone asks you to define your culture, you might choose a narrow definition and respond that you are Catholic, Baptist, American, or German. You might also choose a broader definition of culture and respond that you are a musician, a Southerner, an athlete, or a member of a sorority.

What about race? Is it a social concept used to discriminate against groups of people or is it a biological/genetic concept? There is a lot of controversy in the literature about the definition of race. Pedersen (1994) defines race as "a pseudobiological system of classifying persons by a shared genetic history or physical characteristics such as skin color" (p. x). Race is a topic that people struggle to talk about with one another. Talking about race can be especially challenging due to the political and emotional misapplications of the term. For the first time in the history of the census, respondents in 2000 were given the choice of selecting one or more race categories to identify their racial identity. About 2.4% (6.8 million) of the total population chose more than one category of race. Questions about being Hispanic or Latino were designated a separate category. As pointed out previously, there is often more diversity within a group of people who are regarded as having similar characteristics than there is between different groups.

Ethnicity exists within the broader category of race. Ethnic groups such as Japanese, Cambodian, Chinese, Korean, Filipino, Vietnamese, and Pacific Islander fall under the racial umbrella of Asian. Hispanics, or Latinos, as some people prefer, are Spanish-speaking people. Some Hispanic people may be from Puerto Rico, the Dominican Republic, Mexico, Cuba, Colombia, or Argentina. Hispanics are a very diverse group with varied customs, food, cultural patterns, and politics. People who refer to themself as black might look to Africa, Haiti, Jamaica, or the West Indies for their cultural heritage. People who identify with having a white ethnic background may look to Poland, Australia, Italy, Africa, Ireland, or Germany. Among the American Indian and Alaska native population, you will also find a multiplicity of cultural patterns.

Before you read about suggestions for developing multicultural competencies, in the next section, take a moment to become familiar with some of the terms associated with diversity and multiculturalism.

ableism	prejudice or discrimination against people with mental, emotional, and physical disabilities
ageism	prejudice or discrimination based on age
anti-Semitism	hostility toward Jewish people
classism	prejudice or discrimination based on economic background
culture	group of people bound together by traditions (food, language, religion) and values
discrimination	an action or policy that differentiates one group from another in terms of treatment
ethnocentrism	a belief that one's own culture is more correct or superior
homophobia	an irrational fear of gays, lesbians, or bisexuals
prejudice	preconceived opinion for or against someone or something
privilege	unearned access to resources due to membership in a particular social group
racism	discrimination based on skin color and ethnicity; a belief that a particular race is superior or inferior
sexism	prejudice or discrimination based on gender
stereotyping	overgeneralizing about groups of people based on biased assumptions

DEVELOPING MULTICULTURAL COMPETENCIES

We know that our attitudes and beliefs influence our perceptions. We assimilate attitudes and beliefs throughout our lives, forming assumptions about the way things are and are not, including judgments about people. Unfortunately, we tend to filter out information that does not affirm, or align with, our perception of the world, so we tend to rely on many biased assumptions to guide us through life. Biased assumptions distort the truth and give rise to prejudices that keep us confined in narrowly defined spaces. Is there any way for us to get out of our own little boxes to see what is truly going on around us? The answer is, emphatically, yes! Biases can be intentional or unintentional. They might be based on cultural isolation or ignorance. When you form a belief about an entire group of people without recognizing individual differences among members of the group, you are engaging in *stereotyping*.

We are all guilty of stereotyping because of the way in which the mind stores, organizes, and recalls information to reduce complexity and help us make quick decisions (Johnson & Johnson, 2000). Johnson and Johnson report that the term stereotype was initially used in the eighteenth century to describe a printing process that duplicated pages of type. According to Johnson and Johnson (2000) it was not until 1922 that Walter Lippman used the term to describe the process by which people gloss over details to simplify social perceptions. We tend to stereotype people to whom we do not pay much attention. The practice of stereotyping can lead to prejudice, which can lead to discrimination.

What can you do to overcome biases that cloud your perceptions and create distortions? How do you move beyond intolerance and prejudice? These are questions that have no easy answers. Examining your own attitudes, becoming more aware of other cultures, and developing a multicultural view that will help you communicate, appreciate, and respect people from diverse backgrounds are steps in the right direction.

Examine Your Attitudes

Your culture surrounds you. Culture influences the way you think, feel, and behave. Identities are forged within the cultural context in which you live. Society, the larger culture in which you live, sends both positive and negative messages about the self. Unconscious or conscious beliefs about the way you are suppose to be can create a great deal of pain for those who are excluded and marginalized by the majority members of society. If while you were growing up you received a constant stream of negative messages that you were not okay because your cultural rules were different from those in the dominant culture, you may have internalized feelings that you are not okay. Prejudice has a negative impact on the process of identity formation. Examine some of your own prejudices by answering the questions in Exercise 1.

Attitudes can create barriers to interacting with people from diverse backgrounds. When you see someone walking toward you, what do you tend to notice? Gender? Weight? Skin color? Clothing? Hair? What kinds of assumptions do you make based on your observations? Student? Sorority girl? Nontraditional student? Professor? Athlete? Foreigner? Finally, what assumptions do you make about each kind of person? We all assume things about people. Just remember that your assumptions are often incorrect. Prejudice is a learned habit, and it takes a conscious effort to break it.

Sources of Prejudice

Where do these prejudices come from? They come from a variety of sources.

Economic Competitiveness and Scapegoating. Scapegoating is the process of displacing aggression or projecting guilt onto a group of people. When the economy is bad, accusations like "Those immigrants are taking away all our jobs" increase in frequency. Political candidates sometimes appeal to prejudices among voters. They may scapegoat immigrants, for example, in an effort to win votes from those who feel disempowered or frustrated with the economy.

Parents and Relatives. What messages did your parents send about other people? When you were young and found yourself near a person in a wheelchair, what messages did you receive about how to behave? Did you observe the adult look away or maybe address the person accompanying the person with the disability rather than communicating directly with the person who was disabled? What about when you asked a parent if a friend who was from another socioeconomic or cultural group could come home with you or if you could go to his or her house? Messages can be overt or covert. The effect is the same. When negative messages are attached to differences between people, prejudice takes root.

Institutions. Prejudice is learned through living in a society where prejudices are sustained. Who received the most privileges in your school? Did the gifted students get to engage in more creative learning situations than the other students? What about overweight children in your school? How were they treated? Who participated in sports and organizations with you? Were accommodations made for someone who was mentally or physically disabled? As a child, were you ever conscious of the fact that all U.S. presidents have been white males?

Media. What kinds of messages do you receive from magazines, movies, and television? What prejudices are perpetuated in the media? What groups of people are stereotyped? What types of misinformation about certain groups of people are broadcast? When you watch television or go to a movie, how are women depicted? How often are they depicted as sex symbols? Stereotyping is based on ignorance. Have you heard any disparaging remarks about others lately through the media? What about jokes about religion, sexual orientation, skin color, or weight?

Social Fragmentation. Levine and Cureton (1998) found that undergraduate students across the country described themselves more in terms of differences than similarities. Their study also revealed that students today are more socially isolated than previous generations; increasingly, they voluntarily segregate themselves to form small self-interest groups. Look around you. Do gaps between socioeconomic groups in this country seem to be widening?

The sources that fuel prejudice come together to create a powerful, destructive force that can lead to discrimination and even violence. The number of reported incidents of prejudice and discrimination are reported to be on the rise throughout the country. The Anti-Defamation League and the National Institute Against Prejudice and Violence (NIAPV) record and report incidents of prejudice, discrimination, and hate crimes. The brutal murders of Matthew Shepard, a gay, white man who was a student at the University of Wyoming, and James Byrd, Jr., a black man who was chained to the back of a pickup truck and dragged to his death, outraged the country. Yet *Life* magazine reported that at Matthew Shepard's funeral, a protestor appeared with a sign that read "God hates fags."

The Power of Prejudice

Ableism. Joy Weeber (1999), a person with a disability, has written about being discriminated against and described how painful it is. She wrote that her pain was caused by unconscious beliefs of a society that assume that everyone is, or should be, normal, . . . "capable of total independence and pulling themselves up by their own bootstraps" (p. 21).

She defined ableism as a form of prejudice and bigotry that has as its core a belief in the superiority of being nondisabled and an assumption that those who are disabled wished they could be nondisabled—at any cost.

Laura Rauscher and Mary McClintock (1998) offer the following comments to help educate people about disability and oppression.

- Disability is not inherently negative.
- Becoming disabled involves major life changes including loss as well as gain, but it is not the end of a meaningful and productive existence.
- People with disabilities experience discrimination, segregation, and isolation as a result of other people's prejudice and institutional ableism, not because of the disability itself.
- Social beliefs, cultural norms, and media images about beauty, intelligence, physical ability, communication, and behavior often negatively influence the way people with disabilities are treated.
- Societal expectations about economic productivity and self-sufficiency devalue persons who are not able to work, regardless of other contributions they may make to family and community life.
- Without positive messages about who they are, persons with disabilities are vulnerable to internalizing society's negative messages about disability.
- Independence and dependence are relative concepts, subject to personal definition, something every person experiences, and neither is inherently positive or negative.
- The right of people with disabilities to inclusion in the mainstream of our society is now protected by law, yet they are still not treated as full and equal citizens.

Heterosexism. Heterosexism is the belief that heterosexuality is the only acceptable sexual orientation. In recent years in the United States, there has been increased visibility, via news coverage, movies, advertisements, and television, of gay, lesbian, and bisexual people. Pat Griffin and Bobbie Harro (1997) point out that despite the increased visibility, most Americans continue to have contradictory feelings about gay, lesbian, and bisexual people, and that educators have been uncommonly reluctant to address the issue of homophobia in the schools. Silence about issues that minimize particular groups of people can have devastating effects. The Department of Health and Human Services Report on teen suicide (1989) indicated that lesbian, gay, and bisexual young people are two to three times more likely to commit suicide. Prejudice and discrimination are powerful forces that isolate and marginalize people in society. The first step to getting beyond prejudice and intolerance is to examine your own attitudes and beliefs about people. The second step is to develop an awareness of other cultures.

Developing an Awareness of Other Cultures. Educate yourself about issues related to multiculturalism. Make an effort to get to know people from dissimilar backgrounds. Your college probably hosts a variety of cultural events throughout the year. Many international student organizations sponsor cultural nights, which students and the community are invited to attend. Discover when they are and make a commitment to be there. Develop an open mind, like an anthropologist observing other cultures. As you begin to observe other cultures, be aware of your own cultural filters.

Colleges offer opportunities to study abroad. If your college does not offer a study program in a country you wish to visit, check with other colleges and see what they have to offer. Immerse yourself in different cultures. Ask lots of questions. Learn about different international organizations on campus and in your community. Also check with your local Chamber of Commerce for local cultural celebrations.

You can also educate yourself about other cultures by watching videos. Try renting some international movies the next time you pick up a video at your local video rental store. Having to read subtitles cannot be used as an excuse! Your aim is to become more immersed in another culture. You might also try attending a different place of worship or interviewing other students about their experiences living in a different culture. The more personal information you have about another person or another culture, the less likely you are to stereotype that person or culture.

DEVELOPING A MULTICULTURAL VIEW

Developing a multicultural view requires the motivation to develop better diversity skills to interact with a wider range of people. For some people, the motivation to become multiculturally competent arises from a desire to become a social change agent in the community by helping other people develop more tolerant attitudes. Some people view this as a way of supporting their country, since democracy is a system based on mutual respect and equality of rights. There are things you can do to help build a healthier approach to living in a multicultural society.

Develop Good Critical-Thinking Skills. Learn to think through your assumptions about different groups of people. Remember that your assumptions are based on your experiences. Since your experiences are necessarily limited, your assumptions are going to have many biases where you filled in the gaps. The process of critical thinking can help you get beyond preconceived notions that have been formulated over the years and see the truth.

Part of the process of developing good critical thinking skills is becoming aware of the influence you have on other people. Starting with yourself, think of how you influence friends and family, people at work and school, and your community. What actions could you implement within each one of these spheres to combat sexism, racism, ableism, and other discriminatory isms? How can you change your environment to encourage a multicultural view of the world?

Educate Others about Laws and Policies. There are campus policies and laws to deal with acts of bigotry and discrimination. Become familiar with them. What kind of sexual harassment policy does your college enforce? In 1990 the Americans with Disabilities Act (ADA), a civil rights act for people with disabilities, passed into law. It states that all public facilities, including colleges, are required by law to make a serious effort to provide barrier-free access to all persons with disabilities. When you are eating out in a restaurant, do you ever wonder whether or not the restaurant you are dining in is accessible to all?

Many restaurants and public places are not. How does your college respond to incidents of bigotry? Bigotry can appear in many forms: graffiti, physical violence, written and spoken remarks, and privileges. What about invited or uninvited outside speakers who come to campus to speak with students? Should a student newspaper be allowed to run an advertisement that provides misinformation about a group of people and promotes racism, sexism, anti-Semitism, or any other form of intolerance? What about running a cartoon that is demeaning to people with disabilities in a campus, local, or national newspaper?

The issue of political correctness (PC) has been debated on campuses and throughout society. Pedersen (1994) states, "Philosophically, PC means the subordination of the right to free speech to the right of guaranteeing equal protection under the law. The PC position contends that an absolutist position on the First Amendment (that you may slur anyone you choose) imposes a hostile environment for minorities and violates their right to equal education. Promotion of diversity is one of the central tenets of PC" (p. 5). Are you an advocate or proponent of PC? Why? Or why not?

SOURCES

Barron, W. G. (2002). United States population: Census 2000—The results start rolling in. In W. A. McGeveran (Ed.), *The world almanac and book of facts 2002* (pp. 374–385). New York: World Almanac Books.

Glauser, A., & Bozarth, J. D. (2001). Person-centered counseling: The culture within. *Journal of Counseling & Development, 79,* 142–147.

Glauser, A. (1999). Legacies of racism. *Journal of Counseling & Development, 77,* 62–67.

Glauser, A. (1996). *Dangerous habits of the mind: Getting beyond intolerance and prejudice.* Presentation made at the 1996 World Conference of the American Counseling Association, Pittsburgh, PA.

Goodman, D., & Schapiro, S. (1997). Sexism curriculum design. In Adams, M., Bell, L., & Griffin, P. (Eds.). *Teaching for diversity and social justice: A sourcebook* (pp. 110–140). New York: Routledge.

Griffin, P. & Harro, B. (1997). Heterosexism curriculum design. In Adams, M., Bell, L., & Griffin, P. (Eds.). *Teaching for diversity and social justice: A sourcebook* (pp. 141–169). New York: Routledge.

Johnson, D., & Johnson, F. (2000). *Joining together.* Boston: Allyn and Bacon.

Levine, A., & Cureton, J. S. (1998). *When hope and fear collide.* San Francisco: Jossey-Bass.

Life: The year in pictures, 1998. (1999). New York: Time.

Marable, M. (February 25, 2000). We need new and critical study of race and ethnicity. *Chronicle of Higher Education,* B4–B7.

Pedersen, P. (1994). *A handbook for developing multicultural awareness.* Alexandria, VA: American Counseling Association.

Princeton Language Institute. (1993). *Twenty-first century dictionary of quotations.* New York: Dell.

Rauscher, L., & McClintock, M. (1997). Ableism curriculum design. In Adams, M., Bell., L., & Griffin, P. (Eds.). *Teaching for diversity and social justice: A sourcebook* (pp. 198–230). New York: Routledge.

U.S. Department of Health and Human Services. (1989). *Report of the Secretary's Task Force on Youth Suicide.* Rockville, MD: Author.

Weeber, J. E. (1999). What could I know of racism? *Journal of Counseling & Development, 77,* 20–23.

Wijeyesinghe, C. L., Griffin, P., & Love, B. (1997). Racism curriculum design. In Adams, M., Bell, L. & Griffin, P. (Eds.). *Teaching for diversity and social justice: A sourcebook* (pp. 82–109). New York: Routledge.

NAME: _____ DATE: _____

EXERCISE 1. ASSESSING CULTURAL INFLUENCES

1. When were you first aware of differences among people?

2. When did you become aware of your own racial/ethnic heritage?

3. When did you first experience some form of prejudice? Do you remember your thoughts and feelings?

4. When did you become aware that you had certain privileges, or that you were denied privileges, based on your physical characteristics, socioeconomic background, or ability level?

5. How have others stereotyped you or members of your family?

6. What kinds of messages did you receive as a child that you were inferior or superior to others? Who or what sent these messages?

NAME: _____ DATE: _____

EXERCISE 2. REFLECTING ON RACE RELATIONS

1. Do you think that only certain groups of people are racist? Give examples.

2. How can your college better recruit minorities to enroll at your college?

3. What are race relations like in your community? What about on campus?

4. How can you constructively confront prejudice and discrimination on a personal level?

5. If you were in a position of authority, what could you do to bring your community together to celebrate diversity?

Section 2
Understanding the Learning Process

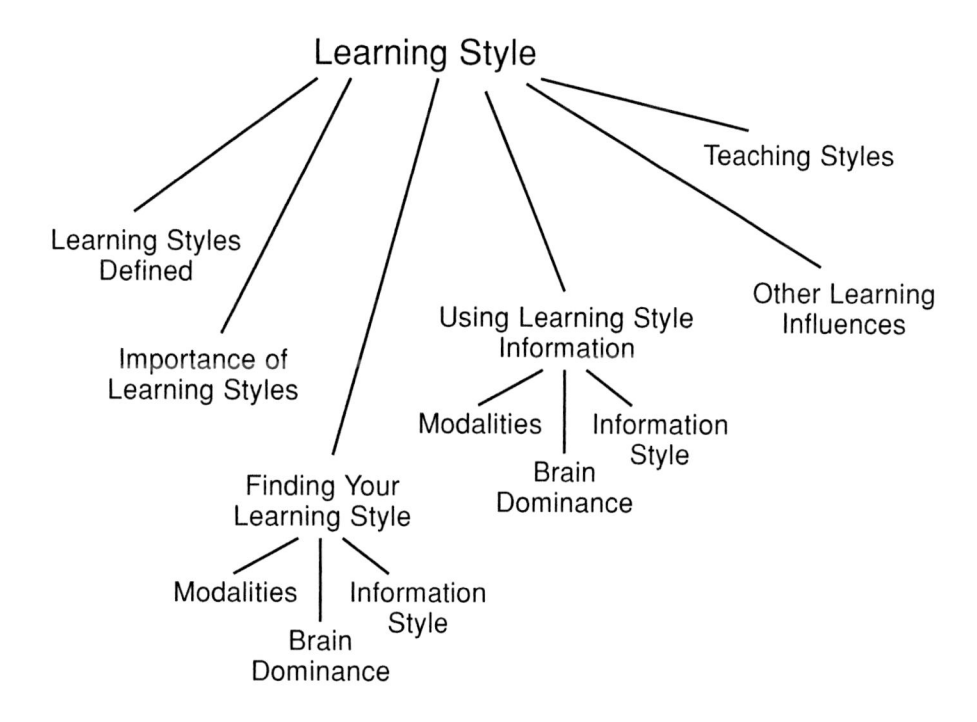

Chapter 8

Learning with Style

This chapter deals with learning styles and how the styles affect your learning. As you read through and do the exercises, keep in mind that there are no right or wrong answers. The goal is to help you find your learning style and use it to your advantage. In the process you will also find out more about your weaknesses. The more you know about yourself and the way you learn, the more effectively you can put that information to use in your college courses. Getting the most information from instructors and textbooks is important to your success. Discovering your learning style can help you be a better, more successful student (if you use the information).

WHAT IS A LEARNING STYLE?

Before continuing, it is necessary to make clear just what is meant by learning style. Scholars have different opinions regarding what should or shouldn't be included in the definition. For our purposes, learning style is the characteristic and preferred way one takes in and interacts with information, and the way one responds to the learning environment. Think of your particular learning style as the way you prefer to learn new or difficult information, and the way you find it easiest and most comfortable to learn.

From Practical Approaches for Building Study Skills and Vocabulary, Second Edition *by Gary D. Funk, Jan Bradley, JoBelle Hopper, Myrna Hite-Walker, and Michele M. Jerde. Copyright © 1996 by Kendall/Hunt Publishing Company. Used with permission.*

To illustrate, suppose that you are given a learning task. What is the first thing you would prefer to do to get the new information—read about it in a book; listen to someone talk about it; or do something with the information to prove that you know it? None of the ways is the right or best way, they are simply examples of different ways to learn. You may prefer one, or a combination of those listed. There is no best way to learn, just different ways. The goal for you is to find your preferred learning style.

Depending on which expert you ask, there are many different ways to consider learning styles and many ways to analyze them. This chapter will only touch on a few. If you feel that you would benefit from a more extensive diagnosis, you should get in touch with your campus counseling or testing center.

Your learning style may be more difficult to determine now than it would have been in elementary school. The reason is that as you get older and become a more mature learner, your learning style becomes more integrated. You have probably learned that you have to use many different ways to get information depending on the learning situation. When you answer the questions on the various learning style inventories given later in this chapter, keep in mind that you want to answer them thinking about your preferences. Answer them based on what you are most comfortable doing, and what's easiest for you. The more accurate the picture of your learning style, the more you can use it to help you.

WHY SHOULD YOU KNOW ABOUT YOUR LEARNING STYLE?

One of the goals of a college education is to make you an independent learner (also, a goal of study skills). There will be many things you will have to learn after you complete your degree, and helping you learn HOW to learn is an important aspect of your education. Knowing how you learn will help you begin to monitor your learning. The more aware you are of the way you learn, the better you can be at determining where you need help and where you don't.

As you study information by reading a textbook for example, if you are not understanding what you are reading, you need to make adjustments in the method you are using. You may try one of several options—reading the material aloud, silently reading it over again, asking someone from your class to explain it, or whatever might work. If you know what your learning style is, you will have a better idea about the one or two strategies more likely to work for you. This makes you more efficient (you don't have to try everything to find a strategy that works) and it makes you more effective because you can change strategies and understand the difficult material more clearly.

Some research indicates that grades are better, and the learner is more motivated when taught using the preferred learning style. The research also indicates a tendency in learners to retain the information better. Although you can't usually make choices about how your instructors will present information to you, you can choose how you will study on your own. This independent studying is the way you will be getting more of your information in college.

Strengths and Weaknesses

Knowing your learning style can also help you understand why certain types of information are easier or more difficult for you to learn. Being aware of weaknesses can help you be prepared for them. For example, if you know that you have trouble with numbers, then you know that your math class (necessary for meeting general education requirements) is going to be difficult for you. You can be better prepared by scheduling the class at a time when you are most alert, finding a tutor early on in the class, or scheduling it during a semester when you can devote the necessary time and effort to it. Your awareness of weak areas will help you be prepared for problems and prevent some, instead of being caught by surprise.

By knowing your strengths, you can overcome the problems and weaknesses. If you know the ways you are most comfortable learning, you can use those to help you learn difficult material. If you know, for example, that you need to read information to really understand it, then you know that you have to read the text chapter before you go to the lecture class. Hearing about something is not your preferred way to get information. You have to prepare yourself to be a better listener by reading first (using a strength).

As indicated earlier, as you mature, your learning style becomes more integrated. This does not mean that you don't have preferences. It only means that you have learned how to get information and use your weaker areas better. You will not always get information in your preferred style, so you must learn to use those styles which are less comfortable for you. Some students learn this easier and more quickly than others. By helping you see your style, you can also find the areas which need attention. The ultimate goal for a student is to use any learning style comfortably depending what's best for the situation. That may not be practical, but you need to be fairly competent getting and using information in several ways. This will help you with instructors who use only one method of getting information across, and will give you more options when faced with difficult material to learn. Most of us learn better when we use more than one modality to get it.

WHAT IS YOUR LEARNING STYLE?

Modality Strength

The first survey is an informal look at whether you prefer the auditory, visual, or kinesthetic modes. Auditory learners like to learn by listening. Visual learners prefer reading or watching, and kinesthetic learners learn by doing (touching or manipulating) or using their hands in some way.

Answer the survey by checking those statements which are MOST like you, or are like you most of the time.

Brain Dominance

The next inventory will help you determine your brain dominance. The results of this inventory and what brain dominance means will be discussed later in the chapter. Answer the questions using the answer sheet given.

Information Style

The final inventory will help you determine your preferences for taking in information and the way you work with that information. Answer the questions according to the instructions given.

Results

Now that you have these results, you can begin to see the way you prefer to learn. The results of the surveys are informal, and if you think you could benefit from a more in-depth diagnosis, you should contact your campus counseling or testing center. They will have other tests which will give you more information.

HOW CAN YOU USE YOUR LEARNING STYLE?

Going back to the checklist for your modality strengths, look at your preferences regarding auditory, visual, and kinesthetic. If you have a strong preference for one over the others, you probably have some idea that you learn better if you receive information in a particular way. You would prefer to work with or react to information in that same mode.

If you don't find that you have a strong preference for one learning style over the others, you may have found that you prefer to receive information one way, but you would rather react to it or work with it in another way. Or you may have found that you are well integrated in these areas, and show no strong preferences in receiving or reacting to information.

The following suggestions will be categorized according to the modality area. It's a good idea to read over all of the suggestions, keeping in mind your strengths and weaknesses. The type of material you are responsible for getting in different classes should also be considered when choosing a strategy to use. Generally, the more senses you can use, the better you learn and remember the information. Sometimes it will be helpful to concentrate on your strong areas especially with difficult material.

Suggestions for Auditory Strengths

General Hints

You will benefit from hearing information—audio tapes, your own voice, or lectures.

You may want to make tapes of reading assignments or class notes.

Pretend that you are teaching someone else the information and explain it out loud.

Reading aloud notes or text material will help you.

Lecture Hints

Use a cassette tape player for pre-testing by asking yourself questions, leaving a 2–3 second blank space, and then giving the answer.

Use a cassette player to record difficult material from your notes and then listen to the information as needed.

Orally test yourself by asking questions from your notes.

Read aloud any difficult material in your notes.

If you can't read aloud, try vocalizing the words quietly.

Textbook Hints

Read aloud summary statements, headings, and subheadings before you begin reading a chapter.

Restate key ideas to yourself as you read material. Keep a "conversation" going with your text as you read (agree or disagree with the author, or question key ideas).

For difficult material, restate in your own words what you have just read.

Read aloud, vocalize, or whisper passages that are difficult.

Read vocabulary words and their definitions before you begin reading.

After reading, quiz yourself (aloud) over the vocabulary.

Orally quiz yourself over selected main ideas.

Tape yourself reading difficult text sections, and then go back and listen to them.

Suggestions for Visual Strengths

General Hints

You will benefit from seeing information—either in print or from videos, charts, or overheads.

It will be easier for you to remember what you read than what you hear.

When given information orally, you should write it down or take some notes.

Lecture Hints

Read the text before attending lectures.

Take notes over lecture material.

For difficult or confusing material, use a mapping technique along with notes (mapping is drawing a diagram of the material read, using only the main ideas, then showing the relationship among the ideas with lines connecting them).

Use white space on your page as a guide when taking notes (skip lines between main ideas).

To learn material, stare off into space and remember what the written information looked like on your page.

Textbook Hints

Preview chapters by reading the headings, subheadings, and outlines before reading the chapter.

Watch for topic sentences. Reread them to help you stay with the material being read. Underline topic sentences.

Draw a diagram, jot down a list, use mapping, or make a chart to help you retain difficult material.

Underline key words and concepts as you read. Marking your text will be very helpful.

Suggestions for Kinesthetic Strengths

General Hints

You learn best by doing. The more involved you are with material, the easier it is for you to learn.

You should try to find practical applications for information. When you can, do projects and experiments using what you learn.

Write information down.

Moving your fingers along the lines as you read may help.

Lecture Hints

Take notes and go back over them, making special marks for important material or material you need to go over more.

For difficult or confusing material, answer practice questions in writing.

Write difficult information in the air with your finger.

Use your hand as a marker as you go through your notes.

Textbook Hints

Use your hand or finger as a guide as you read.

For difficult material, draw a chart or diagram to help you understand what you read.

Underline important words and concepts as you study.

Making and using study cards will help you learn difficult material.

Use 3 x 5 cards with a question on one side and the answer on the other. You can also put charts, lists, and diagrams on small cards to use for studying.

Use your finger to point out summary information, main points, and headings and subheadings as you read.

BRAIN DOMINANCE

Research on the two brain hemispheres began in the 1950s with Dr. Roger Sperry. Dr. Sperry found that the two hemispheres (or halves) of the brain processed information differently, and both were equally important to the whole person. The functions of the hemispheres had previously been found to be different—with speech being a left brain function and spatial (visual) capability being in the right. It was not known until Dr. Sperry's research that the processing of information was different for each of the halves. The left brain is linear and processes in a sequential manner, while the right brain uses a global process.

It seems that schools and their curriculums favor the left hemisphere. In other words, we are given a major dose of left brain learning in school, and the right brain is neglected. Most of us probably learned that success in school depended to a great degree on choosing the proper hemisphere to process information. We didn't consciously make this choice, but we could figure out what would be required of us, and we would do that to be successful. This may have caused many students problems if they were unable to use the left brain easily, or if they couldn't determine what to do to be successful.

Research findings indicate that the learning of most information is better when both the right and left hemispheres are used. If your results from the inventory indicate that you do not have a dominance in the right or the left hemisphere, and that you are integrated, you are achieving the best for learning. You can use both sides of your brain equally well. You can choose one over the other when the situation calls for it.

If you have a strong tendency or preference for either the right or the left hemisphere, you may find yourself having trouble in various learning situations. As with your modalities, integration is the key to becoming a better learner. Use the list of characteristics on the following page to find areas where you can develop or polish your weak areas. Also, use them to help you with difficult material—use your strong areas to compensate for your weak areas. The more integrated you become, the more you are free to choose different ways to process information, depending on what's best for a given situation.

The box on brain dominance characteristics lists some of the characteristics of left brain dominant and right brain dominant people. You will find characteristics in both lists that describe you, but you should find more in the list that corresponds to your results on the survey. If you are an integrated person, you should find that the two lists have about an equal number of characteristics which fit you.

INFORMATION STYLE

In the final learning style inventory, you indicated your preferences for perceiving and processing information. Look at the descriptions on the following page. This will give you a clearer picture of your preferences.

These categories came about as the result of research done by Dr. David Kolb in the early 1970s. The survey that you took is the result of Bernice McCarthy's research of the 1970s. Many other researchers have come up with similar findings over the years. The researchers have been experts in the fields of psychology, education, and business. Their findings are amazingly close when defining characteristics of people in the four areas (although their names for the different styles are different).

Most of us can perceive information either abstractly or concretely and then process it actively or reflectively, but we are more comfortable perceiving and processing in a certain way.

Whether we perceive or process information one way or another is probably the result of heredity, past experiences, and the demands of the present environment on us. We would be better learners if we used each information style equally well, based on what the situation required. When you read over the descriptions of the information styles, think about ways you can build on your strengths and develop your weak areas.

The way you perceive and process information influences the career choices you make, the way you get along with others, the way you solve problems, and the types of subjects you prefer, to mention only a few. You will probably be more comfortable if you follow your natural inclinations. The problem may be that you have had to use one information style so much up to this point, that you have stifled your more natural choice. Again, integration is the key, and the more you can refine your skills in all areas, the better off you will be. You may make some discoveries about your true preferences along the way!

BRAIN DOMINANCE CHARACTERISTICS

Left Hemisphere
Objective
Rational
Sequential and systematic
Like right and wrong answers
Structured
Questioning
Need constant reinforcement
Contract-liking people
Organized
List makers
Time conscious
Follow directions closely
Rely on language in thinking and remembering
Good planners
Accomplish things quickly
See cause and effect
Prone to stress-related ills
Perfectionists
Control feelings
Do one task at a time
Need gentle risking situations
Analytic
Solve problems by looking at the parts
Verbal
Recognize names
More serious
Dislike improvising
Abstract thinkers
Focus on reality
Work on improving the known
Like non-fiction
Learn for personal achievement
Extrinsically motivated
Prefer objective tests

Right Hemisphere
Use visualization
Intuitive
Rely on images for thinking and remembering
Risk-takers
Need neat environment
Long-term memory good
Short-term memory bad
Prefer subjective tests
Random learning and thinking
Short attention spans
Respond to demonstrated instructions
Need touching
Don't read directions
Don't pay attention
Pilers
More flexible
More fun loving
Accident prone
Need to have goals set for them
Multi-tasks needed
Creative
Visual learners
Solve problems by looking at the whole picture
Like humor
Recognize faces
Like improvising
Think geometrically
Dreamers
Assuming
Like fantasy
Inventors
Intrinsically motivated
Learn for personal awareness
Free with feelings

Now that you have some idea of your learning style, you may begin to see how difficult it is to separate the areas. You may have found that you had trouble with some of the questions because you could think of instances when all of the answers fit with your preferences. That's good, because it shows that you can use more than one learning style when faced with a situation calling for one over another.

Refining your skills in weak areas is important to help you become more integrated. The more integrated you are, the more flexible you can be in learning situations. You can use any number of skills and strategies which will help you. Knowing your strengths helps you when you are faced with a difficult learning task because you can use the strategies best suited for your learning style.

WHAT OTHER FACTORS INFLUENCE LEARNING?

In addition to your preferred learning styles, there are other factors which affect your learning. There are factors which affect your ability to study effectively and efficiently. Some of these will affect you more than others. Some may not be an issue for you at all, but you will find some you should consider when planning where, when, how and what to study.

Consider the answers to these questions regarding your preferences. Are writing assignments easier for you than oral ones? Would you rather write a paper or give a talk on a subject? (Tough choice!) Do you feel that you do a better job when you write or when you speak on a subject? Is it easier to get your thoughts down on paper or to talk about them? The answers to those questions will help you determine your preference for oral or written expressiveness. You will have to do some of both, but you can make course choices based on this knowledge.

Another option you may have in some of your classes is whether to participate in study groups. If you are the type of person who is comfortable in a group, then they will help you. Others, who learn better alone, may find a study group a liability. There are times when working with a group can help you understand material because the group can exchange ideas. Material may become clearer as you discuss it among the group members. Know your preferences and study accordingly.

Motivation plays a role in your learning. Are you learning for the pleasure of learning—to become more aware of the world around you, and to broaden your knowledge? Or are you learning with that one goal in mind—a degree? If the achievement of that goal is the only reason you are learning, you are approaching your education differently than the person who is learning to increase knowledge.

Being aware of your locus of control can help you understand your motivation. Locus of control is your perception of what accounts for the successes or failures in your life. It can be either external or internal. If external, then you attribute success or failure to outside forces (family, peers, fate, enemies). If internal, you attribute success or failure to the consequences of your own actions. You probably have a tendency toward one or the other, but do not see everything one way or the other. If this is a problem for you, you may need to work on changing your outlook.

INFORMATION STYLE DESCRIPTIONS*

CONCRETE EXPERIENCE: A high score in this area indicates a receptive, experience-based approach to learning where feeling-based judgments are most important. These individuals tend to be people oriented. Theoretical approaches don't hold much weight with them. They prefer to treat each situation as a unique case, and this is a problem with a theory. They learn best from specific examples and being involved. Individuals who emphasize concrete experience tend to be oriented more toward their peers and less toward authority figures in their approach to learning. They benefit most from feedback and discussion with fellow "concrete experience" learners.

ABSTRACT CONCEPTUALIZATION: A high score in this area indicates an analytical, conceptual approach to learning where logical thinking and rational evaluation are most important. These individuals tend to be oriented toward things and symbols and less toward other people. They prefer to learn in authority-directed, impersonal learning situations. They learn best when theory and systematic analysis are emphasized. They benefit little from unstructured learning approaches where discovery is important. They find these situations frustrating.

ACTIVE EXPERIMENTATION: A high score in this area indicates an active "doing" orientation to learning and processing information. These individuals learn best when they can engage in such things as projects, experiments, and homework. They will prefer small group discussions over passive learning situations such as lectures. They tend to be extroverted.

REFLECTIVE OBSERVATION: A high score in this area indicates a tentative, impartial, reflective approach to learning and processing information. These individuals make judgments based on careful observation. They prefer learning situations such as lectures where they are allowed to be impartial, objective observers in a learning situation. They tend to be introverted.

You can also analyze your "Information Style" one step further by looking at the specific ways that you prefer to perceive or take in information and then the way that you prefer to process or do something with that information. Do this by determining which of the following is your strength: CE or AC _____ and RO or AE _____. This gives you a clearer picture of your preferences, and descriptions follow. You will want to look over each definition, but the one which describes your two strengths as suggested above will be most likely to best describe you.

ABSTRACTLY PERCEIVE (AC) & REFLECTIVELY PROCESS (RO): Look for facts; need to know what the experts think; learn by thinking through ideas; prefer to learn by watching and thinking; more interested in ideas and concepts than people; like to collect data and critique information; thorough and industrious; will re-examine facts in perplexing situations; they enjoy traditional classrooms-schools are designed for them; function by adapting to the experts. Possible careers: basic sciences, math, research, planning.

(continued)

> ABSTRACTLY PERCEIVE (AC) & ACTIVELY PROCESS (AE): Need to know how things work; prefer to learn by testing theories in ways that seem sensible to them; learn by thinking and doing; need hands-on experiences; enjoy solving problems and resent being given the answers; have a limited tolerance for fuzzy ideas; need to know how things they are asked to do will help them in "real" life. Possible careers: engineering, physical sciences, nursing, technical areas.
>
> CONCRETELY PERCEIVE (CE) & ACTIVELY PROCESS (AE): Need to know what can be done with things; prefer to learn by doing, sensing, and feeling; adaptable to change, and love it; love variety and situations calling for flexibility; tend to take risks; at ease with people, but sometimes seen as pushy; often reach accurate conclusions in the absence of logical reasoning. Possible careers: sales, marketing, action-oriented jobs, teaching.
>
> CONCRETELY PERCEIVE (CE) & REFLECTIVELY PROCESS (RO): Look for personal meaning; need to be involved personally; learn by listening and sharing ideas; prefer to learn by sensing, feeling, watching; interested in people and culture; divergent thinkers who believe in their own experience; excel in viewing concrete situations from many perspectives; model themselves on those they respect; function through social interaction. Possible careers: counseling, personnel, humanities, organizational development.
>
> *Source: *Concept & Ideas* created by Bernice McCarthy and David Kolb.

Other factors which may influence your ability to learn or study are given in the following list.

- Noise level—from complete quiet to lots of noise
- Light—from low to bright
- Temperature—from warm to cool
- Time—early morning to late evening (the time you feel most alert)
- Position—sitting to lying down

Try to choose your ideal learning environment taking these factors into consideration. Consider others that impact you. Complete the sentences in the Environmental Factors Worksheet with your preferences for YOUR ideal study environment. Answer with the first thing you think of, and don't spend too much time thinking about them.

Analyze what you have just written. You may want to go back and revise, but you should not change answers unless the new one is definitely a stronger preference. Use the information to set up your study environment. Think about what you can change, and how you can adapt to those you cannot change.

WHAT ARE TEACHING STYLES?

Faculty members are learners from way back (and should still be learning). They also have learning style preferences. Those preferences had something to do with the choosing of their academic fields. The instructors also have teaching styles as a result of personality traits, learning preferences, goals, motivation for teaching, job satisfaction, and other factors.

When you are in a classroom setting where you feel comfortable and everything feels right, you are probably with a teacher whose learning style matches yours. When you are uncomfortable and feel out of place, the teacher may be someone whose learning style is different from yours. Since it isn't always possible to be matched up with a teacher who learns as you do, you must learn to adapt to the teaching style being used by each instructor. The more you can learn to use different styles, the more readily you can identify and adapt to teaching styles.

Many instructors have a tendency to teach the way they learn. You can make some guesses about their preferred learning styles by analyzing the predominant way material is presented and the atmosphere of the classroom. Material can be presented visually—videos, demonstrations, or diagrams on the board or overhead. It can be primarily an auditory presentation with lecture or audio tapes. Hands-on activities and experiments would be kinesthetic. You will find a combination in most classrooms, but look at the predominant one, or the one your instructor seems most comfortable using.

When you are in a classroom that is unlike your preferred style, you will have to work harder at concentrating and understanding. You may have to find extra materials to help you understand. It's imperative that you adapt to be successful.

A number of factors are used to describe teaching styles, and there are different ways of looking at and determining what constitutes a certain style. One area that will be important to you is the way an instructor communicates and interacts with students. At one extreme, there is the instructor who is formal and authoritative, and at the other extreme, the instructor who is very informal and casual. Most teachers fit in somewhere between the two extremes. If you find yourself not getting along with an instructor, think about this aspect and what you are most comfortable with, and you may have a clearer picture of the problem.

Again, you can't always be matched up with someone just like you, but you can ask around about specific teachers' styles. If you prefer a lecture setting, where students work independently and are expected to assume responsibility for learning, then find an instructor who is like that (especially for difficult classes).

However, if you are more comfortable in an informal setting where the instructor uses small and large group discussions and acts as a guide through the learning process, you will want to look for this kind of instructor for the more difficult classes.

You should be aware of teaching styles. You may find it helpful to analyze your teachers a little at the beginning of a class. You will then know whether you are going to feel comfortable in the class or need to adapt somewhat. The earlier you know this, the better your chances for success in the class.

SUMMARY

Learning style has been defined as the way you perceive or take in information, the way you process that information, and the way you react to the learning environment. You were given inventories to determine your modality strengths, brain dominance, and information

Chapter 8 | *Learning with Style* 129

style. Knowing about your learning style is important to you because it can make you aware of your strengths and weaknesses. You can use this information to be a better learner by using your strengths to help you with difficult material. Your weak areas are where you need to develop or improve your skills to become more integrated. Being more integrated means being able to adapt to the best learning strategy for the learning situation.

Many factors influence your ability to learn and study. The more awareness you have of these and your preferences, the better you can set up your learning environment to be the most efficient and effective for you.

Teaching styles of instructors also influence your classroom experience. Being aware of the different teaching styles you may encounter will help you be prepared to adapt when necessary.

Complete the following with what you have found in this chapter.

MODALITY STRENGTH: Auditory

　　　　　　　　　　Visual

　　　　　　　　　　Kinesthetic

BRAIN DOMINANCE:　Left

　　　　　　　　　　Right

　　　　　　　　　　Integrated

INFORMATION STYLE:　Concrete Experience

　　　　　　　　　　Abstract Conceptualization

　　　　　　　　　　Active Experimentation

　　　　　　　　　　Reflective Observation

　　　　　　　　　　(CE or AC) + (AE or RO)

LEARNING STYLE REFLECTIONS:

_____

_____

_____

_____

NAME: _____ DATE: _____

EXERCISE 1. MODALITY CHECKLIST

Check the statements below which are most like you, or like you most of the time.

1. ☐ My emotions can often be interpreted by my general body tone.
2. ☐ My emotions can often be interpreted by my facial expressions.
3. ☐ My emotions can often be interpreted by my voice (quality, volume, tone).
4. ☐ When I'm angry, I usually clench my fists, grasp something tightly, or storm off.
5. ☐ When I'm angry, I usually "blow-up" verbally and let others know I'm angry.
6. ☐ When I'm angry, I usually clam up and give others the silent treatment.
7. ☐ The things I remember best are the things I do.
8. ☐ The things I remember best are the things I hear.
9. ☐ The things I remember best are the things I read.
10. ☐ I remember what was done best, not names or faces.
11. ☐ If I have to learn something new, I like to learn about it by reading books and periodicals or seeing a video.
12. ☐ I like to learn through real experience.
13. ☐ I enjoy learning by listening to others.
14. ☐ I am easily distracted by sounds.
15. ☐ I am easily distracted. I have a short attention span.
16. ☐ I am easily distracted by visual stimuli.
17. ☐ I understand spoken directions better than written ones.
18. ☐ I remember what I have read better than what I have heard.
19. ☐ I like to learn most by building or making things.
20. ☐ I remember names, but forget faces.
21. ☐ I remember faces and forget names.
22. ☐ I tend to be quiet around others, and may become impatient when listening.
23. ☐ If I have to learn something new, I like to learn about it by having it told to me (lectures, speeches, tapes).
24. ☐ I enjoy learning by reading assignments and class notes.
25. ☐ To remember things, I need to write or copy them.
26. ☐ I generally gesture when speaking, and am not a great listener.
27. ☐ I really enjoy talking and listening with people.
28. ☐ When solving problems, I prefer to attack them physically, and often act impulsively.
29. ☐ When solving problems, I prefer to organize my thoughts by writing them down.
30. ☐ When solving problems, I like to talk the problem out and try solutions verbally.

Score by marking the numbers below that you checked. Add up the total number of statements checked in each category. You will find that one area probably had more statements checked than the others. This would be your modality strength. If you do not find one clear strength, you probably are well-integrated in these areas, and can use the modality which best fits the learning situation.

AUDITORY:	3	5	8	13	14	17	20	23	27	30	Total
VISUAL:	2	6	9	11	16	18	21	22	24	29	Total
KINESTHETIC:	1	4	7	10	12	15	19	25	26	28	Total

NAME: _____ DATE: _____

EXERCISE 2. BRAIN DOMINANCE

Check the statements below which are most like you, or are like you most of the time.

1. ☐ I prefer to have things explained to me.
2. ☐ I prefer that someone shows me things.
3. ☐ I don't have a preference for verbal instructions or demonstrations.
4. ☐ I prefer classes where things are planned so I know exactly what to do.
5. ☐ I prefer classes which are open with opportunities for change as I go along.
6. ☐ I prefer both classes where things are planned and open to changes.
7. ☐ I prefer classes where I listen to "experts."
8. ☐ I prefer classes where I try things.
9. ☐ I prefer classes where I listen and also try things.
10. ☐ I prefer to take multiple choice tests.
11. ☐ I prefer essay tests.
12. ☐ I don't have a preference for essay tests or multiple choice tests.
13. ☐ I don't like to play hunches or guess.
14. ☐ I like to play hunches or guess.
15. ☐ I sometimes make guesses and play hunches.
16. ☐ I decide what I think by looking at the facts.
17. ☐ I decide what I think based on my experiences.
18. ☐ I decide what I think based on facts and my experiences.
19. ☐ I respond better to people when they appeal to my logical, intellectual side.
20. ☐ I respond better to people when they appeal to my emotional, feeling side.
21. ☐ I respond equally well to people when they appeal to my intellectual side or emotional side.
22. ☐ I prefer to solve problems by reading and listening to the experts.
23. ☐ I prefer to solve problems by imagining and seeing things.
24. ☐ I prefer to solve problems by listening to experts and imagining things.
25. ☐ I am primarily intellectual.
26. ☐ I am primarily intuitive.
27. ☐ I am equally intellectual and intuitive.
28. ☐ When I remember or think about things, I prefer to think in words.
29. ☐ When I remember or think about things, I prefer to think in pictures and images.
30. ☐ When I remember or think about things, I sometimes prefer words and sometimes prefer pictures.
31. ☐ I am very good at explaining things in words.
32. ☐ I am very good at explaining things with my hand movements and actions.
33. ☐ I am very good at explaining with words and hand movements.

34. ☐ I am almost never absentminded.
35. ☐ I am frequently absentminded.
36. ☐ I am occasionally absentminded.
37. ☐ I am very good at recalling verbal materials (names, dates).
38. ☐ I am very good at recalling visual material.
39. ☐ I am equally good at recalling verbal and visual material.
40. ☐ It is more exciting to improve something.
41. ☐ It is more exciting to invent something.
42. ☐ It is equally exciting to improve something or invent something.
43. ☐ I would rather read realistic stories.
44. ☐ I would rather read fantasy stories.
45. ☐ I don't have a preference for reading realistic or fantasy stories.

Score by marking the numbers below that you checked. Add up the total number of statements in each category. You will probably find that one area had more checks than the others. If so, you have a tendency for that area (left, right, or integrated) to be your stronger learning preference. If you are more integrated than left or right dominant, then you can use either side of your brain. A more detailed description of brain dominance is given later in the chapter.

LEFT BRAIN:	1	4	7	10	13	16	19	22	25	28	31	34	37	40	43	Total
RIGHT BRAIN:	2	5	8	11	14	17	20	23	26	29	32	35	38	41	44	Total
INTEGRATED:	3	6	9	12	15	18	21	24	27	30	33	36	39	42	45	Total

Concepts & Ideas created by David Kolb, Paul Torrance, and Bernice McCarthy.

NAME: _____   DATE: _____

EXERCISE 3. INFORMATION STYLE

This survey is to determine the way you deal with information best. There are no right or wrong answers—just your preferences. Mark the statements which best describe your preferences. Mark the ones most like you, or like you most of the time.

1. ☐ I am energetic and enthusiastic.
2. ☐ I am quiet and reserved.
3. ☐ I tend to reason things out.
4. ☐ I am responsible about things.
5. ☐ I prefer learning to be "here and now."
6. ☐ I like to consider things and reflect about them.
7. ☐ I tend to think about the future.
8. ☐ I like to see results from my work.
9. ☐ I prefer to learn by feeling.
10. ☐ I prefer to learn by watching.
11. ☐ I prefer to learn by thinking.
12. ☐ I prefer to learn by doing.
13. ☐ When learning, I trust my hunches and feelings.
14. ☐ When learning, I listen and watch carefully.
15. ☐ When learning, I rely on logical thinking.
16. ☐ When learning, I work hard to get things done.
17. ☐ I like concrete things that I can see and touch.
18. ☐ I like to observe.
19. ☐ I like ideas and theories.
20. ☐ I like to be active.
21. ☐ I accept people and situations as they are.
22. ☐ I am aware of what is going on around me.
23. ☐ I evaluate things before acting.
24. ☐ I enjoy taking risks.
25. ☐ When I learn I am open to new experiences.
26. ☐ When I learn I like to try things out.
27. ☐ When I learn I like to analyze and break things down into their parts.
28. ☐ When I learn I like to look at all sides of the issue.
29. ☐ I am an accepting person.
30. ☐ I am a reserved person.
31. ☐ I am a rational person.

32. ☐ I am a responsible person.
33. ☐ I am an active person.
34. ☐ I am an observing person.
35. ☐ I am a logical person.
36. ☐ I am an intuitive person.

Score by marking the numbers below that you checked. Add up the total number of statements in each category. You will probably find that one area had more checks than the others. A detailed description of what these areas mean is given later in this chapter.

CONCRETE EXPERIENCE:	1	5	9	13	17	21	25	29	33 Total
REFLECTIVE OBSERVATION:	2	6	10	14	18	22	26	30	34 Total
ABSTRACT CONCEPTUALIZATION:	3	7	11	15	19	23	27	31	35 Total
ACTIVE EXPERIMENTATION:	4	8	12	16	20	24	28	32	36 Total

NAME: _____ DATE: _____

EXERCISE 4. ENVIRONMENTAL FACTORS WORKSHEET

1. The best time for me to study is _____
   _____

2. The best place for me to study is _____
   _____

3. My favorite study position is _____
   _____

4. My preference for noise when studying is _____
   _____

5. My favorite temperature when studying is _____
   _____

6. My favorite light when studying is _____
   _____

7. My preferred class to study first is _____
   _____

8. I can study best when _____
   _____

9. I can't study when _____
   _____

10. List anything else that you know about your preferences for studying. _____
    _____
    _____
    _____
    _____

Chapter 9

Critical Thinking
Developing Critical Skills for the Twenty-First Century

What are we to believe? What should we accept with reservations, and what should we dismiss outright? As we gather information about the world via the media (e.g., television, radio, the Internet, and newspapers and magazines), we tend to take much of the information at face value, ignoring the fact that the information has been selected and organized (shaped and edited) by the person or organization presenting it. People are often lulled into a false sense of security, believing that the sources of information they are basing their decisions on are objective and truthful (Chaffee, 1998). Discovering the answers to the six important questions that reporters are trained to answer near the beginning of every news article—who, what, where, when, why, and how—is not enough to allow us to think critically about complex and sometimes controversial topics. To engage in thinking at this higher level, one needs to know how to ask questions and think independently.

The authors of this chapter view critical thinking developmentally as a set of complex thinking skills that can be improved through knowledge and guided practice. Thinking

From Life Skills for College: A Curriculum for Life *by Earl J. Ginter and Ann Shanks Glauser. Copyright © 2005 by Earl J. Ginter and Ann Shanks Glauser. Used with permission.*

skills are categorized in the problem-solving/decision-making set of life-skills necessary for information seeking. These skills include information assessment and analysis; problem identification, solution, implementation, and evaluation; goal setting; systematic planning and forecasting; and conflict resolution. Presented in this chapter are developmental thinking models, critical thinking and problem-solving models, and information about the construction and evaluation of an argument.

THINKING AS A DEVELOPMENTAL PROCESS

Cognitive psychologists study the development and organization of knowledge and the role it plays in various mental activities (e.g., reading, writing, decision making, and problem solving). What is knowledge? Where it is stored? How do you construct mental representations of your world? The personal answers to these and other questions are often found for the first time in college when students focus their attention on what they know and how they know it.

Models of Knowledge

Different forms of knowledge interact when you reason and construct a mental representation of the situation before you. Joanne Kurfiss (1988) wrote about the following three kinds of knowledge.

- **Declarative knowledge** is knowing facts and concepts. Kurfiss recognizes the considerable amount of declarative knowledge that students acquire through their college courses. To move students to a higher level of thinking, instructors generally ask students to write analytical essays, instead of mere summaries, to explain the knowledge they have acquired in the course.
- **Procedural knowledge,** or **strategic knowledge,** is knowing how to use declarative knowledge to do something (e.g., interpret textbooks, study, navigate the Internet, and find a major).
- **Metacognition** is knowing what knowledge to use to control one's situation (e.g., how to make plans, ask questions, analyze the effectiveness of learning strategies, initiate change). If students' metacognitive skills are not well developed, students may not be able to use the full potential of their knowledge when studying in college.

William Perry

You may have read about the developmental theorist William Perry. In his research on college-age students, Perry distinguished a series of stages that students pass through as they move from simple to complex levels of thinking. Basically, they move from *dualism*, the simplest stage, where knowledge is viewed as a factual quality dispensed by authorities (professors), to *multiplicity*, in which the student recognizes the complexity of knowledge (e.g., he or she understands that there is more than one perspective of the bombing of Hiroshima or the role of the United States in the Vietnam war) and believes knowledge to be subjective, to *relativism*, where the student reaches an understanding that some views make greater sense than other views. Relativism is reflected in situations where a student has made a commitment to the particular view they have constructed of the world, also known as *Weltanschauung*. Constructing a personal *critical epistemology* is an essential developmental task for undergraduates, according to Perry (Chaffee, 1998).

Bloom's Taxonomy of Thinking and Learning

Benjamin Bloom (1956) and his associates at the University of Chicago developed a classification system, or taxonomy, to explain how we think and learn (see Figure 1). The taxonomy consists of six levels of thinking arranged in a hierarchy, beginning with simple cognitive tasks (knowledge) and moving up to more complex thinking (evaluation). Thinking at each level is dependent on thinking skills at lower levels.

```
                    Evaluation
                Assess information
                ─────────────────
                    Synthesis
              Integrate information
              ──────────────────────
                    Analysis
              Connect information
           ─────────────────────────
                  Application
             Construct information
        ──────────────────────────────
                Comprehension
             Interpret information
     ─────────────────────────────────────
                  Knowledge
             Memorize information
```

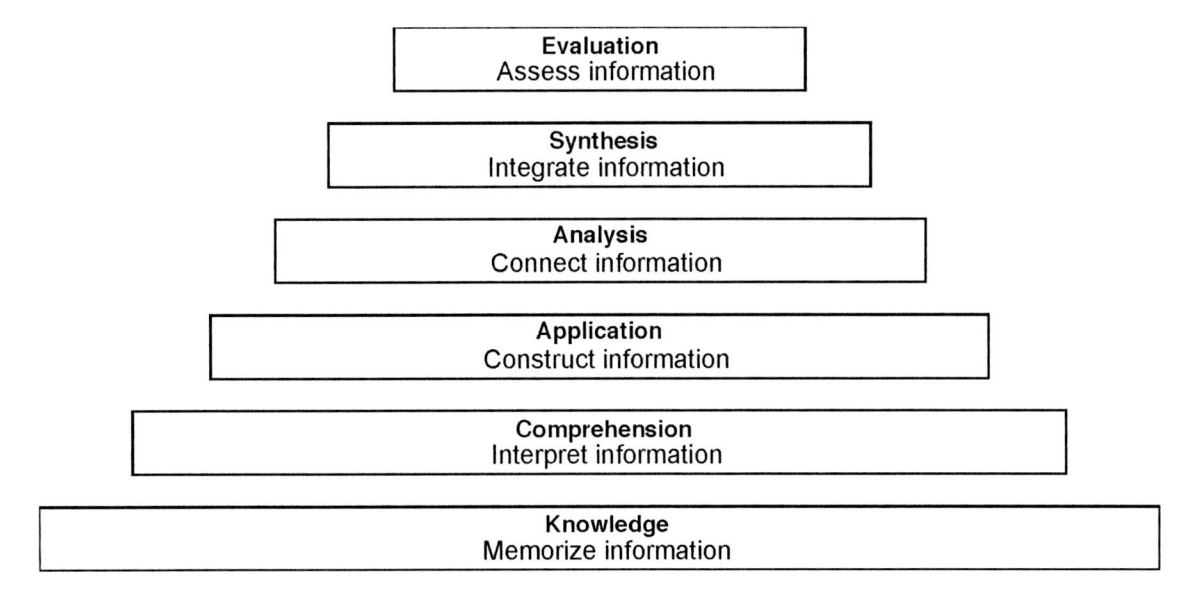

Figure 1 Bloom's Hierarchy of Thinking

One of the reasons that college students often experience difficulty learning and studying during their first semester is that the learning and study strategies from high school are not necessarily effective in the new setting. In high school you are generally asked to memorize, comprehend, and interpret information. In college you are asked to do all that and more. To be successful in a college setting, you need to learn how to apply, analyze, synthesize, and evaluate information. Let's look at Bloom's six levels of learning and thinking.

Knowledge Level. If you are cramming for a test, chances are good that you are thinking at the knowledge level, the lowest level of thinking. You are basically attempting to memorize a lot of information in a short amount of time. If you are asked on the test to identify, name, select, define, or list particular bits of information, you might do okay, but you will most likely forget most of the information soon after taking the test.

Comprehension Level. When you are classifying, describing, discussing, explaining, and recognizing information, you are in the process of interpreting information. At the bottom of your lecture notes for the day, see if you can summarize your notes using your own words. In doing so, you can develop a deeper understanding of the material just covered in class.

Application Level. At this third level of thinking, you are constructing knowledge by taking previously learned information and applying it in a new and different way to solve problems. Whenever you use a formula or a theory to solve a problem, you are thinking at the application level. Some words used to describe how you process information at this level are *illustrate, demonstrate,* and *apply.* To increase thinking at the application level, develop the habit of thinking of examples to illustrate concepts presented in class or during reading. Be sure to include the examples in your notations in your books and notes.

Analysis Level. When you analyze information, you break the information down into parts and then look at the relationships among the parts. In your literature class, if you read two plays from different time periods and then compare and contrast them in terms of style and form, you are analyzing. When you analyze, you connect pieces of information. You *discriminate, correlate, classify,* and *infer.*

Synthesis Level. When you are synthesizing information, you are bringing together all the bits of information that you have analyzed to create a new pattern or whole. When you synthesize, you *hypothesize, predict, generate,* and *integrate.* Innovative ideas often emerge at the synthesis level of thinking.

Evaluation Level. This is the highest level of thinking according to Bloom's taxonomy. When you evaluate, you judge the validity of the information. You may be evaluating opinions ("Is that person really an expert?") or biases.

Answer the following questions to test your understanding of Bloom's taxonomy. According to Bloom's taxonomy of thinking, which level of thinking would you be engaging in if you were asked to

- Read an article about an upcoming candidate in a local election and then summarize the candidate's characteristics?
- View a video about hate and prejudice and then write an essay about how you can confront hate and prejudice on a personal level?
- Determine the most effective way for you to study?
- Identify and define the parts of the forebrain?
- Judge a new campus parking policy created by your college's parking services?

MODELS OF CRITICAL THINKING/PROBLEM SOLVING

Critical Thinking

One of the primary objectives of a college education is to develop the skills necessary to become an autonomous, independent learner. Critical thinking prepares you to be an independent thinker. To ensure that you are thinking critically, you can follow the CRITICAL model developed by the authors (Glauser & Ginter, 1995). This model identifies important steps and key ideas in critical thinking: construction, refocus, identify, think through, insight, conclusions, accuracy, and lens.

Construction. Each of us constructs a unique view of the world. Our construction, or perception, of the world is based on our thoughts and beliefs. Our cultural background influences our perceptions, and they form the basis of our assumptions. For example, you might assume that a college education can help you to get a better job. How do you know this? Maybe you know this because a parent or teacher told you so. If this is the only bit of information on which you are basing your assumption about the value of a college education, you have not engaged in critical thinking. If you had engaged in critical thinking, you would have analyzed and synthesized information that you gathered about the benefits of a college education. If you have based your decision to attend this college on good critical thinking, then you will know why you are here and will more likely be motivated to graduate.

Perceptions of information, behaviors, and situations are often based on unexamined assumptions that are inaccurate and sketchy. The first step in this model is to investigate personal underlying biases that are inherent in your assumptions about any issue before you. For example, let us say that you are with some friends and the topic of surrogate motherhood comes up. Maybe you have already formed an opinion about the issue. This opinion could be based on strong critical thinking, but if not, then your opinion is merely a strong, personal feeling. If you choose to look at surrogate motherhood from a critical-thinking perspective, you would begin by examining your own thoughts and beliefs about motherhood and surrogacy. No matter what issue is before you (e.g., racism, abortion, euthanasia, genetic engineering), the process is the same; begin by examining your own assumptions. As you do this, look for biases and other patterns of thinking that have become cemented over time and are influencing the way you view the issue.

Refocus. Once you have acknowledged some of your own biases, refocus your attention so you can hear alternative viewpoints. Refocus by reading additional information, talking to people with opposing viewpoints, or maybe watching a movie or a video. You are trying to see other people's perspectives. Read carefully, and listen carefully with the intent to learn. Can you think of any books that you have read or movies that have influenced the way you see a particular issue?

To illustrate the effect of refocusing, list three sources of additional information (e.g., book, movie, another person, newspaper, or experience) that changed your mind about something important to you. Explain how it changed you.

1. _____
   _____
   _____

2. _____
   _____
   _____

3. _____
   _____
   _____

Identify. Identifying core issues and information is the third step of critical thinking. After you have gathered all your additional information representing different viewpoints, think over the information carefully. Are there any themes that emerge? What does the terminology related to the issue tell you? Look at all the facts and details. We all try to make sense out of what we hear and see by arranging information into a pattern, a story that seems reasonable. There is a tendency to arrange the information to fit our perceptions and beliefs. When we engage in critical thinking, we are trying to make sense of all the pieces, not just the ones that happen to fit our own preconceived pattern.

Think Through. The fourth step of critical thinking requires that you think through all the information gathered. The task is to distinguish between what is fact and what is fiction and what is relevant and not relevant. Examine premises and decide if they are logically valid. Look for misinformation. Maybe you have gathered inaccurate facts and figures. Check the sources for reliability. Asking questions is a large part of good critical thinking.

This step of the model is where you analyze and synthesize information. You are continually focusing your attention in and out, similar to the way you might focus a camera. This step of the critical-thinking process can be very creative. You are using both parts of the brain. The right brain is being speculative, suspending judgment, and challenging definitions. The left brain is analyzing the information received in a more traditional style, thinking logically and sequentially. While thinking critically, have you detected any overgeneralizations (e.g., women are more emotional and less rational than men are) or oversimplifications (e.g., the high dropout rate at the local high school is due to an increase in single-parent families)?

Insight. Once key issues have been identified and analyzed, it is time to develop some insight into some of the various perspectives on the issue. Sometimes some of the best insights come when you can sit back and detach yourself from all the information you have just processed. Often new meanings will emerge that provide a new awareness. You might find that you have developed some empathy for others that may not have been there before.

When you hear the term "broken home," what images do you conjure up? How do you think a child who resides with a single parent or alternates between divorced parents' homes feels when hearing that term applied to his or her situation? A lot of assumptions are embedded in such concepts.

Conclusions. If you do not have sufficient evidence to support a decision, suspend judgment until you do. An important tenet of critical thinking is not to jump to conclusions. If you do, you may find that you have a fallacy in your reasoning. A fallacy is an instance of incorrect reasoning. Maybe you did not have sufficient evidence to support your decision to major in biology, or maybe your conclusions about the issue of euthanasia do not follow logically from your premise. Also look at the conclusions you have drawn, and ask yourself if they have any implications that you might need to rethink? Do you need to consider alternative interpretations of the evidence?

Accuracy. You are not through thinking! In addition to looking for fallacies in your reasoning, you also need to consider some other things.

- Know the difference between reasoning and rationalizing. Which thinking processes are your conclusions based on?
- Know the difference between what is true and what seems true based on the emotional attachment you have to your ideas and beliefs.
- Know the difference between opinion and fact. Facts can be proven; opinions cannot.

Lens. In this last step of critical thinking, you have reached the understanding that most issues can be viewed from multiple perspectives. These perspectives form a lens that offers a more encompassing view of the world around you. Remember that there are usually many solutions to a single issue.

Problem Solving

Problem solving involves critical thinking. Are problem solving and critical thinking the same? Not really. Problem solving is about having the ability and skills to apply knowledge to pragmatic problems encountered in all areas of your life. If you were trying to solve a financial problem or decide whether or not to change roommates, you probably would not need a model of thinking as extensive as the one previously described. The following steps offer an organized approach to solving less complex problems.

1. Identify the problem. Be specific and write it down.
2. Analyze the problem.
3. Identify alternative ways to solve the problem.
4. Examine alternatives.
5. Implement a solution.
6. Evaluate.

Identify the problem. What exactly is the problem you wish to solve? Is it that your roommate is driving you crazy, or is it that you want to move into an apartment with your friend next semester? Be specific.

Analyze the problem. Remember, analysis means looking at all the parts. It is the process by which we select and interpret information. Be careful not to be too selective or simplistic in your thinking. Look at all the facts and details. For example, suppose you want to move into an apartment with your friends. Do you need permission from anyone to do so? Can you afford to do this? Can you get a release from your dorm lease? Your answer to all the questions might be yes, with the exception of being able to afford it. You want to move, so now the problem is a financial one. You need to come up with the financial resources to follow through on your decision.

Identify alternative ways to solve the problem. Use convergent and divergent thinking. You are engaging in **convergent thinking** when you are narrowing choices to come up with the correct solution (e.g., picking the best idea out of three). You are engaging in **divergent thinking** when you are thinking in terms of multiple solutions. Mihaly Csikszentmihalyi (1996) says, "Divergent thinking leads to no agreed-upon solution. It involves fluency, or the ability to generate a great quantity of ideas; flexibility, or the ability to switch from one perspective to another; and originality in picking unusual associations of ideas" (1996, p. 60). He concludes that a person whose thinking has these qualities is likely to come up with more innovative ideas.

Brainstorming is a great way to generate alternative ways to solve problems. This creative problem-solving technique requires that you use both divergent and convergent thinking. Here are some steps to use if you decide to brainstorm.

- Describe the problem.
- Decide on the amount of time you want to spend brainstorming (e.g., 10 minutes).
- Relax (remember some of the best insights come in a relaxed state).
- Write down everything that comes to your mind (divergent thinking).
- Select your best ideas (convergent thinking).
- Try one out! (If it does not work, try one of the other ideas you selected.)

Students have successfully used the process of brainstorming to decide on a major, choose activities for spring break, develop topics for papers, and come up with ideas for part-time jobs. Being creative means coming up with atypical solutions to complex problems.

Examine alternatives. Make judgments about the alternatives based on previous knowledge and the additional information you now have.

Implement a solution. Choose one solution to your problem and eliminate the others for now. (If this one fails, you may want to try another solution later.)

Evaluate. If the plan is not as effective as you had hoped, modify your plan or start the process over again. Also look at the criteria you used to judge your alternative solutions.

Think of a problem that you are currently dealing with. Complete Exercise 1 ("Creating Breakthroughs") at the end of the chapter. This is an opportunity to try to solve a problem using this six-step problem-solving model.

ARGUMENTS

Critical thinking involves the construction and evaluation of arguments. An argument is a form of thinking in which reasons (statements and facts) are given in support of a conclusion. The reasons of the argument are known as the **premises**. A good argument is one in which the premises are logical and support the conclusion. The validity of the argument is based on the relationship between the premises and the conclusion. If the premises are not credible or do not support the conclusion, or the conclusion does not follow from the premises, the argument is considered to be **invalid** or fallacious. Unsound arguments (based on fallacies) are often persuasive because they can appeal to our emotions and confirm what we want to believe to be true. Just look at commercials on television. Alcohol advertisements show that you can be rebellious, independent, and have lots of friends, fun, and excitement by drinking large quantities of alcohol—all without any negative consequences. Intelligence is reflected in the capacity to acquire and apply knowledge. Even sophisticated, intelligent people are influenced by fallacious advertising.

Invalid Arguments

It is human irrationality, not a lack of knowledge, that threatens human potential.
—RAYMOND NICKERSON, IN J. K. KURFISS, *CRITICAL THINKING*

In the book *How to Think About Weird Things,* Theodore Schick and Lewis Vaughn (1999) suggest that you can avoid holding irrational beliefs by understanding the ways in which an argument can fail. First, an argument is fallacious if it contains **unacceptable premises**, premises that are as incredible as the claim they are supposed to support. Second, if they contain **irrelevant premises**, or premises that are not logically related to the conclusion, they are also fallacious. Third, they are fallacious if they contain **insufficient premises**, meaning that the premises do not eliminate reasonable grounds for doubt. Schick and Vaughn recommend that whenever someone presents an argument, you check to see if the premises are acceptable, relevant, and sufficient. If not, then the argument presented is not logically compelling, or valid.

Schick and Vaughn abstracted from the work of Ludwig F. Schlecht the following examples of fallacies based on illogical premises.

Unacceptable Premises

- **False dilemma** (also known as the either/or fallacy) presumes that there are only two alternatives from which to choose when in actuality there are more than two. For example: You are either with America or against us. You are not with America, therefore you are against us.
- **Begging the question** is also referred to as arguing in a circle. A conclusion is used as one of the premises. For example: "You should major in business, because my advisor

says that if you do, you will be guaranteed a job." "How do you know this?" "My advisor told me that all business majors find jobs."

Irrelevant Premises

- **Equivocation** occurs when the conclusion does not follow from the premises due to using the same word to mean two different things. For example: Senator Dobbs has always been *patriotic* and shown a deep affection and respect for his country. Now, though, he is criticizing the government's foreign policy. This lack of *patriotism* makes him unworthy of reelection.
- **Appeal to the person** (*ad hominem,* or "to the man") occurs when a person offers a rebuttal to an argument by criticizing or denigrating its presenter rather than constructing a rebuttal based on the argument presented. As Schick and Vaughn note, "Crazy people can come up with perfectly sound arguments, and sane people can talk nonsense" (1999, p. 287).
- **Appeal to authority** is when we support our views by citing experts. If the person is truly an expert in the field for which they are being cited, then the testimony is probably valid. How often do you see celebrities endorsing products? Is an argument valid just because someone cites an article from the *New York Times* or the *Wall Street Journal* for support?
- **Appeal to the masses** is a type of fallacy that occurs when support for the premise is offered in the form, "It must be right because everybody else does it." For example: It's okay to cheat. Every college student cheats sometime during their undergraduate years.
- **Appeal to tradition** is used as an unsound premise when we argue that something is true based on an established tradition. For example: It's okay to drink large quantities of alcohol and go wild during Spring Break. It's what students have always done.
- **Appeal to ignorance** relies on claims that if no proof is offered that something is true, then it must be false, or conversely, that if no proof is offered that something is false, then it must be true. Many arguments associated with religions of the world are based on irrelevant premises that appeal to ignorance.
- **Appeal to fear** is based on a threat, or "swinging the big stick." For example: If you don't start studying now, you will never make it through college. Schick and Vaughn remind us, "Threats extort; they do not help us arrive at the truth" (1999, p. 289).

Insufficient Premises

- **Hasty generalizations** are often seen when people stereotype others. Have you noticed that most stereotypes are negative? When we describe an individual as pushy, cheap, aggressive, privileged, snobbish, or clannish and then generalize that attribute to the group we believe that person belongs to, we are committing a hasty generalization.
- **Faulty analogy** is the type of fallacy committed when there is a claim that things that have similar qualities in some respects will have similarities in other respects. For example: Dr. Smith and Dr. Wilson may both teach at the same college, but their individual philosophies about teaching and learning may be very different.

- **False cause** fallacies occur when a causal relationship is assumed despite a lack of evidence to support the relationship. Do you have a special shirt or hat that you wear on game days to influence the odds that the team you are cheering for wins?

CLOSING REMARKS

Belgian physicist Ilya Prigogine was awarded the Nobel Prize for his theory of dissipative structures. Part of the theory "contends that friction is a fundamental property of nature and nothing grows without it—not mountains, not pearls, not people. It is precisely the quality of fragility, he says, the capacity for being shaken up, that is paradoxically the key to growth. Any structure—whether at the molecular, chemical, physical, social, or psychological level that is insulated from disturbance is also protected from change. It becomes stagnant. Any vision—or any thing—that is true to life, to the imperatives of creation and evolution, will not be 'unshakable'" (Levoy, 1997 p. 8).

Throughout this textbook you will read about how change affects you now as a student in college and throughout the rest of your life. Education is about learning how to look and how to listen to what instructors, books, television, and other sources of information are saying, and to discover whether or not what they are saying is true or false.

In reference to education and learning, the philosopher Jiddu Krishnamurti said that there should be "an intent to bring about change in the mind which means you have to be extraordinarily critical. You have to learn never to accept anything which you yourself do not see clearly" (1974, p. 18). He said that education is always more than learning from books, or memorizing some facts, or the instructor transmitting information to the student. Education is about critical thinking, and critical thinking is the foundation of all learning.

Critical thinking is thinking that moves you beyond simple observations and passive reporting of those observations. It is an active, conscious, cognitive process in which there is always intent to learn. It is the process by which we analyze and evaluate information, and it is how we make good sense out of all the information that we are continually bombarded with.

Marcia Magolda believes that critical thinking fosters qualities such as maturity, responsibility, and citizenship. "Both the evolving nature of society and the student body has led to reconceptualizations of learning outcomes and processes. In a postmodern society, higher education must prepare students to shoulder their moral and ethical responsibility to confront and wrestle with the complex problems they will encounter in today and tomorrow's world. Critical, reflective thinking skills, the ability to gather and evaluate evidence, and the ability to make one's own informed judgments are essential learning outcomes if students are to get beyond relativity to make informed judgments in a world in which multiple perspectives are increasingly interdependent and 'right action' is uncertain and often in dispute." (Magolda & Terenzini, 1999, p. 3)

SOURCES

Bloom, B. (1956). *Taxonomy of educational objectives: The classification of educational goals. Handbook I: Cognitive domain.* London: Longmans.
Chaffee, J. (1998). *The thinker's way.* Boston: Little, Brown.
Csikszentmihalyi, M. (1996). *Creativity.* New York: HarperCollins.
DiSpezio, M. (1998). *Challenging critical thinking puzzles.* New York: Sterling.
Glauser, A., & Ginter, E. J. (1995, October). *Beyond hate and intolerance.* Paper presented at the southeastern Conference of Counseling Center Personnel, Jekyll Island, GA.
Johnson, D., & Johnson, F. (2000). *Joining together.* Boston: Allyn and Bacon.
Krishnamurti, J. (1974). *Krishnamurti on education.* New York: Harper & Row.
Kurfiss, J. G. (1988). *Critical thinking: Theory, research, practice, and possibilities. Critical thinking, 2.* Washington, DC: ASHE-Eric Higher Education Reports.
Levoy, Gregg. (1997). *Callings.* New York: Three Rivers Press.
Magolda, M. B., & Terenzini, P. (1999). Learning and teaching in the twenty-first century: Trends and implications for practice. In C. S. Johnson & H. E. Cheatham (Eds.), *Higher education trends for the next century: A research agenda for student's success.* Retrieved November 30, 1999, from http://www.acpa.nche.edu/ seniorscholars/trends/trends.htn
Perry, W. (1970). *Forms of intellectual and ethical development during the college years: A scheme.* New York: Holt, Rinehart and Winston.
Schick, T., & Vaughn, L. (1999). *How to Think About Weird Things: Critical Thinking for a New Age.* Mountain View, CA: Mayfield.

NAME: _____ DATE: _____

EXERCISE 1. CREATING BREAKTHROUGHS

Select a problem related to being a student at your college.

1. State the problem.

2. Analyze the problem.

3. Brainstorm alternative solutions.

4. Examine your alternatives. Pick the five best options from your brainstorming and record them below.

   a. _____

   b. _____

   c. _____

   d. _____

   e. _____

When you consider your problem and the list of options that you have created, what kind of criteria do you want to use in judging your options? For example, let us say that you stated your problem as needing money to stay in school. The best five options you came up with for getting money to stay in school were to work full time and go to evening school, alternate between going to school for a year and then working for a year, take out a student loan, study hard and raise your GPA to obtain a scholarship, and beg your family for money. The criteria you choose to judge your options might be that you do not want to be really stressed out, you want your plan to be reliable, and you want to owe as little as possible upon graduation.

List three criteria you will use to evaluate your options.

   C1. _____

   C2. _____

   C3. _____

Now, using a scale from 1–5, rate each option using your criteria, with 5 being the highest rating.

OPTIONS	C1	C2	C3	TOTAL (C1 + C2 + C3)
a.				
b.				
c.				
d.				
e.				

NAME: _____ DATE: _____

EXERCISE 1 (continued)

What are your two best options?

_____

_____

5. Implement a solution. Which option will you choose to act on?

   _____

   What kinds of resources will you need? (List four.)

   _____

   _____

   _____

   _____

   List some of your planning steps.

   _____

   _____

   _____

   _____

   _____

   _____

   _____

   _____

   _____

6. Evaluate. Look over what you have listed as resources and planning steps, and decide if you forgot something important. Indicate below if you believe the plan you have come up with is feasible, and whether you left something out that now should become part of your solution.

NAME: _____ DATE: _____

EXERCISE 2. CRITICAL-THINKING PUZZLE

Without lifting your pencil from the paper, draw six straight lines that connect all sixteen of the dots below. To make things more challenging, the line pattern that you create must begin at the X.

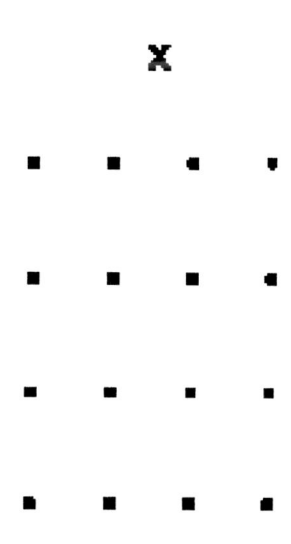

X

■ ■ ■ ■

■ ■ ■ ■

■ ■ ■ ■

■ ■ ■ ■

(The solution can be found at the end of this chapter.)

Source: DiSpezio, M. (1998). *Challenging critical thinking puzzles.* New York: Sterling.

Solution to Exercise 2

Critical-Thinking Puzzle

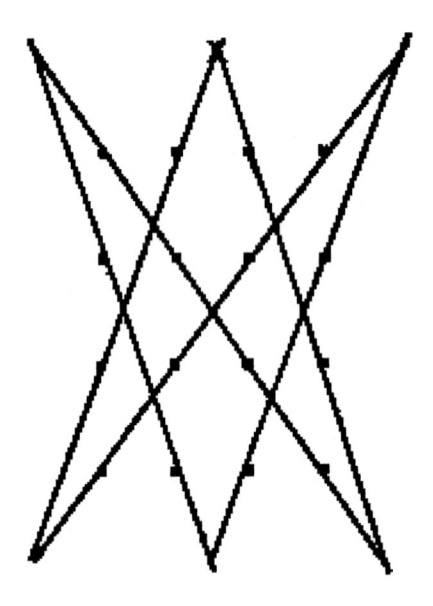

DiSpezio, M. (1998). *Challenging critical thinking puzzles.* New York: Sterling.

Chapter 10

Becoming a Better Notetaker

CASE STUDY
Carlos

Carlos was offered a management position in his company, provided he completes his degree. Back when he was in high school and first starting college, Carlos earned above average grades, so he wasn't too worried about returning to school. However, after the first month of classes, he is beginning to realize that he may have underestimated the academic demands of his courses.

He never used to take notes. As an auditory learner, Carlos could absorb enough information just by sitting through the lecture. Because most of his high school teachers taught directly from the textbook, whatever he missed he could pick up from the reading. He had a good memory and usually did well on tests.

Now that Carlos is an adult student with a full-time job and family, he is taking night classes that meet one evening per week for three hours. After a long day at work, it is very difficult to concentrate. He keeps thinking about things he needs to get done the next day, how

From The Community College: A New Beginning Fourth Edition *by Linda S. Aguilar, Sandra J. Hopper, and Therese M. Kuzlik. Copyright © 2005 by Kendall/Hunt Publishing Company. Used with permission.*

to resolve problems at the office, and a lot of other things about which he didn't have to worry when he was young and single.

His first major exam is next week. The professor told the class that anything and everything covered so far is fair game for test questions. "Everything" includes five chapters in the textbook, two in-class videos, the four weekly lectures, and some supplemental material posted on the course Web site.

In looking over his notes, Carlos notices that he missed a lot of material, especially from the fast-paced videos. He tended to write things down as the professor was talking, and now his spiral notebook is a mass of unorganized points that he has tried to connect with arrows. In between the lines he squeezed information that was added later in the class. What a mess! As a linear thinker, Carlos is frustrated trying to study from these notes and is ready to throw the whole notebook out.

Reflections

- What mistakes did Carlos make?
- Why is reading the textbook not enough?
- What advance preparations can Carlos use to make sure he records the most critical information?
- What notetaking method would he find effective?

INTRODUCTION

Perhaps you have not been concerned about your notetaking skills in the past. You may have managed to get by without even taking notes. However, now that you are in college, your instructors will hold you responsible for knowing the course content and the concepts presented in class. Your tests may cover several chapters at a time. In some courses, the only tests are a midterm and a comprehensive final exam that includes material from the entire semester. It is difficult to remember everything that is said in class. That is why you need to have good notes.

Academically successful college students are not necessarily the most intelligent students in the class but are students who use effective study skills. Many students who made good grades without too much effort in high school don't do as well in college. Becoming a better notetaker is a big step toward increasing your success in the classroom. Developing good notetaking skills requires *being prepared for class, actively listening* to the lecture material, *selecting a notetaking style,* and learning to *use your notes* as a part of your total study system.

This chapter will help you to check your notetaking strengths and weaknesses and will introduce several notetaking systems for you to try. You'll also learn how to identify your instructor's lecture style and to develop the notetaking style that works best for you.

Pretest: Assessing Your Notetaking Skills

Check Yes or No for each item that describes your notetaking habits.   Yes   No

1. I check my course syllabus before each class to make sure I'm ready for each assignment.
2. I read the text chapter(s) before class to make sure the lecture material will be familiar.
3. I use a three-ring binder and loose-leaf paper for notetaking.
4. I pay attention in class even if the instructor wanders from the point or makes remarks with which I don't agree.
5. I ask questions if I don't understand the material presented in class.
6. I identify introductory and concluding statements and recognize transition words and phrases when the instructor is lecturing.
7. I pick out the main ideas and supporting details without difficulty.
8. I understand my notes when I look them over several days or weeks later.
9. I take notes in my own words rather than trying to write down everything the instructor says.
10. I use abbreviations and symbols so that I can note all of the important information.
11. I make sure to include examples and all key information the instructor puts on the board.
12. I leave enough space to fill in or add to my notes later.
13. I review and edit my notes on a daily basis.
14. I use my notes to think of possible test questions.

Look over your responses to the pretest. Can you honestly say that you practice most of these notetaking habits? If not, use the information provided in this chapter to better your notetaking skills.

PREPARATION FOR CLASSROOM NOTETAKING

Preparation for notetaking starts before you actually begin the class. When you purchase supplies at the beginning of the semester, don't buy a spiral notebook! Why not? Spiral notebooks are limiting; they don't offer the flexibility for using your notes in study sessions that a three ring binder and loose-leaf paper will provide. In addition, write on only one side of the paper. Our sample notes provided later in this chapter will show you how to use your loose-leaf notes for test review.

Recognizing Instructor "Signals"

Once you get to class and the lecture starts, you have to decide quickly what information needs to be recorded. In addition to having read the material ahead of time, you need to be able to follow the instructor's lecture. She/he will use *verbal and nonverbal signals* or clues to help you pick out the information you should record.

Non-Verbal Signals include:

- *Visually Presented Information:* If the instructor puts information on the board, projects it on the screen, or distributes handouts, she/he is giving you a signal that the information presented is important. Remember that some instructors just jot down key words or phrases. Be sure to write enough information to prompt your memory later.
- *Instructor Mannerisms:* Frequently when instructors are about to introduce a new topic, they will pause for a minute or glance down at their notes to gather their thoughts. This is a clear signal that you should skip a line or two and get ready for a new topic.

Verbal Signals include the following:

- *Definitions:* Terms or definitions frequently show up as test questions, whether in multiple choice, matching, or true/false formats.
- *Repetitions:* You can usually assume information is important if it's repeated. Make a notation in the margin, like a circled R, to show that the information was repeated.
- *Examples:* Examples help you to understand the material when you review it later.
- *Enumerations:* Your instructor may use signals like "Five characteristics of . . .," or "The three steps in the process are . . . ." Make sure you clearly identify the topic and write down each item listed.
- *Transitional Words:* Be alert for words like "consequently," "furthermore," or phrases like "another reason for . . . ." These words and phrases are clear signals to record the information provided.
- *Direct Announcement:* Some instructors may simply tell you up front that something is important with a lead-in like, "Pay attention to . . .," "This is important," or literally, "Write this in your book or put it in your notes."

Some instructors are not great lecturers and tend to stray from the point, but paying attention to the clues they provide can help you to record the information you need.

Notetaking Short-Cuts

In addition to using a loose-leaf binder and learning to "read" your instructor's signals, advance preparation includes developing some personalized notetaking short-cuts. Most instructors speak at a rate of about 125–150 words per minute when giving a typical lecture. You can't possibly record every word, but you do want to write down as much information as possible. Using a system of abbreviations and symbols will help you increase your notetaking speed. Some common abbreviations and symbols are listed in Table 1.

Table 1

WORD OR TERM	ABBREVIATION OR SYMBOL	WORD OR TERM	ABBREVIATION OR SYMBOL
About	~	Introduction	Intro.
Amount	Amt.	Months	Mo(s.)
And	&	Number or Pound	#
Chapter	Ch.	Organization	Org.
Company	Co.	Page(s)	Pg., p., pp.
Continued	Cont'd.	Psychology	Psyc.
Decrease	Decr.	Principal	Princ.
Definition	Def.	Significant	Sig.
Economic	Econ.	Social or sociology	Soc.
Example	Ex. or X or e.g.	Summary/summarize	Sum.
General	Gen.	Versus	Vs.
Government	Gov.	Volume	Vol.
Hour/hourly	Hr./hrly.	Year	Yr.
Illustrate	Illus. or e.g.	Equal/Not Equal	= and ≠
Important	Imp.	Less than/more than	< and >
Increase	Inc.	Positive/negative	+ and −
Information	Info.	With/without	w/ and w/o

Other personalized short cuts include using a ? any place where you think you missed something important, using a B to indicate work from the board, and an X for examples. Using abbreviations can become especially important in later semesters when you develop a specialized terminology for your major.

Active Listening

How do we listen actively? What does this term mean? For now, we'll use the term to mean paying attention to what the speaker *means* as well as to what she/he *says*.

In the classroom, you are given directions and assignments, and you listen to presentations and lectures. How well you understand the material will help determine the grade you will receive in the class. When working, you listen to instructions that will help you do your job. In your personal life, you listen to the concerns and problems of your friends and family members. Listening, therefore, is an essential life skill, and developing that skill can make you a better student.

We can improve our listening skills for classroom use by practicing the following strategies:

- **Read the Text:** Make sure you know the topic for upcoming lectures and that you've completed the reading assignment. Your instructor gives you a course syllabus for just this reason! Being familiar with the topic can help you follow the instructor's lecture.

- **Concentrate:** We all know it's easy to "drift off," so you need to concentrate on paying attention. Many instructors test primarily from lecture notes rather than from the book, so you need to keep focused. Make sure you record all main points and supporting ideas. You need to be actively involved in listening to the lecture, and writing will help you keep your concentration.
- **Respond to the Message, not the Messenger:** Don't let your instructor's appearance, mannerisms, or lecture style detract you from your task—writing down the relevant information.
- **Be Accepting of Different Ideas and Viewpoints:** Many college classes will introduce you to new ideas or to value systems that differ from yours. While questions are always appropriate, the classroom is not intended for personal arguments. Don't be defensive or aggressive in class if the instructor is presenting material that differs from your beliefs. You're responsible for learning the information presented in class—not for arguing with the instructor or monopolizing class time. If you have an honest difference of opinion on an issue, make an appointment to discuss it with your instructor during his/her office hours.
- **Pay Attention to Instructional Clues:** As discussed earlier, your instructor will use "signals" or clues to guide you through the lecture. Keeping up with these transitions will help you to write down the important facts.

NOTETAKING STYLES

You've spent a number of years taking classroom notes already and may have a format or style that really works for you. Many students use a formal numbered outline format, grouping main ideas or topics, secondary topics, and supporting details. This is one of the oldest notetaking systems in use, and it can be very effective if the instructor is well organized and presents the information in an easy-to-follow, step-by-step manner.

Our sample notes will present information regarding the stages of memory in two variations of the formal outline system. We'll also take this same information and present it in a visual format that may work very well in certain classes or for certain topics in a given class. Remember that you don't need to use exactly the same notetaking style for every class or even all the time in the same class.

The Informal Outline

The Informal Outline (also known as the indented topic system) identifies major topics and lists secondary points and supporting details by indenting them under the major topics without using a numbering system. This format leaves a 2^1/$_2$-inch margin on the *right* side of the paper. (Left handed people may want to put their margin on the left.) After class, you can jot down key words or terms in this space for use as memory prompts when you review your notes. The following student notes use the *informal outline*.

3/14/2007
Psych

Stages of Memory

A. Sensory Memory
- First point of information intake—sight, sound, touch
- Lasts for a few seconds as exact copy

B. Short-Term Memory
- Temp. storage of small amts. of info.—5-7 "bits" avg. Digit-span experiment (in text)
- "Chunking" helps us to remember more—e.g. S.S. #'s are 3 digits, 2 digits, and 4 digits
- Provides a "working" memory—e.g. -looking up phone #'s
- Sensitive to interruption—phone # lost if someone interrupts us before we dial
- After 18 secs the info. is lost w/o coding or rehearsal— e.g. Meaningless syllables experiment (in text)

C. Long-Term Memory
- Permanent storage
- Rehearsal process (repetition, etc.) required
- Limitless storage capacity
- Info. stored on basis of meaning & imp.

Bit-piece of info./digit
Digit-span exp.

Chunking—grouping bits together

Sensitive to interruption

Info. lost after 18 secs.

Permanent
Requires rehearsal
Limitless

The Cornell System

The Cornell System, developed by Dr. Walter Pauk of Cornell University, is a widely-used notetaking system. The example below shows a blank notebook page divided into the three sections of the Cornell System, and the next page shows our "Stages of Memory" notes recorded using this system. As the sectioned paper shows, this format leaves a blank column on the *left* side of the page. This space is used to develop questions about the material presented for later review. The horizontal column across the bottom of the page is used to jot down a quick summary of key points.

Cornell Page Set-Up	
2½" for questions	Notes
Summary	

3/14/07 Psych	
How does the process of chunking help us to remember? What happens to info. entering STM? How does info. get moved from STM to LTM?	Stages of Memory Sensory Memory 1. First point of information intake—sight, sound, touch 2. Lasts for a few seconds only as exact copy Short-Term Memory 1. Temp. storage of small amts. Of info.—5-7 bit avg.—digit span experiment 2. "Chunking" like bits of info. together makes it easier to remember—e.g. S.S. # has 3/ 2/4 bits grouped 3. Info. from sensory memory is selected for attention—phone # you've looked up, etc. 4. Serves as working memory 5. Sensitive to interruption—someone interrupts before you make phone call, & # is gone 6. After 18 secs. w/o rehearsal, info. is lost & doesn't get to LTM. 7. Coded, rehearsed info → LTM Long-Term Memory 1. Perm. storage 2. Limitless storage capacity 3. Rehearsal process (repetition, etc.) required 4. Info stored on basis of meaning & Imp.
Info. must go through 3 stages—sensory, S/T, and L/T. Rehearsal process <u>required</u> for retention. Info. stored on basis of meaning & Imp.	

Charting, Mind-Mapping, and Clustering

These three methods of notetaking allow you to "picture" the information visually. Mind-mapping and clustering usually begin with the main topic circled in the middle of the page, with arrows or smaller circles radiating out from the middle to show supporting topics or details. Charting is a more linear format, using horizontal or vertical arrows or lines to show a sequence of events. The figure below shows our memory notes in a horizontal chart, with the process moving from left to right and top to bottom across the page.

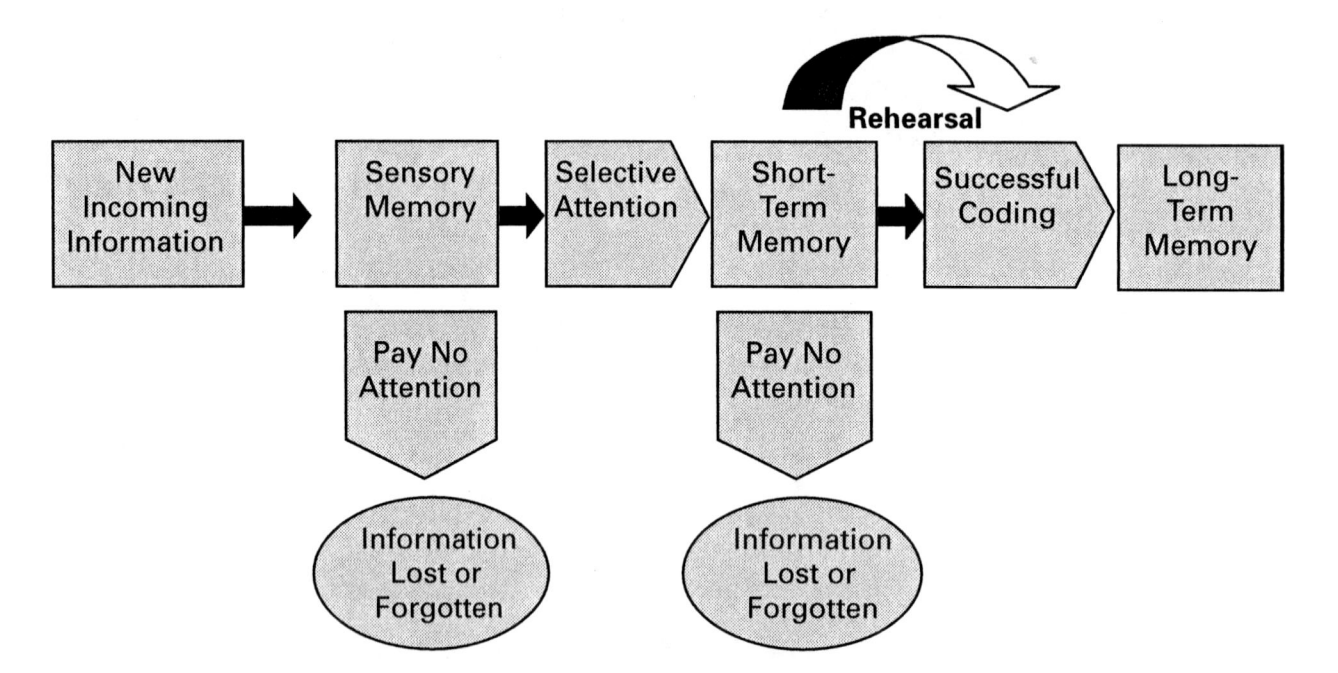

```
New Incoming Information → Sensory Memory → Selective Attention → Short-Term Memory →(Rehearsal)→ Successful Coding → Long-Term Memory
                              ↓                                      ↓
                           Pay No                                  Pay No
                           Attention                               Attention
                              ↓                                      ↓
                           Information                            Information
                           Lost or                                Lost or
                           Forgotten                              Forgotten
```

Choosing a Notetaking Style

We've looked at three different styles of taking notes. How do you know which method will work the best for you? Look over some of your previous notes. How are they arranged? Do they seem to match one of the styles we've discussed, or do you have an original style? Have your notes provided you with the information you needed? Are you comfortable with the system you've been using? If so, you don't need to change. On the other hand, like Carlos from our case study, if you are frustrated because your notes do not meet your needs, identify a style that suits you and try using it.

As you reviewed the descriptions of these three notetaking systems, you probably thought one of them seemed easier to use than the others. Many psychologists and neurologists think that we are primarily either linear or holistic thinkers. By understanding how we tend to organize and process information, we can learn to develop a notetaking style and study system with which we feel comfortable.

Linear thinkers like things to be logical and use rational, step-by-step problem-solving techniques. Holistic thinkers, on the other hand, like to see the whole picture and respond strongly to visual stimuli. Look over the characteristics identified with primarily linear or holistic thinkers and see if one pattern seems to describe the way you work.

LINEAR THINKERS	HOLISTIC THINKERS
• Make lists • Keep track of time • Prefer to work alone • Like a neat, orderly desk • Plan and organize work & study schedules • Usually take linear, outline format notes • Take notes that clearly identify main ideas and supporting details • Complete one task or assignment before beginning another • Are comfortable with deadlines and work according to a schedule • Use facts and reasoning to come up with answers and solutions	• Use visuals and colors when getting down ideas • Are not worried about time—concentrate on the present • May have a messy desk or work area but feel comfortable with the mess • Like to study or review with others • Study whenever time allows; sometimes have energy bursts and work non-stop • May use arrows or lines in their notes to show connections and relationships • Sometimes work on several projects at once • Use intuitive feelings and "hunches" to problem solve

If you identify with the style described in the linear column, you'll probably feel comfortable with either the indented outline format or the Cornell method of notetaking. If the holistic style seems to describe you better, you might want to try one of the more visual notetaking methods. With these systems, you can easily add symbols and diagrams and can color code information to show relationships between ideas.

You may feel comfortable with several items from either side of the chart. If you seem to have a balance between both styles, you have strengths in both areas and can use those strengths to your advantage. For example, you may usually plan your work and follow an organized schedule like a linear thinker. However, you may occasionally get a burst of energy and work non-stop until you finish a job like a holistic thinker. Remember, too, that you may need to change your notetaking style depending upon the demands of a particular class, so be flexible. It's also a good idea to find a study partner of the opposite thinking style so that you can each add creative input to a study session.

USING YOUR NOTES

Developing a good notetaking system isn't enough. You must also learn to use your notes as a part of your total study system. Follow the steps below to maximize the usefulness of your class notes.

- *Editing:* Your first review of your notes should take place as soon as possible after class. Use this time to rewrite illegible words, finish incomplete thoughts or ideas, clarify any abbreviations you used that you may not remember, and fill in any information you might have missed getting down.

This first review is a repetition step that serves as a rehearsal, and it will help you move the information into long-term memory.

- *Weekly Review:* At the end of each week, you should complete a second review of your notes. Concentrate on relationships, time sequences, and organizational patterns at this point. Think about how your notes and your text material overlap. This second review is critical to processing the information for long-term memory storage.

- *Test Preparation:* If your instructor has notified you of the test format, try to predict both objective and essay-type questions. For math class, try straight calculating as well as word problems. Remember to look over your notes for information that was put on the board or that the instructor announced was important.

Questions developed from the Cornell notetaking system can be especially useful if you've followed our advice to use loose-leaf paper for your notetaking. Remove your one-sided notes from your binder and overlap them so you can only see the question or key word column as shown in the example that follows.

Use a blank sheet of paper to cover your notes from the top sheet. Quiz yourself by answering the questions listed. If you're not sure, flip the page to find the correct answer. Once you're sure you know the material, put those notes back in your binder. Continue working on the material you still haven't mastered.

Which memory stage holds information for only a few seconds? Describe the effect of interruptions on short-term memory. How does the digit-span test affect memory?	Why can you remember your social security number when shorter strings or numbers or information may be forgotten? What process is necessary to transfer information from S/T to L/T memory?	What did the meaningless syllable experiment prove? How is information in LTM stored?
Pg. 1	Pg. 2	Pg. 3

- *After the Test:* Your final review should come after your test has been returned. Was the test the kind you expected? If not, what kind was it? Were you prepared? Were your notes adequate? If not, what kind of information was missing from your notes? What percentage of test questions seemed to come from lectures? What percentage came from the text? Think about what you need to do to improve your test scores next time.

SUMMARY

This chapter stressed that taking good notes requires being prepared for class, actively listening to the lecture, selecting a notetaking style, and using your notes as a part of your total study system. You learned to key in to the verbal and nonverbal signals your instructors will use to guide you through the lecture, and you were encouraged to use abbreviations, symbols, and other short-cuts to help you record as much information as possible.

Remember that your notes are only as good as the information you record and the way in which you use them. Students who test well have usually practiced the editing and review techniques covered in this chapter.

NAME: _____ DATE: _____

JOURNAL QUESTIONS

1. What are the major notetaking problems experienced by Carlos in the case study?
2. What should he do to resolve these problems?
3. Describe how you actually take notes in class and how you use your notes.
4. Identify **at least three** *specific* changes you can make in your notetaking. These changes can be from any part of the notetaking process: advance preparation, active listening, notetaking style, or use of notes as part of a total study system.

If you receive notes from a note-taker or use a tape recorder instead of taking notes in class, identify which style of notetaking you prefer. List **three or more** reasons why you prefer this style in relation to your study habits and the type of course for which the notes are being taken. Describe your own advance preparation for class, what you do in class to ensure that you are getting all of the correct information, and how you use and adapt the notes to help you study more effectively.

NAME: _____ DATE: _____

EXERCISE 1. CHECKING OUT YOUR INSTRUCTOR'S LECTURE STYLE

Directions: Use the statements below to evaluate the lecture style used by one of your instructors for this semester.

Course Name _____

                                                                                                                                 Yes   No

1. My instructor begins each class with a quick review of the last session.
2. My instructor is well organized and clearly introduces each new topic.
3. My instructor lectures at a comfortable pace; she/he doesn't speak too slowly or too fast.
4. My instructor speaks clearly and at a voice level I can understand.
5. My instructor is focused and doesn't wander off the topic.
6. My instructor includes illustrations and examples that help me to understand the material she/he is presenting.
7. My instructor uses a vocabulary that I can understand and defines new terms when needed.
8. My instructor is open to questions and encourages classroom discussion.
9. My instructor frequently provides visual input by his/her use of the board, projection equipment, or handouts.
10. My instructor uses the last few minutes of the period to summarize main ideas and/or to clarify new assignments.

How easy does this instructor make it for you to take notes? If your responses cluster on the "No" side, the notetaking strategies presented in this chapter are especially important. They should help you to make the most of your classroom time.

NAME: _____ DATE: _____

EXERCISE 2.

Directions: Complete *one* of the assignments listed below:

1. Photocopy at least two pages of notes you've taken in this class or another one. Using the editing technique described in this chapter, rewrite any illegible or incomplete words or phrases, fill in any gaps, and clarify any abbreviations used. **Do this with a different colored pen so your editing changes stand out.**

2. Photocopy **at least two** pages of notes you've taken in this class or another one. Use the margin of the paper to develop questions from the main ideas and topics presented in class. Develop *at least five study questions,* concentrating on "How" and "Why" questions. Write your questions in a different color so they are obvious.

Special Instructions

Please do not submit your original notes from another class unless you have a copy to use for study.

You may use notes taken by a note-taker to complete this assignment as long as the editing changes or study questions are your own. The purpose of this assignment is for you to demonstrate that you can apply and use the notetaking techniques described in this chapter.

Chapter 11

Studying Effectively

Leadership and learning are indispensable to each other.
—JOHN F. KENNEDY

LEARNING STYLES

How do you learn? You've probably discovered by now that you have a certain way of learning and understanding what you hear and read. You probably also have a certain time of day when you prefer to study. It is a fact that there are "morning people" and "night people" when it comes to studying. This explains why some people are always up at the crack of dawn, take their classes as early as possible, and try to complete all of their homework assignments before dinner. On the other hand, there are those who stay up until dawn, schedule classes in the afternoon or at night, and prefer to study long after everyone else has gone to bed.

Where you choose to study can be as important as the time of day to successful studying. Where do you like to study? Are you a "library" person or an "in my room" person? Do you like absolute quiet or background noise? So, how do you learn? What is your learning style?

Let's begin our exploration of study skills with an assessment of your basic habits and preferences. Take a few minutes to complete items one through twelve in Exercise 1. BE HONEST WITH YOURSELF! How do you **usually** behave in the situations described?

From The First Year: Making the Most of College Fourth Edition *by Glenda A. Belote and Larry W. Lunsford. Copyright © 2003 by Kendall/Hunt Publishing Company. Used with permission.*

You now have some information that can be used in planning your approach to studying and learning. Let's develop a quick summary of your preferences so that you can refer back whenever you need a reminder. In the section provided in the exercise, write a brief summary statement which describes your preferred learning style.

ACTIVE LEARNING

We all have different ways of learning the content presented in any class. Some of us learn best by listening, while others learn best by reading or by discussing. It is not coincidental that the three most popular teaching strategies in a university involve these three modes of learning.

Many students do not think about learning as an active process, one that requires some involvement on their part. Listening and reading are often considered passive activities, yet each requires active participation in order to provide maximum learning. Just as you have a preference for where and when you study, you also have a preference for how you study.

How do you learn best? What is your preferred learning preference or "style?" Take a few minutes to complete Exercise 2 about learning preferences. As you complete this exercise, consider how your learning preferences influence how you study and how you learn.

READING

When we ask students to tell us the title of the last book they read for fun, they seem to consider this a trick question. The words "read" and "fun" do not, from their perspective, fit logically together in the same sentence! The sad truth is that many students do not enjoy any form of reading including newspaper, magazines, and light fiction. We know, however, that "light" reading is a foundation for vocabulary development, understanding how a sentence and a paragraph are constructed, and expanding one's own imagination.

Many students, and even many who consider themselves effective readers, are overwhelmed by the amount of assigned reading and the complexity of ideas presented in their college texts. New vocabulary, new theories, and new concepts are presented in textbooks which provide the foundation for class discussion and understanding the professor's lectures. It is essential, therefore, to keep up with reading assignments; more important, it is necessary to approach reading as an active process that you engage in on a daily basis.

How many of the active strategies identified in Exercise 3 do you use when reading a text? Do you vary your approach to reading depending on the subject matter? At the end of the term, does your text look as if it has been used? Or is it still in pristine condition, containing little more than your name on the inside cover?

Active readers write in their books; active readers highlight, underline, and make notes in the margins; active readers write down questions to ask in class, either to clarify a point or seek additional information. In short, active readers are engaged in the process of reading.

When you read assigned materials before attending class, lectures will begin to make more sense. You will find that you understand more about the concepts and theories presented;

terminology will seem familiar. Because the professor's lectures usually augment the text, your understanding of the topic expands if you are doing the reading assignments. A person who uses listening as a primary learning mode will more quickly pick up on critical points and increase his/her understanding of the materials. Those who enjoy the give and take of class discussion will have more to offer and will better understand the points made by others if the reading assignments are completed in advance.

LEARNING CENTER

Location: _____
Telephone: _____
Hours: _____

There are many reading strategies and techniques designed to improve your reading skills if you find it difficult to keep up with assignments or do not fully understand the materials presented. Most campuses have a learning center or study skills center where a reading specialist can provide you with a diagnostic test and assist you in improving your reading speed and comprehension.

LISTENING TO LECTURES

Lectures are an efficient way for a professor to present new information not found in the text or to elaborate on materials that may have been covered superficially. While some professors may appear to repeat verbatim what is written in the text, most do not. Missing a lecture can mean missing important information which may appear later on a quiz or final exam. It has been said that 80 to 90 percent of the material on the average college exam is based on materials covered in class lectures and discussions. Attending class regularly is the most effective way to master subject materials. The notes you take will augment the readings and class discussions, and will serve to clarify ideas and concepts.

Listening to a lecture is not a passive activity. While sitting in a chair in a classroom is fairly passive, the process of sitting and **listening** is not. The first and most important step in developing good listening skills is to attend every class session on time! Or, as one student was fond of saying, "You snooze, you lose!"

The most visible activity during a lecture is note taking. Less obvious to the casual observer is the thinking process which determines which words or phrases finally appear in a student's notes. Try the following experiment with one of your friends in a class you take in common. See how the two of you "hear" the same lecture!

Critical listening requires careful attention to what is said. It goes beyond hearing words and requires an understanding of the meanings behind what is said. If terminology is unfamiliar or concepts are unclear, your level of learning will be reduced. In fact, it is not uncommon to hear a student say after a lecture, "I didn't understand anything she said." An important part of effective listening is asking for clarification when you don't understand something.

Many students are reluctant to ask questions in class because they don't want to appear unknowledgeable, "uncool," or, even worse, foolish. In fact, every time you have a question, you may safely assume that at least 30 percent of the class has a similar question in mind. How often has someone asked a question that you, too, were considering? This leads to the importance of class discussion in the learning process.

CLASSROOM DISCUSSION

Most college professors welcome and encourage class participation. In many classes, discussion plays a vital part in the learning process. It is also the mechanism used by professors for identifying and exploring points which are unclear to students. Discussion provides an opportunity to examine different perspectives or points of view.

As we mentioned earlier, students are responsible for asking questions when information is unclear. If you have read your assignment, listened attentively, and still do not understand, ask questions of the professor. Most professors enjoy answering questions and view them as a sign of student involvement.

If you find it difficult to ask questions in class, make it a point to talk with the professor after class or during his office hours. Seeking clarification is the student's responsibility. A professor cannot tell by looking at you whether or not you understand the subject under discussion; if you wait to see how you do on the exam, it may be too late!

This active approach applies to other types of class participation. Many professors structure their classes in such a way that participation is required. This allows the professor to see students in action and promotes a lively learning environment. While there are some students in every class who will not participate, and there are students who participate without being adequately prepared, most seem to enjoy and benefit from an active involvement in the learning process.

In a class where participation in discussions is a part of the grading system, it is important to find ways to contribute to each and every class session. While you do not have to talk all the time, contribute your thoughts and ideas as appropriate.

INTEGRATED LEARNING

The most successful students are those who learn to integrate the three primary learning modes. They read, listen, and participate, using each mode as needed for the subject and structure of the course. These students develop habits that fit their individual learning style and increase their chance for success in the classroom. While each successful student has a dominant or "preferred" approach to learning, each has learned to use the other modes in support. Let's consider some specific strategies and techniques to improve learning.

NOTE TAKING EXPERIMENT

During one of your class sessions, each of you take notes as you usually do. After class, have a cup of coffee together and compare your notes to see what information each of you thought was important. Compare the format of your notes for clarity and future use as a study tool in preparing for exams.

What did you learn from this experiment? Is one of you a better note taker? Did you "hear" the same information? Could you benefit from exchanging notes on a regular basis? More on note taking later!

FIVE WAYS TO IMPROVE YOUR ACADEMIC PERFORMANCE

1. Read a good novel for an hour each day instead of watching TV. It will improve both your reading and writing skills.
2. Write all of your papers on a computer with spell check. **Use spell check!**
3. Let a paper sit for at least three days before preparing a final copy. Careless errors will become more visible.
4. Learn three new words a week and use them. Just using a dictionary is helpful.
5. Don't let a job or your social life become more important than school. If school is not your number-one priority right now, why are you here?

DEVELOPING STUDY SKILLS

Do you have one or two friends who never seem to study but always manage to get good grades? They are probably brilliant or lucky, or maybe they have developed effective study habits. Possibly all three conditions apply! In fact, many successful students have developed such good study habits that they never appear to study at all. They have time for a social life, participation in activities, and, perhaps, even a job. How do they do it?

Assuming you have identified a place or two where you feel comfortable studying and you have some ideas about which modes of learning you prefer, the next challenge is actually sitting down and doing it. This is the point at which students begin to have difficulties. Let's examine a few of the reasons why effective studying can be so difficult.

DISTRACTIONS

No matter how carefully you've selected that ideal study location and how motivated you are, there will be some distractions every time you prepare to study. These may be self-created: daydreaming, thinking about other things you need or want to do, feeling overwhelmed by the amount of studying you have to get done. Or the distractions may be external: background noises, other people entering the area, not having on hand the information or materials you need.

Distractions often become an excuse for not making good use of study time, so you have to become aware of what distracts you and develop ways to address these distractions as they occur. Good study habits begin with an ability to focus on the task at hand, no matter what.

ATTITUDE

Do you view studying a "chore" to be done? A punishment? If you see it this way, studying will not seem enjoyable in any way. If all study time is viewed as unpleasant, you will resent being put in this situation and will, at some level, resist.

Students who resist or resent time spent preparing for classes, reviewing notes, and reading are probably negative about school in general. They find studying as one more "chore." If you are a student who has this

> Five characteristics consistently demonstrated by successful managers working for the Xerox Corporation were, in no particular order:
>
> Creativity
>
> Inquisitiveness
>
> Idealism
>
> Ability to change
>
> A sense of values and ethics

attitude about studying, then perhaps attending college may not be the right thing for you right now! However, if you want to be in college and have goals that include a college degree, then it is time to consider your attitudes about studying.

MOTIVATION

Effective students are usually highly motivated people. They have set clear goals for themselves and are excited and challenged by the process of learning. College is viewed as an opportunity to explore exciting new interests and ideas.

Motivation is something that is intrinsic. No one else can motivate you, although others in your life may support and encourage your efforts. Sometimes another person, perhaps a professor or another student, will challenge or inspire you, but that's different from the basic motivation to learn, which has to come from within.

COMPETING DEMANDS

Most students do have a life outside of attending classes and studying, but what is that "life?" If too many things are competing for your time and attention, studying and attending class may begin to drop off your list of priorities. The "big three" competitors for students' time are jobs for pay, friends, and family. If the time required for any (or all) of these interferes with your study time and going to classes, it is likely you will never become as successful a student as you might like to be.

How do you say, "No" to family and friends? How do you give up all those things that your job allows you to buy or pay for? The answer is simple: it takes practice, a willingness to make changes in your life, and a commitment to planning for the future rather than living only in the here-and-now.

A FEW STUDY TIPS

Now that we've looked at some of the factors in your life that might interfere with serious, productive study, let's examine some of the basic skill areas required to be a successful student. Mastery of basic study skills is the second major problem area for students after the intrinsic issues are addressed. Entire books have been written on each of the following topics. This is a brief starting point for you to begin developing your skills as needed.

THE THREE "Rs"

It may seem simplistic, but the foundation of all successful academic work is mastery of those skills you were first taught in your earliest education: reading, writing, and mathematics. If you are not a good reader, cannot write effectively, and shy away from anything mathematical, you are in for a challenging experience in college!

Very few college classes, for example, are taught without a designated textbook or two. Often, several additional books will be assigned as reserved reading in the library. To cover this amount of written material, you must read quickly and with reasonable levels of comprehension. Students who are not strong readers might benefit from taking a course designed to improve reading speed and comprehension. Such courses may be taken at a community college or you might want to schedule time with a reading specialist in the university's learning center.

Writing is another major requirement in most college courses. Many universities now insist that all students demonstrate a mastery of basic writing skills as a requirement for graduation. This may mean taking a specific sequence of writing courses or it may mean passing a test of your English writing skills.

You will write papers in almost every course you take. Some professors will reduce your grade if a paper is poorly written from a technical perspective. If you don't use proper sentence structure, punctuation, and spelling, your grade may be dropped significantly. While you will focus much of your attention on a paper's content, it cannot be the sole consideration in preparing college-level written assignments. You need to learn to write clearly, concisely, and correctly.

If you don't own a basic style manual, buy one. There are several available and in general use including the *Chicago Manual of Style*, the *Modern Language Association Manual of Style*, and the *American Psychological Association Style Manual*. A style manual will provide you with the correct technical information required to write a strong paper.

Mathematics is another subject required for graduation from most universities. While the number of required courses may vary, it is not uncommon for students to fulfill both basic math and computer literacy requirements. Many academic majors require more. Students whose math background is weak need to take lower-level preparatory courses before tackling college-level courses if they hope to be successful. Math is one of those areas where there is no substitute for mastery of the basic skills!

USING PLACEMENT TEST SCORES

At Orientation, you took placement tests that provided some information about your preparation for college-level math and/or writing courses. You may have taken one or more Advanced Placement (AP), International Baccalaureate (IB), or College Level Examination Program (CLEP) tests before coming to the university. These tests may have provided you with credits for college-level course work in one or more areas and allow you to immediately move on to higher level courses.

If you took a placement test, however, you may dislike the results and want to take more advanced courses than the recommended placement level. We're not sure whether this reluctance to accept placement results is "ego" or just difficulty in admitting a weakness in earlier academic preparation. The reasons are irrelevant. What is important to understand is that students who ignore placement test results and individually choose to enroll in higher-level courses often fail those courses.

Placement tests can help identify areas where you may need additional work to become as effective in the classroom as you might like to be. Don't ignore the results of these tests because of your vanity!

LISTENING SKILLS

When you are not reading or writing, the odds are you will be in a classroom listening. You will listen to lectures, class discussions, and speeches by guest lecturers. Each form of oral communication will reinforce or add to what you've read and researched. Listening effectively is a critical and difficult skill to develop. It is related to a number of factors including your ability to focus and concentrate.

Where do you sit in class? What is your in-class "attitude?" Are you attentive? Do you follow what is going on? Are you day-dreaming? Dozing? Worrying about what you'll be doing after dinner? These things all influence your ability to focus and learn from what you are hearing.

NOTE TAKING

There are many different systems of note taking. Any basic study skills book can provide you a "system" for taking notes during class and when you are reading the text. There are, however, some common elements in all systems.

A first step is to develop and use a system of note taking that you understand and can interpret. There is nothing worse than looking at notes a week or two later and discovering that you have no idea what they mean! Individual note taking systems often include:

1. Developing a set of abbreviations that you can use as a form of "shorthand." This saves time when taking notes, but is only effective if you can remember what your symbols mean.

&	=	and	<	=	less than	w/	=	with
%	=	percent	♀	=	woman, female	w/o	=	without
>	=	greater than	♂	=	man, male	=	=	equals

Figure 1 Common Abbreviations

2. Not writing down everything. Look for key words, definitions, terms, and new concepts. Most professors work from an outline while lecturing, even if they sometimes digress. Try to follow and take notes in an outline format.

3. Leaving space to add new information or continue points on a topic that may appear at a later time in the lecture.

4. Reviewing your notes within 24 hours after the class. It is easier to make additions and clarifications while the information is still fresh in your mind. You can also identify questions to ask at the next class session.

One popular system of note taking which many students use is outlined in Figure 2. There are notebooks and note paper which are formatted to use this type of note taking approach.

TEST TAKING

Tests take on a new meaning in college. In some ways, universities still follow the old academic tradition in which tests were the primary mechanism for determining who received a degree and who did not. Students attended lectures until they (and their "tutor") decided they were ready to take examinations. Those who passed were awarded a degree; those who failed left the university. Some students attended lectures for years without ever taking their examinations or earning a degree!

INSTRUCTORS AND TESTING

Taking tests is one of the most challenging parts of any course. No matter how well you read or how precise your notes might be, tests and quizzes will make up a large part of your grade in most classes. And, unfortunately, there will be fewer tests upon which your grade is based than you were accustomed to in high school. Some professors may give only two exams, a mid-term and final. Other professors may give several quizzes in addition to a mid-term and final. Then there is that occasional class when the only test is a final!

Professors may also weigh tests or quizzes differently. A final may count for as much as one-half of the course grade or it may be weighed the same as any other test or quiz given during the course. Some professors count every test grade, while others allow students to "throw out" their lowest grade. Some professors allow make-up tests if you miss an exam; others do not.

As a student, you have to learn each professor's testing system, expectations, and requirements. Unlike high school, there are few acceptable excuses for missing a test or quiz. You must negotiate with each instructor if something happens and you miss a test; however, don't expect much sympathy if you were not in contact *before* the test was given.

TYPES OF TESTS

Three common types of tests are essay, short-answer, and multiple-choice/true-false. Which type of test is given depends on the individual professor's preferences and, to some extent, the course material. Each test type requires a different strategy and study method. Knowing what type of test the instructor gives will allow you to better prepare yourself.

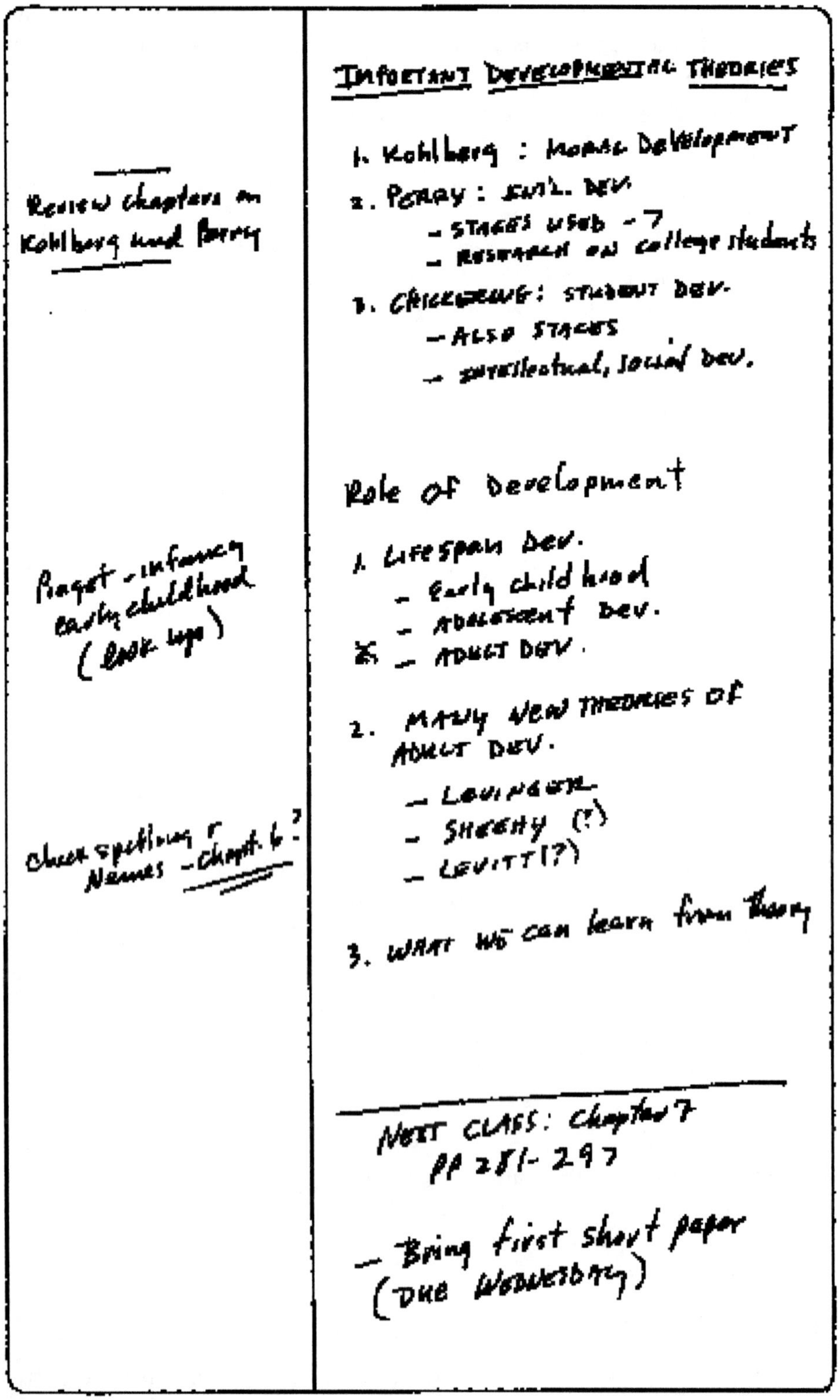

Notes (left margin):

Review chapters on Kohlberg and Perry

Piaget — infancy, early childhood (look up)

Check spellings of Names — Chapt. 6?

Main notes (right):

INPORTANT DEVELOPMENTAL THEORIES

1. Kohlberg : Moral Development
2. Perry : Intel. Dev.
   - Stages used - 7
   - Research on college students
3. Chickering : Student Dev.
   - Also stages
   - Intellectual, Social Dev.

Role of Development

1. Lifespan Dev.
   - Early childhood
   - Adolescent dev.
   - Adult Dev.
2. Many new theories of Adult Dev.
   - Loevinger
   - Sheehy (?)
   - Levitt (?)
3. What we can learn from theory

NEXT CLASS: Chapter 7
pp 281-297

- Bring first short paper (Due Wednesday)

Figure 2 Important Developmental Theories

Essay tests are often given in courses where students are expected to analyze and compare or contrast information. When preparing for an essay test, keep the following points in mind:

1. Read each question carefully and understand what is required in your response. More points are deducted for not understanding directions than for any other reason. Look for key words and phrases like "compare," "contrast," and "describe," which suggest how your answer should be framed.
2. Take time to make some notes or a brief outline of ideas before you begin writing. Think about key points or concepts you want to include in your answer. Don't be in too big a hurry to begin writing.
3. Keep track of time if you have more than one essay question to answer. If points are evenly distributed for the questions, distribute your time evenly.
4. Use your best writing skills. Write in complete sentences using correct punctuation and spelling. Many instructors will deduct points for poor writing, regardless of how well you may cover the topic.
5. Leave enough time to review your answers. It is likely that you will recall additional information when you do this.

Short-answer tests are used most frequently in courses where clusters of information are important. Questions usually call for recollection of facts, dates, names, or lists of items. Short answer tests may also involve filling in blanks and writing one or two sentence responses.

In responding to questions on this type of test, consider the following points:

1. Read the sentence stem or question carefully. Be sure you understand what type of information is sought. Ask yourself what you recall from readings and lectures about the topic.
2. Be brief and focused in your responses. That's why this is called a "short-answer" test!
3. Jot down ideas in the margin or on the back of the test before you start responding. Organize your ideas by looking at all of the questions and making some notes before you start writing.
4. Start with the items you know best and leave the more difficult questions until last. Successfully completing one or two questions will relax you and probably help you recall additional information.

Multiple-choice tests are often used in large lecture sections and for common departmental exams. These tests are usually machine scored and make use of standard computer answer sheets. When taking a multiple choice or true-false test, the following suggestions may be helpful:

1. Read the directions carefully. If a computer answer sheet is used, examine the format and know which way the numbers go. Some use horizontal and some use vertical numbering. A quick way to fail a test is to bubble in the right answer next to an incorrect number!

2. Don't panic if you don't know the answer to the first item or two. Keep reading and begin with those answers you do know.
3. Unless there is a penalty for guessing, answer every item on the test. With true-false questions, you have a 50-50 chance of guessing correctly; with multiple choice responses, you can often rule out some of the response options and narrow your choices.
4. As you work through the test, look for information that may assist you in answering other questions.
5. As a rule of thumb, don't change answers unless you are certain the new answer is correct. Your first choice is usually the better choice if you are not 100 percent certain.

USING STUDY GROUPS

In many courses, forming a study group is an effective way to master subject material. There are some distinct advantages to study groups as well as some potential drawbacks.

On the positive side, study groups offer support, a chance to hear others' ideas, and an opportunity to test your own knowledge through the give-and-take of group discussion. On the down side, study groups can become an excuse for not keeping up with assignments, a social rather than a work group, or a mechanism for letting others do the work. Study groups are definitely not for everyone.

Groups are best used in courses where there is much reading. Discussing a reading assignment can be helpful in developing a deeper understanding of the material. Groups are also helpful in courses where memorization and repetition may be required. Group members can "coach" one another, develop practice questions, and quiz one another.

Follow these basic guidelines for a successful group experience:

1. Know who is joining the group. Every member should be willing to make a commitment of both time and effort. If not, you may be the one doing all the work!
2. Establish a regular meeting time and place. Try to avoid areas where people are socializing (the cafeteria, the student center lounge).
3. Agree on how the group will function. Will members each take special responsibility for some aspect of the assignment? Will everyone come prepared to discuss the entire assignment? Will someone lead the discussion?
4. How will the group deal with non-participation? With people who don't do their part of the work?
5. Will you share and discuss writing assignments in the group? (Remember, written work you submit as part of a class assignment must be your own, but the group can give feedback on what you've written.)

MORE THAN JUST BOOKS

Books, magazines, a place to study or meet friends—that's what most students think of when they think about libraries. But university libraries are much more: research collections of all kinds and in various formats; services to help you do your assignments and write your papers; and people who are detectives at finding information and committed to teaching you how to become information literate. The library is the heart of academic life and your gateway to the world of information.

SUMMARY

Being a good student requires time and effort on your part. It begins with knowing yourself and how you best learn information. Good students also develop basic skills and strategies that allow them to manage their workload successfully. Assess your study habits now and begin to make the kinds of changes that will enhance your performance in the classroom.

NAME: _____ DATE: _____

EXERCISE 1. LEARNING STYLE INVENTORY

Write the letter of the best answer in the space.

1. I study best when I'm working
    a. alone.
    b. with a friend.
    c. in a group.

2. My energy level is highest
    a. early in the morning.
    b. in mid-afternoon.
    c. late at night.

3. I concentrate best
    a. in total silence.
    b. with the radio or television on.
    c. with normal noise and confusion around me.

4. I learn best if I
    a. highlight or underline important material in the text.
    b. say or make important points aloud.
    c. write important information in my own words.

5. I study best when I'm
    a. reclining in bed.
    b. sitting at a table or desk.
    c. relaxing in a comfortable chair.

6. I learn best when I study
    a. in long blocks of time.
    b. in several short blocks of time with short breaks.
    c. in no set pattern.

7. I study best when the room is
    a. warm and cozy.
    b. a little cool.
    c. about normal temperature.

From Developing Power in Reading *by Roe and Ross. Copyright © 1993 by Kendall/Hunt Publishing Company. Used with permission.*

8. I usually work best
    a. with dim lighting.
    b. with bright lights all around me.
    c. with normal lighting.

9. After studying a long time, I find I relax best by
    a. reading something light.
    b. exercising.
    c. visiting with friends.

10. I function best if I
    a. get eight or more hours of sleep a night.
    b. get only a few hours of sleep and nap occasionally during the day.
    c. vary the amount of sleep I get in relation to my activities.

11. I work best
    a. under pressure.
    b. when relaxed.

12. I can handle well
    a. only one thing at a time.
    b. many projects simultaneously.

Summary of my learning style: _____
_____
_____
_____
_____
_____
_____
_____
_____
_____
_____

NAME: _____ DATE: _____

EXERCISE 2. SELF-AWARENESS INVENTORY

Choose the answer that is usually true for you, even though more than one answer might be appropriate sometimes. Write the letter in the space.

1. When taking notes from a lecture, I usually
   a. try to write down everything.
   b. randomly select some of the ideas.
   c. identify and write down the important points.

2. When studying for an exam from my class notes, I usually find the notes
   a. incomprehensible.
   b. incomplete.
   c. adequate.

3. When I study, I usually
   a. need to get up and get supplies (dictionary, paper, pencil, etc.) frequently.
   b. have everything I need but get up because I'm restless.
   c. get down to work without frequent breaks because I have everything I need.

4. If I don't understand something, I usually
   a. avoid it, hoping I'll get by.
   b. ask someone about it.
   c. try to figure it out.

5. When I read a chapter in my textbook, I usually
   a. read it straight through, giving my equal attention to each word.
   b. skip through it and read the parts that interest me.
   c. try to pick out the major points.

6. When I come to illustrations or other graphic aids in the textbook, I usually
   a. skip over them.
   b. glance at them casually.
   c. try to relate them to the narrative portion of the text.

7. When I try to remember material for an exam, I usually
   a. rely on memory tricks.
   b. make silly associations.
   c. relate new material to what I already know.

From *Developing Power in Reading* by Roe and Ross. Copyright © 1993 by Kendall/Hunt Publishing Company. Used with permission.

8. I prepare for exams by
   a. cramming the night before the exam.
   b. completing each assignment when it is due.
   c. completing assignments when due and reviewing periodically.

9. On an exam, I usually
   a. answer each question as I come to it.
   b. concentrate on the most difficult questions.
   c. work quietly through the exam, answering questions I'm sure of first.

10. When taking a test, the questions are usually
    a. a complete surprise.
    b. some that I expected and others that I did not anticipate.
    c. about what I expected them to be.

11. If I want to find a specific topic in my book, I am likely to
    a. flip through the pages hunting for it randomly.
    b. look in the table of contents.
    c. look in the index.

12. When I go to the library, I
    a. seldom know how to find what I need.
    b. usually ask for help in locating materials.
    c. usually find what I want.

13. When I need to study but I'm tempted to do something else, I usually
    a. give in to temptation.
    b. compromise—do a little of both.
    c. study.

14. I work best when
    a. someone tells me exactly what to do and checks up on me.
    b. I follow the same plan for every assignment.
    c. I work at my own pace and in my own way.

15. When the teacher calls on me unexpectedly during class, I usually
    a. guess at the answer.
    b. go blank.
    c. give the right answer.

16. When studying for an exam, I usually
    a. run out of time.
    b. have time left over.
    c. have about the right amount of time.

17. If I want to get good grades, I have to
    a. study nearly all the time.
    b. give up my social life.
    c. carefully balance my time between studying and extra-curricular activities.

18. If I have a term paper to write, I
    a. wait until the last minute.
    b. am not sure how to proceed.
    c. organize the assignment and meet self-imposed deadlines.

19. When I think about my course work, I generally feel
    a. that it is a waste of time.
    b. discouraged and depressed.
    c. that I'm learning something worthwhile.

20. When the teacher assigns homework, I usually
    a. try to get out of doing it.
    b. resent the assignment but do it anyway.
    c. do it because it will probably help me learn what I need to know.

21. When it's time to go to class, I usually
    a. dread going.
    b. go because attendance is required.
    c. go to learn something.

22. When I don't understand an assignment, I'm likely to
    a. not do it.
    b. do it any way I can.
    c. ask for clarification.

Answers to Exercise 2

The "a" response indicates poor approaches to learning, while the "c" responses indicate good approaches. The "b" responses are neither good nor bad indicators. In evaluating your learning habits, consider that 10 or more "a" responses suggest you need to review and revise your approach to studying. Ten or more "c" responses suggest you already employ some effective habits.

The Inventory items are divided into several categories. In analyzing your answers by category, you may identify some areas where change will be helpful. The items and categories are:

1–4	Study skills
5–6	Textbook reading
7–10	Exams
11–12	Reference skills
13–14	Self-discipline
15–16	Stress
17–19	Time management
20–23	Attitude

NAME: _____ DATE: _____

EXERCISE 3. ACTIVE READING STRATEGIES

Reading a textbook is not like reading a novel; reading a novel is not like reading the newspaper. Much of the reading you'll do in the next few years will be linked to textbooks and assignments for college courses, so let's assess your level of skill for this type of reading.

As you read each of the following statements, mark your response using this key:

1 = I seldom or never do this.
2 = I occasionally do this, depending on the class.
3 = I almost always or always do this.

1. I write notes in the margin of the text.

2. I underline or highlight important phrases and passages.

3. Before I begin reading, I glance through the chapter and note section headings.

4. I read the summary of the chapter before reading the chapter.

5. I take notes in my notebook for future study as I read.

6. I keep up with reading assignments on a daily basis.

7. I re-read chapter summaries before tests.

8. I plan reading time for each class in my weekly schedule.

9. I review reading assignments and lecture notes after class to be certain I understand everything.

10. If a chapter has study questions, I use them as a guide.

TOTAL POINTS:

Scoring Key: 25–30 points   You're a skilled reader!
               20–24 points   You're good but keep improving.
               15–19 points   Some changes are needed.
               10–14 points   Major improvements are needed.
               0–9 points   Seek assistance!

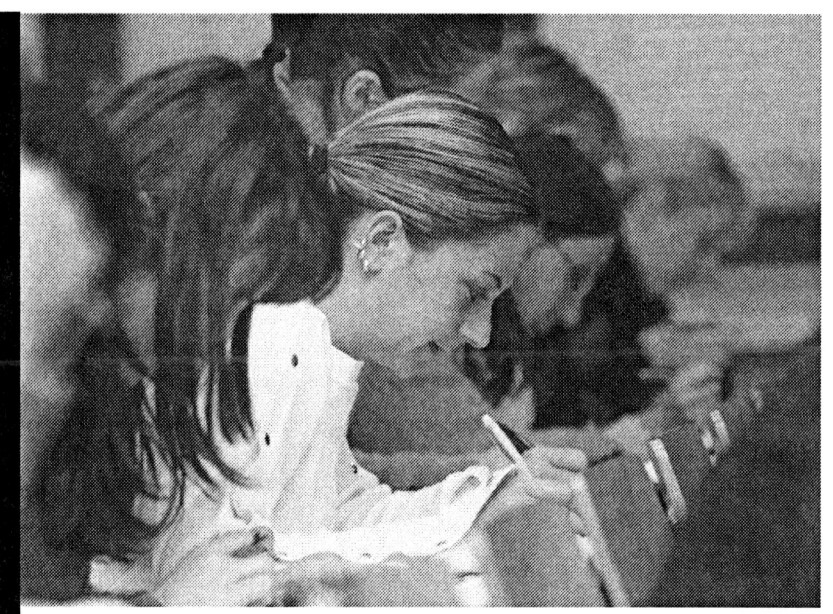

Chapter 12

The Art of Test Taking

INTRODUCTION

Testing is the age old method of finding out what students know about assigned course information and/or how well they have mastered a skill. Examinations force students into learning material and provide the instructor with feedback on how well they have been taught a subject and whether they need to modify their delivery of course information. Test results also provide students with information on how well they are progressing in the course. This information should tell students if they need to modify their method of studying in order to successfully pass the course.

Since testing is such an important college survival skill, you need to know just how it is done and what the rules are for succeeding. Therefore, this chapter will provide tips and strategies on how to effectively prepare for and take tests. It will also emphasize the importance of preparing for tests.

Taking tests is a four part process that requires a lot of work on the part of the student. Testing is a skill. Therefore, it must be practiced in order to learn it. You have to work at

From Keys to Excellence, Seventh Edition *by Carol Cooper. Copyright © 2004 by Kendall/Hunt Publishing Company. Used with permission.*

being a successful test taker just as you must practice and rehearse any other skill you want to learn. The four part process consists of the following:

- General Preparation
- Test Specific Preparation
- Taking the Test
- Reviewing After the Test

You must be a smart student if you want to pass the test. The smart student is sufficiently motivated and understands why he or she must pass the test. Remember, it is not always the most intelligent, organized, or the best students who do well on a test and earn good grades. It is those students who have developed good study skills in test preparation and are committed to passing a course. These are generally the students who perform well at exam time. They are committed, time conscious and, once again, organized and are willing to put in a sufficient amount of time in test preparation to make the grade. Here are some **tips** to help you understand this process.

GENERAL PREPARATION—PART I

Tip 1: Know the planning rules for effective studying.

Start studying for exams from the first day of class. When talking with the instructor after you have received the course syllabus, be sure to ask the following questions:

a. What are the major goals of the course?
b. What kinds of exams do you normally give? Do you have any copies of some of your old exams I may use to help me prepare for your exams?
c. How many units or chapters are usually covered on an exam if it is not already in the syllabus?
d. Does the instructor expect you to remember general or specific detail, deduction, and/or opinions?
e. Will the tests normally cover class texts, lecture and other assigned materials such as films, periodicals, etc.?
f. Will make-up exams be allowed if I fail or miss a test?
g. How much will each exam count toward passing the course?

Tip 2: Develop a systematic method of studying.

If you do not develop this system, it will be difficult for you to be a successful test taker. Use the following rules to develop your system.

a. Learn the vocabulary of the course. Many students fail because they do not understand the vocabulary on exams.
b. Establish a study group or find a study partner from the class. Never go through a class without connecting with at least one other person in that class. You will have

Chapter 12 | *The Art of Test Taking* 201

a built-in system for getting class notes you missed or for cross-checking information. In a study group, each person is responsible for units of information which they must share/teach to others in the group. This is good because when you have to teach information to someone else, you are more likely to learn it.

c. Always scan your chapter before you read. Then read the introduction and summary. These two parts of the chapter should help you to zero in on what you need to know. Do not read your textbooks as if you are reading a suspense or romance novel. Read with the knowledge or understanding of what is on the next page. Make connections.

d. Always read with a question and/or objective in mind. Never read aimlessly. Take the information in like your exam is tomorrow. Know the objectives your instructor wants you to cover. For each unit covered, ask the instructor to share the *must know* items.

e. Always do a quick review before going to class.

f. Take good notes from lecture and/or assigned readings.

g. Immediately after each lecture/reading assignment, organize your information the way it should be remembered. Rewrite your notes if necessary. Preferably a rewrite should be done within 24 hours of the class/review.

h. Once material is organized, master it before you go back to class and take in new information. **Mapping** is a method that can help you organize material. See the example "Kinds of Examinations" in Table 1. Why don't you try making one for all of your courses.

i. It is a good practice to take weekly tests on new information. This will help in moving information from short-term to long-term memory.

j. This is the time to develop mnemonics if necessary.

k. Use flash cards. You may use these cards to review or test. You can take them places where you are not allowed to take books or tablets. A flash card is a 3" x 5" card with the question on one side and the answer on the opposite side.

TEST SPECIFIC PREPARATION—PART II

Tip 3: Know how to "Get Ready."

a. Ask the instructor for the format of the test. Format refers to kinds of test such as **objective**—true/false, multiple choice, matching, fill in the blanks—and **subjective**—essay and short answer. Objective exams require precise information. Subjective exams usually are not as precise, but require you to support the data. The test formats are discussed later in this chapter. **Remember,** smart students test themselves before the instructor tests them. In preparing for an exam, they develop a test similar to what they think the instructor will give in class and take it under what they perceive as the same classroom testing conditions. Test preparation can be demanding but its the smart thing to do.

b. Ask the instructor what areas/chapters the test will cover. If you ask, some instructors will even tell you what questions will be on the test. Make sure you have all information from which the test questions will be taken.

c. Study with a classmate whom you know does well in the course. It makes no sense to study with someone who is failing and cannot help you.

d. Establish the test date and how much time you will have to complete the test when it is given.

e. Set up a time schedule of pre-exam activities based on the date of the exam and your other life tasks (cooking, housekeeping, working, sharing). In preparing for the exam, you may have to sacrifice social, domestic, and some sleeping time.

f. Develop test questions from lecture notes and assigned work.

g. Equally divide your objectives and/or anticipated test questions so that you learn and review a certain portion each day. Remember to consider the complexity of each question/objective. Learning a portion each day or over a period of time is called spaced learning. **Do not cram.** If you have not done so already, turn all objectives for the units or areas to be covered on the exam into questions. Write out your answers for all of them. If you are studying for a skill class such as mathematics, practice the processes until you are able to work them without guessing and/or repeatedly looking at your notes. You need to be able to clearly distinguish formulas and/or rules. **SKILL CLASSES REQUIRE A LOT OF PRACTICE.**

h. When you sit down to study, always review all information previously studied before moving on to new study questions.

Nicole is enrolled in Psychology and Professor Cooper has just announced a test for next Friday. He has given them thirty items to study and has indicated that the test will be a combination of objective and essay questions. Nicole works 12–16 hours a day on weekends. The only time she has for studying is during the week. So today she needs to make sure she has all of the notes and information from which the test will be drawn. Based on the test information, she has 4 days to prepare. She must also begin to determine which items may be asked objectively or in essay form.

Mon.	Tues.	Wed.	Thurs.	Fri.
10 items	10 items	10 items	Test/Rev	Test Day

Day One Master the 1st 10 items/test yourself
Day Two Review the 1st 10 items
         Master the 2nd 10 items/test yourself
Day Three Review the 1st 20 items
           Master the 3rd 10 items/test yourself
Day Four Retest yourself on all items/review
Day Five Arrive early enough to relax/then take test

Note: You should use a realistic time table that takes into consideration your daily responsibilities and the difficulty of the material to be learned.

i. Ideally, the day before exams should be for briefly reviewing materials and not trying to take in new data. Get a good night's rest and get to class early so you can have time to relax before the exam. **Do not** use this time to cram in new information. Knowing the testable information is one of the greatest deterrents to test anxiety. Knowing the information really inspires confidence.

Tip 4: Know how to "Get Set."

a. Anticipate test questions and their format if you don't already have them.

b. Design a test on how you think the instructor is going to test you. Now test yourself with your notes and book closed just as they do in most class settings. Try to approximate the classroom environment. Set a timer or have someone call you when the time is up.

c. Grade your test through the eyes of your instructor. Review again if necessary.

TAKING THE TEST—PART III

Tip 5: Know how to "Go." You are in the classroom and have the test in your hand. You are now going to take the test.

a. Read the directions. Make sure you understand them. Now is the time to ask for clarifications. Do not argue with the tester.

b. Scan the entire test before you begin.

c. Dump data as quickly as possible by lightly writing it on the back of your test or wherever it's feasible. This data refers to information that you are still holding in short term memory or that you have had difficulty retaining. **This may include acrostics and acronyms.**

d. Pay attention to qualifiers and absolute words.

e. Underline key words in directions and questions.

f. Now take a deep breath.

g. Develop a time strategy based on the number or questions and their point value.

h. Focus on your exam and do not let the behavior of other students distract you. For instance, some students panic when they see other students passing their papers in before them or busily writing when they are not.

i. If you are asked to do an essay, develop a brief outline first beginning with the main points.

j. When completing objective questions and you are using a scantron answer card, be sure to line up the questions and answers.

k. Read questions carefully and answer the easy ones first.

l. When reading questions, watch for grammatical agreements. This may help you in answering some of the items.

m. Look for answers in other questions.

n. Look for clue words.

o. Use the guessing or "bulling" rule if you don't know the answer. Bulling refers to coming as close as you possibly can with your answer. Be creative. Try to respond to all questions whether objective or essay. The only time you should leave a question unanswered is when there is a penalty and you are definitely unsure.

p. Make time to look over your test before passing it in to the instructor.

REVIEW AFTER THE EXAM—PART IV

Tip 6: Take a deep breath, review and modify if necessary.

a. Reward and praise yourself if you did well on the test.

b. Review answers to all questions you did not know and/or had to guess on before coming to the next class.

c. Analyze what you did right and what behaviors *you must modify* before the next test.

d. If you believe you did everything right and still did not pass the test, visit your instructor and let him or her give you analysis of the test items. It will help you to focus on weak areas.

e. Immediately put into practice your new behaviors.

Table 1 KINDS OF EXAMINATIONS

TYPE	RULES
Multiple-choice	1. Consist of stems, choices, distracters. 2. Read the entire stem and choices. 3. Eliminate the distracters. 4. Select your answer from the remaining choices. 5. When more than one choice is correct, look for the choice "all of the above," or certain other designations. 6. When more than one choice is incorrect, look for the choice indicating some of the choices or none of the choices. 7. It saves times to answer the easy ones first. 8. There are few situations in which something is always or never true.
True/False	1. True/false tests are not the easiest. Don't be fooled. 2. Make sure you understand what is being asked. 3. You always have a 50-50 chance of getting the item correct. 4. For a true/false statement to be true, the entire statement must be true. 5. Conversely, if any part of the statement is false, the statement is false. 6. Beware of absolute words such as all, none, every, and always. 7. Statements containing qualifiers such as some, sometimes, most, or often are frequently true.

Table 1: KINDS OF EXAMINATIONS (continued)

TYPE	RULES
Completion	1. You must know the correct information. 2. Sometimes clues are placed in the question. 3. Pay attention to words that precede the blank(s). 4. The grammatical structure of the sentence can help in determining what the instructor is looking for in an answer.
Matching	1. It is critical that you pay attention to directions. 2. Sometimes within the directions you will find that an answer may be used twice or only once. 3. If an item has only one correct answer, look for the more correct or complete answer. 4. As you collect responses (answers) cross them out so you don't waste time re-reading them again.
Essay	1. Outline what you plan to cover. 2. Present your information in a clear, concise, neat, and organized manner. This includes writing legibly. 3. Deal with the aspects of the topic the instructor has requested. 4. Pay attention to Key words since they tend to tell you how you are to deal with the topic. 5. Remember that most essay questions measure your depth of the knowledge of the subject and expect you to integrate and apply that knowledge. 6. State main points and use examples to support them. 7. Please refrain from excessive verbiage. Long answers do not equate to good grades.

Key Words

Discuss or explain	Examine in detail. Give facts, reasons, pros, cons.
Compare	Explain similarities and differences.
Contrast	Only explain the differences.
Critique/Evaluate	Give your opinion on the good and bad aspects of the facts as presented.
Describe	Present a mental picture consisting of the characteristics and/or how something really is.
Define	Give the meaning (not your opinion).
Enumerate	State points and briefly explain one by one.
Illustrate	Use examples to explain.
Interpret	Use your own words to explain.
Identify	Be specific in listing/naming items in a category.
Outline	Describe the major facts/ideas that are relevant to a subject.
Prove/Justify	Use evidence or logic based on facts to support an argument/idea.
Relate	Show the connection between ideas and points.
Summarize	Present the main ideas usually in paragraph form.
Trace	Describe the progress or development of an event.

Practice Test

Practicec your test-taking skills by taking the following timed quiz. Please follow directions. Before you begin, read all the items carefully. Each question is worth ten points.

1. Write your name here. _____

2. Identify one concept that you know you have learned well in this course.

   _____

   _____

3. Briefly explain it. _____

   _____

   _____

4. When you compare and contrast, you are

   _____

5. In a true/false question, there is always a _____ percent chance that the item is true.

6. Multiple choice questions consist of the _____ , _____ and _____ ,

7. In true/false items, in order for it to be _____ the entire statement must be true.

8. In true/false questions, be aware of _____ .

9. Once you receive your test in hand, the first rule is to _____ .

10. Add the date beside your name in item number one and do not complete the other nine items.

How did you do? Question number one should be the only one answered with your name and today's date. The rest of the blanks should be empty. Subtract ten points for every one you attempted to answer.

TEST ANXIETY

"I really studied for this test but when I got in there, I couldn't remember a thing." "When I looked at the first question and couldn't answer it, I knew I was a goner." "I'm always afraid of exams because I never do well." "I'm so nervous, my hands sweat. I can't think and when I look around, everybody is working away but me."

Most of you have probably heard some of these statements before. They reflect how these persons are responding to test anxiety. Test anxiety is stress related to testing. Stress is defined as "the body's response to any demand made on it." The demand in this case is a combination of the test preparation and the test itself. On the one hand, you need to know that a little anxiety is good for everybody. It keeps us alert and on our toes. It keeps us from being too relaxed. If we are too relaxed, sometimes we take things for granted and don't prepare as we should. On the other hand, too much worry/anxiety keeps us from performing as we should. When one's anxiety level is very high, we know that it interferes with your memory and as a result drives information from your mind that you know you are more than familiar with.

Anger, depression, and a lack of confidence are other emotions that can also block memory. According to Atkinson and Longman, "test anxiety is a cycle in which self-doubt—even by a well-prepared student—causes the panic that results in a poor grade. The poor grade reinforces the feelings of self-doubt, which causes more panic and again self failure." When grades are tied to fear of loss and expectations of others, the anxiety level increases and once again causes one not to perform as is desired. Another factor to be considered is one's inability to concentrate on test preparation and the test once it is placed in your hands. You are not able to control your thoughts. Having counseled many students, I have found that the number one problem is really a lack of adequate preparation for the test. Most students simply are not test smart. An example of this would be the student who never tested himself/herself prior to the test under similar conditions as the instructor would do—closed book and timed. How do you respond to anxiety? Do you know the causes?

In the following exercises, think about what happens to you when you are anxious and what you think are the causes. For instance, a symptom might be a migraine headache. Working in a small group, complete the exercise on your own paper and then share information. Once you have made your list of symptoms and causes, discuss ways to overcome them. See exercise 3.

If you know that you have prepared well for the exam and you are failing, you may need to make an appointment with your school counselor. If you are one of those students who get ill at the thought of a test or upon walking into the test room, run to a professional counselor. You need help. If the reason you worry is because you have not studied, began to do so now and eliminate your anxiety. Refer to the information on how to prepare for tests. However, the basic rule to rid oneself from normal test anxiety, is to learn to relax. Professionals try to teach you how to desensitize yourself to anxiety through a form of relaxation. The theory is that you cannot be tense and relaxed at the same time. Hence, if you know the information and you can get rid of thoughts that are blocking your memory and causing panic, you can get back control of your thoughts and memory. It sounds simple, right?

During preparation and the exam itself, use deep breathing and muscle relaxing techniques to calm yourself. Close your eyes momentarily and breathe in and out focusing on something other than the exam. Focus by imagining a relaxing scene or situation. If that does not work, tense and relax your muscles while sitting in the chair with your feet flat on the floor and with your hands holding on to the sides of the chair. Tense and let go. Tense and let go. Do this four to five times while breathing in and out. To relax your hands, make tight fists and slowly release them. Do this a few times. In exercise 3, using your own paper, preferably the same one you used in Exercise 2, tell us some of the things you do to calm your anxiety level.

SUMMARY

This chapter has covered the reasons instructors give tests, the four parts of the test taking process and offered ideas on why we have test anxiety and how to cope with it.

Instructors give tests to assist the student in: mastering skills, learning course information, understanding how well they are progressing and whether they need to modify their method of studying for the course. Instructors also give tests to gauge how well they are teaching and getting the information over to students and whether they need to modify their method of delivery.

The four parts of the test taking process consist of: (1) *general preparation,* (2) *test specific preparation,* (3) *taking the test, and* (4) *reviewing immediately after the test.*

Test anxiety is stress related to testing, and this feeling is caused by physical and mental symptoms. Some are lack of confidence, inability to concentrate, fear of failure and the expectation of others. Being prepared for tests along with breathing and muscle relaxation exercises are some of the ways to cope with test anxiety.

REFERENCES

Atkinson, Rhonda Holt and Longman, Debbie G. *Getting Oriented.* West Publishing Company: New York, 1995.
Blerkom, Diana L. *College Study Skills: Becoming a Strategic Learner.* Wadsworth Publishing Company: Belmont, CA, 1994.
Cirlin, Alan. *Simple Rules for Success in College.* Kendall/Hunt Publishing Company: Dubuque, IA, 1989.
Elliot, Chandler H. *The Effective Student: A Constructive Method of Study.* Harper & Row, Publishers: New York, 1966.
Hawes, Gene R. and Hawes, Lynne Salop. *Hawes Guide to Successful Study Skills: How to Earn High Marks in York Courses and Tests.* New American Library: New York, 1981.
Herlin, Wayne R. and Albrecht, Laura J. *Study and Learning: The Development of Skill, Attitude And Style.* Kendall/Hunt Publishing Company: Dubuque, IA, 1990.
Huff, Darrell. *Score: The Strategy of Taking Tests.* Appleton-Century-Crofts: New York, 1961.
Kanar, Carol C. *The Confident Student,* 4th edition. Houghton Mifflin Company: New York, 2001.
Kessel-Turkel, Judi and Peterson, Franklynn. *Test Taking Strategies: How to Raise Your Score on All Types of Tests.* Contemporary Books, Inc.: Chicago, 1981.
Landsberger, Joe, site coordinator. Test Preparation and Taking Website, University of St. Thomas, St. Paul, Minnesota. 2004. http://www.iss.stthomas.edu/tstprp1.htm.
Maring, Gerald H., Burns, J. S. and Lee, Naomi P. *Mastering Study Skills: Making It Happen In College.* Kendall/Hunt Publishing Company: Dubuque, IA, 1988.
Starke, Mary C. *Strategies for College Success, Second Edition.* Prentice Hall: Englewood Cliffs, NJ, 1993.
Test Taking Strategies Website. Paul Treur, coordinator, University of Minnesota, Duluth. http://www.d.umm.edu/student/loon/acad/strat/test_take.html. 2004.

NAME: _____ **DATE:** _____

JOURNAL QUESTIONS

1. Now that you have reviewed this chapter, share your current methods that you use in preparing for tests. What methods do you need to modify and/or change? Remember, it's one thing to say and another to do.

2. Within the past week, how much time did you devote to test preparation? If you devoted any time at all to test preparation, what strategies did you use and why?

3. If you suffer from test anxiety, what strategies will you employ to reduce them. Discuss your plan of action.

NAME: _____ DATE: _____

EXERCISE 1. TEST TAKING AWARENESS CHECK

Directions: Please place an "X" in the appropriate box.

YES NO

1. ☐ ☐ Tests are given to determine your intelligence.
2. ☐ ☐ Cramming is more likely to keep the test information fresh in our minds for the test.
3. ☐ ☐ Students who pass tests are the most intelligent.
4. ☐ ☐ Taking daily notes is a part of test preparation.
5. ☐ ☐ There are basically only two kinds of formats for testing.
6. ☐ ☐ Multiple choice tests usually consist of the stem and the distracters.
7. ☐ ☐ Absolute words and qualifiers in test questions usually will tell you the answer.
8. ☐ ☐ In an essay question when you are asked to do a contrast, you must explain the similarities and differences.
9. ☐ ☐ Test preparation begins on the first day of class.
10. ☐ ☐ One of the key reasons for test anxiety is that some students cram for exams.

NAME: _____ DATE: _____

EXERCISE 2. HOW DO YOU KNOW WHEN YOU HAVE TEST ANXIETY?

Symptoms	Causes
1. _____	_____
2. _____	_____
3. _____	_____
4. _____	_____

NAME: _____ DATE: _____

EXERCISE 3. THINGS I DO (OR SHOULD DO) TO GET RID OF TEST ANXIETY

1. _____

2. _____

3. _____

4. _____

NAME: _____ DATE: _____

EXERCISE 4. THE ART OF TEST TAKING

Directions: Answer the following questions based on chapter information.

1. List three reasons why instructors give examinations and briefly explain your answers.

    a.

    b.

    c.

2. Identify the four parts of the test taking process and explain key elements of each.

    a.

    b.

    c.

    d.

3. Briefly define the following terms:

    a. Critique and/or evaluate

    b. Enumerate

    c. Discuss

    d. Illustrate

    e. Compare

4. Enumerate three reasons for test anxiety.

   a.

   b.

   c.

Section 3
Understanding the Field of Education

Chapter 13

Vocation

More than a Job, More than a Career

Alan Weber (2000) interviewed business psychologists Timothy Butler and James Waldroop about differences between the words *job, career,* and *vocation.* Although people tend to use the three words interchangeably, the words do not share a common definition. A **job** has to do with specific tasks and responsibilities that someone is employed to carry out. The word *career* "comes originally from the Latin word for cart and later from the Middle French word for racetrack" (p. 13). A **career** is a line of work such as teacher, nurse, botanist, or author. But one's career may not be one's vocation. According to Butler and Waldroop, **vocation** is derived from the Latin *vocare* (to call) and describes what one does that brings meaning and purpose to one's life via work. Some callings are to do something while others are to be someone. Gregg Levoy in his book *Callings* (1997), recounts how the mythologist Joseph Campbell reminds us that we are continuously having experiences that hint at our calling. By listening to these hints and learning to recognize them, it is possible to choose the right vocation that can bring further meaning and purpose to life.

Vocational planning is a developmental process that involves self-exploration, career exploration, and occupational exploration. It can be an enjoyable, creative journey, but it does require purposeful planning to discover the kinds of opportunities needed to build life-skills for optimal growth. Zen masters inform us that every journey in life begins beneath

From Life Skills for College: A Curriculum for Life *by Earl J. Ginter and Ann Shanks Glauser. Copyright © 2005 by Earl J. Ginter and Ann Shanks Glauser. Used with permission.*

our feet, even a 2,000-mile journey. Finding the right vocation is a journey that begins right beneath your feet. Choosing the right vocational path and identifying the college major and opportunities that can lead you to your calling are important steps in vocational planning, but not the only steps. The first step comes during the freshman phase of your college experience. This step's goal is to become more aware, through self-exploration, of your interests, values, skills, and aptitudes, and how your personality relates to career choice.

SELF-EXPLORATION

Who are you? What do you want? If you know the answers to these two questions, and are willing to put forth the time and effort needed to answer your calling, you are off to a successful start. The definition of success is a personal one. For some students, success is synonymous with making a lot of money, owning a business, having a prestigious career, or being elected to public office. For other students, altruistic endeavors and relationships may define success. Success can also be a combination of all these values and many more. Being able to identify precisely what you want in life is not necessarily an easy task.

Marsha Sinetar (1987) writes about discovering the right livelihood. She believes that choosing the right livelihood is based on making conscious choices. Sinetar acknowledges that this, too, is a difficult task because "unfortunately, since we learn early to act on what others have to say, value, and respect, we often find ourselves a long way down the wrong road before realizing we did not actually choose our work" (p. 11). Where you are today has a lot to do with decisions you have made in the past. Decisions that you make now create new directions that will determine your future. When you are conscious of the choices you make, you are choosing to be responsible. You are choosing to accept the consequences of decisions that you make, and in doing so, you learn to make better decisions.

At different periods in life, people make vocational decisions based on different sets of motivations. According to Butler and Waldroop, the decisions you make in your twenties are related to creating opportunities for yourself. You are trying to enlarge your world to find all the channels for getting what you think you need and want. In their thirties, people tend to make decisions based on the realization that there is limited time available to accomplish everything, so decisions become more focused. As you become aware of your own mortality throughout your forties and fifties, the gap between your dreams and reality narrows as you search for meaning and purpose. People tend to become more conscious of the choices they are making.

Why wait until later, until your forties and fifties, to discover meaning and purpose? It sometimes takes courage to make clear vocational choices that are reflective of who you are and what you want. Being courageous is often worth the risks involved. Courageous actions can significantly lessen the amount of time required to create meaning and purpose in our lives. The more you know about yourself, the easier the task of finding meaning and purpose becomes. Knowing your values is an important piece of your vocational puzzle. Values are what ultimately guide our behavior and give us direction in life.

Values

Do you ever wonder why it is that you feel strongly about some issues, like abortion, the environment, or capital punishment, but not so strongly about other issues? The intensity of your feelings and thoughts on various issues is related to the strength of your values. Values are different from opinions and facts. **Values** are standards, reference points that guide your behavior, thoughts, and feelings. All your values together form your **value system**. Goals based on your value system will be stronger than ones that are not, and you will be more motivated to spend the necessary time and effort needed to reach them. If your career choice is firmly aligned with your values, you will be more enthusiastic and passionate about your career. Do you value competition? recognition? wealth? excitement? security? friends? volunteering? success? Where do these values come from? Did they choose you (inherited) or did you choose them (assimilated over a lifetime)? Your values may be similar to ones held by significant people in your life, but values adopted without engaging in critical thinking are not as strong as ones that have survived being examined and then accepted as your own.

Do values ever change? Yes, experiences can modify and change them. For example, someone who values material wealth, prestige, and power may when faced with a life threatening illness begin to value health, family and spirituality more. In college as you meet new people, have new experiences, and are exposed to different perspectives, your values will most likely be challenged.

Considering the following questions can help you identify your own set of personal values: What is the most exciting thing you have done? What do you value most about another person? Whom do you most admire? Answers to these questions may point to underlying values. Another way to identify values is to complete Exercises 2 and 3 at the end of this chapter.

Personality

When we talk about **personality**, we are referring to a set of motivations, beliefs, attitudes, traits, and response patterns that are consistent over time and distinguish one person from another. Each person is a unique composite of physical, biological, mental, emotional, and spiritual traits and potentials.

Personality factors influence vocational exploration. *Thinking types* prefer to systematically gather facts about interesting majors, weigh the pros and cons of each major, and then make an objective decision. *Feeling types* tend to make subjective decisions based on how they feel about particular majors. If they do not feel personally engaged in the curriculum of a particular major, they are apt to switch majors to find one they feel more in tune with. When it comes to acting on the decision about a major and investigating various careers, *judging types* tend to reach closure quickly and begin to investigate specific career options, whereas *perceiving types* may resist closure and hesitate to become focused on one particular career path because they see so many options.

How does personality affect career choice? It is much nicer to be in an environment that affirms and supports, rather than one in which you have to continually explain and defend yourself. When your personality traits match up with a career, you will tend to find more support for challenges that you undertake and greater understanding for failed attempts. Let us explore some personality attributes associated with careers.

Extroversion and Introversion. *Extroverts* tend to define themselves by how others recognize and respond to them, whereas *introverts* tend to be private and may not share what is significant and valuable about themselves with colleagues. In working situations extroverts prefer to be around people and seek opportunities to interact with others. Introverts need time and space to think through their thoughts carefully before answering a question or giving an opinion. A person with an extroverted personality generally prefers a job that offers a lot of variety activity and can become impatient with long, tedious tasks.

Intuition and Sensation. Intuitive types in the workplace want to be appreciated for generating ideas and theories, whereas *sensing types* wants to be appreciated for all the details and facts they can bring to the work situation. People who rely on sensing prefer to use skills that they have already developed. They prefer work environments that have standardized procedures, and they do well in work that involves precision. Intuitive types are the opposite. They tend to dislike repetitive tasks and prefer careers that offer numerous opportunities to learn a variety of new skills.

Thinking and Feeling. Feeling personality types like to work in harmonious environments, generally enjoy pleasing people, and are genuinely interested in the people they work with. *Thinking personality types* respond more to ideas than people at work and are good at analyzing situations. They tend to be firmer in their decisions and seek careers that encourage the use of logical reasoning.

Judging and Perceiving. In a work situation, *judging types* are most productive when they have lists and plans to follow as well as the necessary resources (supplies, tools, and people) needed to begin work. *Perceiving types* are good at adapting to changes that arise at work and prefer to start projects rather than finish them. People who rely mostly on judging seek careers that require organization, whereas people who rely mostly on perceiving prefer work situations in which they can create their own schedule.

While no combination of preferences is inherently better than any other type, knowing your personality type can help you understand not only your behavior in a work environment but also those around you. Understanding how your values and personality influence your career choice is important knowledge to have when constructing a picture of your right livelihood, or calling. Next, let us connect some more dots and explore how interests influence vocational choices.

Interests

Most people are more likely to feel motivated to accomplish a task if they are interested in the task. Chances are good that if your interests are congruent with your occupational environment, you will achieve more job satisfaction. A student we know attended a large college for a year, intending to major in psychology. After his first semester, he started feeling apathetic about attending classes and studying. At the end of his second semester, he returned home and began thinking about what he "would like to be when he grew up." He realized that his major interests focused on food: cooking, creating new recipes, observing people cook, reading cookbooks, going to restaurants. He decided to become a chef. Now having successfully graduated from a culinary institute, he is working as a chef and enjoying the work even though the hours are long and the work is demanding. What changed? He is now motivated to work hard because he is doing what he likes! Your interests can be a good predictor of job satisfaction. Think of times in your life when you were deeply engaged in what you were doing. It is during these times that your interests are activated, and you feel a sense of satisfaction and completion in what you are doing. Can you identify your interests? Are you aware of which jobs match up to your interests?

The things that overwhelm one person in terms of challenge and supervision can stimulate and energize someone else. John Holland, a vocational psychologist, has proposed that our interests define our personality. He believes that different personalities cluster together in society, and that personalities can be differentiated from one another according to interests. Holland identifies six clusters of personality traits: realistic, investigative, artistic, social, enterprising, and conventional. According to Holland's vocational theory, career satisfaction and achievement are based on the degree of congruence between a person's interests and personality and his or her vocational environment (Holland, 1966). A popular career test based on Holland's theory of personality, which is found at most college counseling and career centers, is the Strong-Campbell Interest Inventory (SCII). It consists of 325 items concerning occupations, school subjects, activities, people, and characteristics. During the assessment you make decisions about likes and preferences. Results provide information about occupations you might wish to pursue based on your profile of interests.

Skills and Aptitudes

The ability to acquire a proficiency is called *aptitude*. Someone may have an aptitude to play a violin, but if that person is never given the opportunity to play, that skill may never be realized. Many students have the capacity to learn many things, but if the environment is not conducive to learning or students do not avail themselves of the opportunity, they may not learn. Do you have any aptitudes that you have not developed into skills? Skills are things you do well. Perhaps you are mechanically gifted, have good communication skills, are good at problem solving, or have a particular artistic skill like drawing, playing a musical instrument, or dancing. Some people have skills that are easily identifiable because they are observable. Others have skills that are harder to identify, like being able to analyze and synthesize information, mediate, and inspire others. Some people are better with data and information, and some are better with people. How quickly you learn and understand new information and engage in good critical thinking is based on skills.

When you have assessed your values, personality, interests, and skills, you have completed the first step in vocational exploration. Self-exploration will continue throughout your college experience (and life). As you become engaged in different activities and experiences, your beliefs, interests, values, skills, and even your personality may change. The picture that you create of yourself is likely to be revised along the journey. When you "connect all the dots," what picture do you have of yourself? Do you have a clear, accurate vision of what you want to do and who you are? Not only do you need a clear vision, but you also need a systematic plan on how to get there. Part of this plan is choosing the right major and the right career. The next stage of vocational exploration is career exploration.

CAREER EXPLORATION

In addition to engaging in self-exploration, which should begin as a freshman, get curious about all the possible career options out there for you. Talk with parents, professors, parents of friends, and whoever else might provide you with information about careers. Become familiar with career services on campus. At your college counseling or career center you can find information about choosing a major and future career (e.g., information about jobs, career seminars, career planning courses). Be sure to attend career decision-making workshops (if offered), take some vocational tests, sign up for a class on choosing a major if one is available, sign up for internships, attend career fairs and seminars, go on informal interviews, and make a list of careers that interest you and review it often.

Based on what you know about your values, personality, interests, and skills and aptitudes, what career do you think is the best fit for you?

_____

_____

What major will help you get there? _____

During your sophomore year, you should continue to obtain information about careers, seek out volunteer opportunities and work experience, talk to people about their work, and check out memberships in different clubs, committees, and organizations that can provide you with opportunities to develop leadership skills and other life-skills. Visit your career center and read about careers, or go online and find information. Explore every career possibility you can. Consider taking an elective class in a major you are interested in. If you have not done so already, gather information about future employment and firm up your choice of a major. The following resources provide an enormous amount of information about careers and jobs.

Computer-Assisted Career Exploration Programs

SIGI Plus. This computer program is designed to help you identify your interests, skills, and values, find careers that match your personal preferences, and prepare for an occupation. There are eight sections from which to gather information related to careers, and you can use them in any order.

Discover. This computer program can also help you organize your interests and experiences into probable careers. There are nine sections that cover topics ranging from self-assessments and job characteristics to identifying training and finding financial planning.

State-Specific Career Information. Information relating to your state or the state where you will work after graduation can be used to match your interests and abilities with specific occupations. Current information is provided about occupations in different areas of the specific state, including working conditions, hiring requirements, and job outlook. For example, the Georgia Career Information Services (GCIS), which is updated every year, provides information about specific fields of study, financial aid, military careers, and other colleges throughout the United States.

Books

Guide for Occupational Exploration (GOE). In this book, put out by the U.S. Department of Labor, information is provided about interests, aptitudes, and adaptability for over 2,500 jobs. Jobs are clustered by major interest area. This is a good tool to use to analyze whether or not your interests and skills match up with specific jobs. Information about job preparation is also included.

Occupational Outlook Handbook (OOH). Published by the U.S. Department of Labor, Bureau of Labor Statistics, OOHInfo@bls.gov. This resource provides information on more than 300 jobs. Information is provided about training, qualifications, outlook, earnings, and working conditions. A good supplement to the Handbook is the *Occupational Outlook Quarterly,* published about every two years, which has important articles and information about aspects of career planning. For more information about these publications and others, you can contact the Bureau of Labor Statistics through its website at http://www.dol.gov.

Dictionary of Occupational Titles (DOT). This resource offers descriptions of about 20,000 jobs and is updated periodically. The Bureau of Labor Statistics also publishes this book. A good use for this book is to look at the job clusters to see related occupations. It may be that you think of a career and want to know about related professions (counselor, social worker, and psychologist). The *DOT* can help you discover various job options.

OCCUPATIONAL EXPLORATION

Is there a perfect job out there for you? Without the right career guidance, finding the perfect job might be akin to finding a needle in a haystack. After all, most jobs are not advertised. In fact, only about 20% are well advertised. There are plenty of jobs out there if you know how to find them and are able to convince an employer to hire you. According to Richard Bolles, author of *The 1997 What Color Is Your Parachute?*, mailing out resumes to employers at random, answering ads in professional journals and newspapers, and going to private employment agencies for help are the *least effective* ways to find a job.

As a junior, there are specific occupational exploration tasks that you can engage in to increase your likelihood of finding that perfect job. You will want to increase your work experiences, continue attending career fairs, develop a resume, develop career contacts, network, take on leadership roles in organizations to which you belong, and do some serious research about careers (including learning about entry-level positions). Other steps you can take are to participate in Cooperative Education Programs (co-ops) if possible, try to get jobs that are related to your major, do some mock interviews, and begin to gather information about graduate schools if you are planning to pursue a graduate degree. Check with your campus or counseling center to find the most comprehensive resources available to help you find the right job, or go online. You should be able to locate information concerning cooperative educational experiences, internships, student employment, mock interviews, interviews with recruiters, and a variety of other experiences. Executive, managerial, administrative, and other positions can be highly competitive. Different kinds of work experiences, including internships and specialized training, can help you secure a position.

Having a good resume is essential to getting a good job. Many career centers can help you write a resume (and show you how to create an online one), set up a credential file, and educate you on how to secure government employment. Many campus career centers have a variety of books, as well as people, to help you write your resume.

Resume

There are plenty of books on the market about resume and cover letter writing. Besides career centers and counseling centers, check with campus and off-campus bookstores as well as libraries for books on resume writing. The resume is a screening device intended to get you an interview. Remember, the receiver will probably invest very little time in looking over your resume; therefore, it must look great. Here are some general guidelines for developing a resume.

- Your resume needs to be well organized, neat, and easy to read. (No smudges!) Make sure your grammar, punctuation, and spelling are correct. Use a good-quality paper in either white or ivory and use a clear typeface and type size (10 to 14 point). Double-space above and below each heading.
- Learn how to format your resume to enhance specific information about yourself. The reader should be able to form a clear image of you and be motivated to meet you. When choosing a format for your resume, choose one that best suits your purposes. Become familiar with different formats. Know when it is best to use a chronological format (highlighting work history) and when to use a functional format. For example, if you have had little work history, you might want to focus on your skills using a functional resume format.
- Give identifying information at the top of your resume: name, address, and phone numbers where you can be reached. Be sure to get an answering machine or use voice mail to record messages if you are going to be away from your phone for long periods of time.
- Some people like to put an objective in their resume (e.g., "public relations position with a nonprofit agency"). If you include an objective, create it before you begin writing your resume. An objective can help you stay focused while developing your resume. Be sure that you support the objective throughout your resume.
- List your education in reverse chronological order. Make sure you include the year, the type of degree (BA, BS), and name of the school you will graduate from. Include your overall grade point average if impressive, as well as professional affiliations and training seminars. Also include career-related experiences; the name and location of the company, the title of the position you held, and the month and year you started and ended employment. List work experiences from most recent to least recent. You may also want to include school and community-related activities, honors and transferable skills, achievements, and a statement that references will be furnished upon request. Make statements specific, using words that convey action (e.g., *organized, supervised, developed, implemented, generated,* and *eliminated*). Each sentence should convey information about you that you want the reader to notice. Do not put down anything that you cannot later substantiate in an interview.

Occupational exploration tasks during your senior year include reviewing and updating your resume, requesting letters of reference, completing course requirements, signing up for interviews, sending out resumes, setting up interviews, taking qualifying examinations for your profession (e.g., a teacher exam), and participating in campus recruiting efforts. If you have not done so already, register with your career center so you can access a variety of career services. Check their schedules to see what workshops and career fairs are being offered and when. Tell everyone you know that you are looking for a job and describe the type of job. This may also be the time to send out graduate school applications and begin buying a professional wardrobe. Let's assume you have made your contacts, networked through your career center, sent out your resume, and have been asked to interview for a position. There are some general interview guidelines that are important to know.

Job Interview

A job interview serves two purposes. It is a way for the prospective employer to decide if you are the person for the job, and it is a way for you to see if you want the job. This may be an opportunity for you to get farther down the path to attaining your goals. Campus career centers often work with recruiters to set up on-campus interviews, which are usually screening interviews, with students. Spend as much time preparing for your interview as you did writing your resume. Additionally, here is a list of tips to help you successfully navigate your way through an interview.

- Dress neatly and appropriately.
- Be punctual and communicate your appreciation for the opportunity to meet with whomever is interviewing you.
- Job interviews generally start off with personal introductions and a bit of small talk. Do not forget to make good eye contact.
- During the interview try to appear confident and relaxed. You will probably be asked to
  - Describe yourself (qualifications including strengths and weaknesses) and your professional goals.
  - Explain how your education and experience are related to the particular job that you are interviewing for. (Whoever is interviewing you is most likely assessing you to see if your goals match up with the organization.)
  - Explain why you are interested in working with the organization. Knowledge of the organization is vital. Do your homework before the interview. Research the nature of the organization, where it currently is, and where it is heading. It will demonstrate your interest in the position.
  - Explain why you are leaving your current job, if you are doing so.
  - Ask questions. You can always ask about the organization's expectations for its employees as well as future challenges and directions.
- Communicate to the interviewer your skills and accomplishments. (Do not make outlandish claims. Dishonesty will not impress future employers.)
- Before you leave, ask when you can expect to hear from the interviewer again. After the interview, take time to make notes about the interview. Include in your notes people's names, ideas presented, further questions, and changes to make before the next interview. A few days after the interview, follow up with a note thanking the interviewer for the opportunity to meet with him or her and learn more about the organ-

ization. If you are interested in the position you interviewed for, say so, and state that you are looking forward to hearing from the interviewer should he or she have any further questions.

Employment Projections

Every year in the United States millions of new jobs are created. Although not everyone in this country attends college, 63% of the high school graduating class of 2000 was enrolled in a college or university, according to Bureau of Labor Statistics (BLS). Employment that generally requires a college degree or other post-secondary award is projected to grow faster than any other category of occupation. It is projected that the civilian work force in the United States will reach 158 million in 2010, an increase of 17 million from 2000. The overall job outlook for university graduates in the United States looks good, according to the BLS. The Bureau of Labor Statistics analyzes factors that influence economic trends in the United States (e.g., technology, foreign competition, demand for goods and services) to create projections about employment. The BLS projections for 2000–2010 were released in December 2001, but they were completed prior to the September 11 terrorist attacks. Although the lasting impact of this tragedy on the economy is unclear, projections for 2000–2010 include the following.

- Among the ten occupations with the *largest job growth* are registered nurses, office clerks, food preparation and service workers, customer service representatives, retail salespersons, computer support specialists, cashiers, security guards, computer software engineers, and waiters and waitresses.
- The top ten industries with the *fastest wage and salary employment growth* are computer and data processing services, residential care, health services, cable and pay television services, personnel supply services, warehousing and storage, water and sanitation, miscellaneous business services, miscellaneous equipment rental and leasing, and management and public relations.
- The top ten occupations with the *fastest employment growth* are computer software engineers, computer support specialists, network and computer systems administrators, network systems and data communication analysts, desktop publishers, database administrators, personal and home care aides, computer system analysts, and medical assistants.

CLOSING REMARKS

The earlier you begin the process of vocational exploration, the more successful you will be in finding the perfect job, the right livelihood, your calling, or the answer to what you want to be "when you grow up." The right vocation is one that reflects your values, interests, personality, and skills. Marsha Sinetar writes about *vocational integration,* a term used to designate a person who is so completely congruent with and committed to his or her vocation that he or she has no doubts about whether or not to invest the energy required to get the job done. Some students feel that once they have chosen a major, that's it. In fact, many students change majors as their interests change, and as their values change. Remember that vocational exploration is a life-long process. Most people change careers several times, so throughout your life you will be making career decisions. Congratulate yourself for the steps you have already taken, and motivate yourself to take the necessary steps to continue on your career path. Plan for your future now.

SOURCES

Bolles, R. N. (1996). *The 1997 what color is your parachute?* Berkeley, CA: Ten Speed Press.
Employment Outlook, 2000–2010: A summary of BLS projections. (2001). Washington, DC: U.S. Department of Labor, Bureau of Labor Statistics, Government Printing Office.
Kendall/Hunt Publishing (1999). *First-year experience sourcebook.* Dubuque, IA: Author.
Levoy, Gregg. (1997). *Callings.* New York: Three Rivers Press.
Holland, J. L. (1966). *The psychology of vocational choice.* Waltham, MA: Blaisdell.
Sinetar, M. (1987). *Do what you love and the money will follow.* New York: Dell.
Webber, A. (2000, January). Is your job calling? *Fast Track,* pp. 13–16.

NAME: _____ DATE: _____

EXERCISE 1. ASSESSING INTERESTS

Read over the descriptions of the six personality clusters developed by John Holland. Then answer the questions that follow.

R = Realistic. People who are classified as realistic deal with their work environment in an objective, concrete manner. They prefer working with tools and machines rather than people and ideas. Realistic people are often characterized as being practical. They often enjoy working outdoors. Occupations that are primarily realistic in nature include those in athletics, construction, technical fields, forestry, agriculture, and skilled trades.

I = Investigative. Investigative types can be described as analytical, logical, scholarly, creative, and independent. Occupations characterized as being investigative tend to be related to scientific activities. Investigative people tend to be less conventional and less practical than realistic types. People closely aligned with this cluster would usually prefer to work alone rather than with other people. They prefer jobs where they can investigate and engage in critical thinking and logical analysis. Some specific jobs within the investigative cluster are ecologist, biologist, college professor, mathematician, physician, and computer programmer.

A = Artistic. Artistic types describe themselves as being independent, artistically inclined, creative, and unconventional. They dislike rigid situations with rules and regulations that are enforced. Some artistic jobs include actor, journalist, musician, photographer, media specialist, and interior decorator.

S = Social. Others generally see people who score high in the social cluster as sociable, nurturing, helpful, and responsible. These people have a lot of concern for human welfare and tend to be more optimistic than pessimistic. Social people have good verbal skills and enjoy working with others in groups to solve problems. Jobs that involve these personality attributes include teacher, counselor, social worker, minister, travel agent, nurse, and recreational leader.

E = Enterprising. Enterprising individuals can be characterized as enthusiastic, assertive, and extroverted. They prefer occupations that involve sales or other situations where they are in a position of leading or persuading others. People who score high in this cluster are generally good at public speaking and interviewing. They prefer jobs in the fields of marketing, retail merchandising, health administration, real estate sales, law, television production, and politics.

C = Conventional. Conventional people tend to prefer jobs that are structured and predictable. They can be characterized as conscientious, neat, conservative, controlled, and persistent. They thrive on order and prefer systematic jobs such as banker, accountant, office manager, legal secretary, statistician, and dental assistant.

1. Which personality cluster fits you the best?
2. Rank the personality clusters based on how well each reflects your interests and personality traits, with 1 being the best fit.

   1. _____
   2. _____
   3. _____
   4. _____
   5. _____
   6. _____

NAME: _____ DATE: _____

EXERCISE 2. VALUES CLARIFICATION

Look over the list of values below and on the next page. Identify 15 values that are significant to you. Rank them from 1 to 15, with 1 being most important.

- Spiritual well-being
- Relationships
- Respect
- Empathy/compassion
- Sense of humor
- Autonomy
- Competition
- Security
- Wealth
- Good job
- Success and achievement
- Happiness
- Courage
- Strength
- Acceptance
- Appreciation of nature
- Adventure
- Learning/education
- Diversity
- Loyalty
- Freedom
- Intelligence
- Health
- Endurance
- Intimacy
- Creativity
- Love
- Challenges

    Altruism (helping others)

    Appreciation of beauty

    Recognition

    Ambition

    Pleasure and joy

    Other

    a.

    b.

    c.

1. What are your top three values?
2. How are these values reflected in your life?

NAME: _____ **DATE:** _____

EXERCISE 3. WORK VALUES

Work values are qualities about a job that are most significant and meaningful to you. Without them the job would not be satisfying. Identify 10 work values that are important to you and rank them from 1 to 10, 1 being most important.

- Great salary
- Recognition from others
- Security
- Fun
- Autonomy
- Variety
- Excitement
- Lots of leisure time
- Leadership role
- Helping others
- Prestige
- Creativity
- Improving society
- Influencing others
- Continuity
- Professional position
- Flexible work schedule
- Working outside
- Having an office
- Congenial workplace
- Competition
- Travel
- Affiliation
- Decision making
- Supervising others
- Work flexibility

Public contact

Working alone

Others

a.

b.

c.

1. What are your top three work values?
2. Describe why each of these values is important to you.

3. Will your career choice satisfy these values? Explain.

NAME: _____ DATE: _____

EXERCISE 4. GREATEST ACHIEVEMENTS

Think about all the goals you have set for yourself thus far in your life and all of your achievements. List five achievements that you consider to be the most significant.

1. _____
2. _____
3. _____
4. _____
5. _____

Identify five *skills* that were used to reach your achievements.

_____
_____
_____
_____
_____

Identify five *values* that are reflected by your achievements.

_____
_____
_____
_____
_____

Identify five *interests* that are reflected by your achievements.

_____
_____
_____
_____
_____

Congratulations! You have completed the first step in vocational exploration: self-exploration. You have assessed and identified your values, personality, interests, and skills. Now look for patterns and themes among them all. What have you learned about yourself?

NAME: _____ DATE: _____

EXERCISE 5. VOCATION

Career decisions are influenced by what people learn about themselves and various professions. Research indicates that having a specific career goal in mind is related to a student's academic performance at a college. Uncertainty about a major has been linked to poor performance and frequency of dropping out. Answer each question.

1. Review John Holland's six personality types: realistic, investigative, social, conventional, enterprising, and artistic (Exercise 1). Discuss which type describes you best. Be sure to indicate traits or characteristics you have that make you believe this particular type fits you.

2. List occupations that match the type you selected above. Then explain why you think they match this type. Are there any careers you are interested in that do not exactly fit your personality type (e.g., your type is realistic, but you are interested in banking and accounting)? If the answer is yes, list these careers and indicate how you found out about the careers that do not fit your type (e.g., friend, family member, career assessment). Finally, explain what attracts you to the careers that do not match your type.

NAME: _____ **DATE:** _____

EXERCISE 5. (continued)

3. Select two careers that you are most interested in. Gather information about both careers using a career-exploration software program or printed source (e.g., *GOE, OOH, DOT*). The instructor of your course will specify whether he or she wants you to use a certain source.

   How might the information you gathered concerning these two occupations be used to move you closer to finding a career that will prove satisfying and rewarding? Refer to the list of work values on Exercise 3. When you respond, discuss the work values that are of importance to you.

Chapter 14

Understanding Educational Philosophy and Your Professional Beliefs

CLASSICAL PHILOSOPHIES

The *philosophy* of education is the study of the purpose, nature, and content of education. Other questions that philosophy answers include the nature of the knowing mind and the human subject, problems of authority, and the relationship between education and society (Murphy, 2005; Nodding, 1995). Philosophers have proposed a number of purposes for education:

From Learning to Teach *by Billie J. Enz, Bette S. Bergeron, and Michael Wolfe. Copyright © 2007 by Kendall/Hunt Publishing Company. Reprinted by permission.*

1. The success of any society depends on educating its young to become responsible, thoughtful, and productive citizens. In addition to understanding children and the role of children in society, educators must consider the far-reaching outcomes of the curriculum, including ethical principles and moral values.
2. Progress in all aspects of society—cultural, economics, religious, agriculture—depend upon having capacities that schooling can educate. Education thus is a means to fostering the individual's, society's, and even humanity's future development and prosperity.
3. An individual's development and the ability to reach a personal goal often depends upon an appropriate and sufficient education in childhood and preparation in adulthood. Education can provide a firm foundation for future achievement and personal fulfillment.

While there are many philosophers and philosophies, there appear to be four dominant schools of philosophical thought, which have strong support in American education today. We will briefly discuss these philosophies to help you build a framework from which you can better understand the type of schooling you received as an elementary and secondary student, and then help you develop your own educational philosophy and practices.

- *Essentialism* assumes there is a core body of knowledge that must be mastered in order for a person to be considered "educated." It focuses on the "essentials" and is subject oriented. Essentialism could be summed up in this phrase: "Information is the key to a good education" (see Box 1).
- *Perennialism* is more "idea" oriented, and considers education to consist of becoming acquainted with the great writing and thinking throughout history. To perennialists, "understanding is the key to a good education" (see Box 2).
- *Progressivism* seeks to make education practical and applicable to the needs of students and society. It assumes that making knowledge and skills meaningful are the keys to a good education (see Box 3).
- *Existentialism* stresses "authenticity"—the commitment to finding true being. To the existentialist, discovering one's own meaning in life is the key to a good education (see Box 4).

Figure 1 summarizes these major philosophies. On the following pages, we provide more information about the goals of each philosophy and profile the major founder philosopher for each system of thought. We also will offer our thoughts on how these philosophies "look" inside today's classrooms.

Philosophies in the Classroom

How do these common philosophies relate to classrooms, or classroom practice? The philosophy that is held by a teacher, administrator, or even a community will directly mold what teachers implement and how they deliver their lessons. Let's take a closer look at how this philosophical impact relates to classrooms today.

BOX 1 MORE ABOUT ESSENTIALISM

Essentialism refers to the "traditional" approach to education. It is so named because it strives to transmit the "essentials", such as traditional moral values and intellectual knowledge students need to become model citizens. While the term essentialism as an educational philosophy was originally popularized in the 1930s by the American educator **William Bagley** (1874–1946), the philosophy itself had been the dominant approach to education in America from the beginnings of American history (Wesley-Null, 2003; Bagley, 1909).

American essentialism is grounded in a conservative philosophy that accepts the social, political, and economic structure of American society. It contends that schools should not try to radically reshape society. Rather, essentialists argue that American schools should instill such traditional American virtues such as respect for authority, perseverance, fidelity to duty, consideration for others, and practicality (Nodding, 1995; Pring, 2005).

BOX 2 MORE ABOUT PERENNIALISM

Perennial means "everlasting," like a flower that blooms year after year. Perennialists support the view that some core ideas have lasted over the millenniums and are as important today as when they were first conceived. A major proponent of the perennialist philosophy, **Robert Hutchins** (1899–1977), believed these eternal concepts should be the focus of education.

The *Great Books of the Western World* (published by Encyclopedia Britannica) is a series originally published in 1952. The series contains sixty volumes and forms the basis of the perennialist curriculum (Mayer & Hicks, 1992). The series began when the University of Chicago's president, Robert Hutchins, collaborated with Mortimer Adler (chairman of the board of Encyclopedia Britannica).

Perennialists believe students, who are engaged in learning profound and enduring ideas, will come to appreciate learning for its own sake. Like an Essentialist, Hutchins believed schools should focus on these ideas rather than practical or applied knowledge. However, unlike an Essentialist, he believed schools should not teach values. He believed that this effort would weaken the intent and outcome of learning (Ashmore, 1989).

BOX 3 MORE ABOUT PROGRESSIVISM

John Dewey (1859–1952) is the person most responsible for the success of the Progressivist educational philosophy. A social reformer and professor of philosophy and psychology at the University of Chicago, Dewey founded the famous Laboratory school as a place to pilot his educational ideas. This work has had a major impact in American schools since the 1920s (Martin, 2003; Hook, 1995).

The progressive movement encouraged schools to broaden their curriculum to reflect the needs and interests of the students. Dewey believed children learned best through active interactions and play with others. He believed children learned best when they were engaged in activities that had meaning to them. Dewey believed children acquire knowledge when they applied their previous experience to solving new, meaningful problems and he developed a five-step method for solving problems (Nodding, 1995).

BOX 4 MORE ABOUT EXISTENTIALISM

Educational existentialism sprang from a strong rejection of the traditional essentialist approach to education. Existentialism rejects the existence of any source of objective, authoritative truth. Instead, individuals are responsible for determining for themselves what is "true" or "false," "right" or "wrong," "beautiful," or "ugly." For the existentialist, there exists no universal form of human nature; each of us has the free will to develop as we see fit.

Søren Aabye Kierkegaard (1813–1855) was a nineteenth century Danish philosopher and theologian generally recognized as the first existentialist philosopher. Kierkegaard was deeply influenced by the work of the writer Rousseau.

In the existentialist classroom, subject matter takes second place to helping the students understand and appreciate themselves as unique individuals who accept complete responsibility for their thoughts, feelings, and actions. The teacher's role is to help students define their own essence by exposing them to various paths they may take in life and creating an environment in which they may freely choose their own preferred way. Since feeling is not divorced from reason in decision-making, the existentialist demands the education of the whole person, not just the mind (Garff & Kimmse, 2004).

Jean Jacques Rousseau (1712–1778) was a Franco-Swiss philosopher of Enlightenment period whose political ideas influenced the French Revolution. His revolutionary legacy is perhaps best demonstrated by his most famous line in *The Social Contract*: "Man is born free, and everywhere he is in chains." His career began in 1749, when Rousseau won first prize in a contest, held by the Academy of Dijon, on the question: "Has the progress of the sciences and arts contributed to the corruption or to the improvement of human conduct?" Rousseau took the negative stand, contending that humanity was good by nature and had been fully corrupted by civilization. His essay made him both

BOX 4 MORE ABOUT EXISTENTIALISM (continued)

famous and controversial. Few people have equaled Rousseau's influence in politics, literature, and education. Many attribute his writing to influencing the Existentialist philosophy of education (Damrosch, 2005).

Rousseau illustrates his views on education in Émile, a story describing the growth of a young boy of that name, presided over by Rousseau himself. He brings him up in the countryside, where he believed humans are most naturally suited, rather than in a city, where we only learn bad physical and intellectual habits. The aim of education, Rousseau says, is to learn how to live, and this is accomplished by following a guardian who can point the way to good living. He minimizes the importance of book-learning, and recommends that a child's emotions should be educated before his reason. He placed a special emphasis on learning by experience. Rousseau views education as the "drawing out" of what already exists in the child—the fostering of what is native—allowing the freed development of the human potential (Starobinki, 1988).

Essentialist Theories Essentialists urge that essential academic skills and knowledge be taught to all students. Traditional disciplines such as math, natural science, history, foreign language, and literature form the foundation of the essentialist curriculum. Essentialists frown upon vocational content (e.g., learning skills needed to be an auto mechanic or hygienist).

Students are required to master a body of information and basic techniques, gradually moving from less to more complex skills and detailed knowledge. Only by mastering the required material for their grade level are students promoted to the next grade.

Essentialist programs are academically rigorous, for both slow and fast learners. It calls for more core requirements, a longer school day, a longer academic year, and more challenging textbooks. Moreover, essentialists maintain that classrooms should be oriented around the teacher, who ideally serves as an intellectual and moral role model for the students. The teachers or administrators decide what is most important for the students to learn and place little emphasis on student interests, particularly when they divert time and attention from the academic curriculum. Essentialist teachers focus heavily on achievement test scores as a means of evaluating progress (Murphy, 2005).

In an essentialist classroom students are taught to be "culturally literate," that is, to possess a working knowledge about the people, events, ideas, and institutions that have shaped American society. Reflecting the essentialist emphasis on technological literacy, *A Nation at Risk* recommends all high school students complete at least one semester of computer science. Essentialists hope that when students leave school, they will possess not only basic skills and an extensive body of knowledge, but also disciplined, practical minds, capable of applying schoolhouse lessons in the real world (Wesley-Null, 2003; Bagley, 1909).

Perennialism Theories While both perennial and essentialist philosophies believe in rigorous intellectual curriculum and accept little flexibility, the perennialist differs in the belief that factual knowledge is more important than conceptual understanding. For example, science is not about the current facts, but rather the act of investigation (Murphy, 2005).

Figure 1 Comparison of Educational Philosophies

PHILOSOPHIES	PERENNIALISM	ESSENTIALISM	PROGRESSIVISM	EXISTENTIALISM
Basic Belief	The acquisition of knowledge of the great ideas of western culture	Core body of basic knowledge and skills	As society is ever changing; new ideas are important	There exists no universal form of human nature; all humans have free will
Curricular Emphasis	Curriculum should remain constant over time	Emphasis on intellectual and moral standards	Student interest and motivation are important	Individual student interest drives the learning
Teaching Method	Teachers should directly instruct and guide students' understanding	Teachers transmit instruction in a logical and systematic manner	Hands-on inquiry, field trips; integration on thinking, feeling, and doing	Learning is self-paced, self-directed; teacher is co-learner
Character Development	Cultivation of the intellect is the highest priority of education	Students should be taught respect for discipline, hard work, and authority	Schools should help students develop personal and social values	Schools help students appreciate themselves as unique individuals who take responsibility for their actions

In classroom practice, the teacher who follows a perennial philosophy conducts seminars where students and teachers engage in mutual inquiry sessions—called Socratic dialogues—to develop an understanding of history's most critical and timeless concepts.

Existentialist Theories Although many existentialist educators provide some curricular structure, existentialism, more than other educational philosophy, affords students great latitude in their choice of subject matter. In an existentialist curriculum, students are given a wide variety of options from which to choose (Garff & Kirmmse, 2004).

Vocational education is regarded more as a means of teaching students about themselves and their potential than of earning a livelihood. In teaching art, existentialism encourages individual creativity and imagination more than copying and imitating established models.

Existentialist teaching methods focus on the individual. Learning is self-paced, and self-directed. It also includes a great deal of individual contact with the teacher, who relates to each student uniquely and freely. Although elements of existentialism occasionally appear

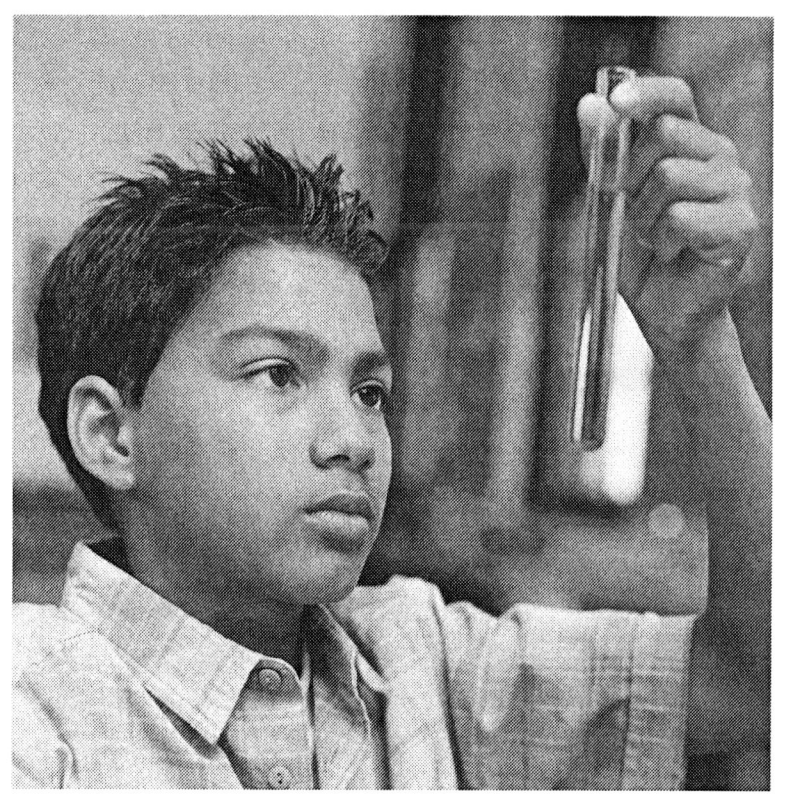

Teachers who believe in the Progressivist Theory use hands-on experiences to stimulate interests and opportunities to learn.

in public schools, this philosophy has found wider acceptance in private schools and alternative public schools founded in the late 1960s and early 1970s (Pring, 2005).

Progressivist Theories Progressivists believe education should be a perpetually enriching process of ongoing growth, not merely a preparation for adult lives. They stand in direct contrast to essentialists and perennialists in the belief that the study of core-traditional subject matter is appropriate for all students. Progressivists believe that the home, workplace, and schoolhouse can ideally blend together to generate a continuous and fulfilling learning experience in life.

Today's progressivists center the curriculum on the experiences, interests, and abilities of the student. Teachers plan lessons that encourage curiosity and guide students' greater levels of learning. Teachers use games and hands-on experiences to stimulate interests and opportunities to learn. Children work together to solve problems, generate ideas, and create new knowledge for themselves.

GROUP TALK

The Influence of Educational Philosophy on Your Current Thinking

In a small group, discuss your educational background using these questions to guide your discussion.

1. What classic philosophy best represents the education you received?
2. How has this philosophy influenced your thinking about education?
3. You may have attended more than one school system as you grew up. Were these systems different in philosophical stance? If so, did that have an impact on your education?

TEACHING STYLES IN PRACTICE

When you are asked about your philosophy of education, most people asking this question are referring to your personal notions about how you plan to teach and why. In most cases we do not explicitly consider learning theory or classical philosophies as we form our own teaching philosophy; instead, teaching philosophies begin at a much more personal level and are usually formed by the experiences we have had in classrooms as we were going to school. In most cases, we are responding to the teaching styles of our past teachers. Use the following two "processing activities" to consider your own former influential teachers.

NAME: _____ DATE: _____

PROCESSING ACTIVITY—THE BEST TEACHER

Directions: Take a few moments to consider your schooling experience. Please respond to the following questions.

Who was your favorite teacher?

What grade or subject did they teach?

Why was this particular teacher your favorite?

What type of adjectives did you and your classmates use to describe this teacher?

What specific practices did this teacher use to motivate students?

What did this teacher do to help you learn?

NAME: _____ DATE: _____

PROCESSING ACTIVITY—THE WORST TEACHER

Directions: Take a few moments to consider your school experience. Please respond to the following questions.

Who was your worst teacher?

What grade or subject did they teach?

Why was this particular teacher your least favorite?

What type of adjectives did you and your classmates use to describe this teacher?

What specific practices did this teacher use to motivate students?

What did this teacher do to keep you from feeling successful in their class?

Chapter 14 | *Understanding Educational Philosophy and Your Professional Beliefs* 257

Hopefully, most of us have had several teachers we considered as we completed this exercise. However, our experiences as students, and our discussions with pre-service teachers over the last forty years, suggest that nearly all of us have had a negative experience with a teacher. These individuals may also cause us residual feelings of frustration, anger, and self-doubt. Take a few moments to consider the *worst* teacher you have had during your schooling experience.

Our prior experiences in school continue to have both positive and negative influences on our lives long past childhood and adolescence. Likewise, these experiences may also impact your views of teaching and the teaching style you adopt for your own classroom (Steffy, Wolfe, Pasche & Enz, 1997).

As a **preservice professional**, your philosophy of education is still being formed; yet, these early beliefs have a profound influence on your everyday classroom practices. Take a moment to complete the Instructional Beliefs Survey (Figure 2), then add your points. The Special Feature by Jill Stam (Box 6), which follows this survey, will provide you with insight regarding your choices and philosophies.

BOX 6 EXPLORING TEACHING STYLES IN PRACTICE

Special Feature by Jill Stamm

After you have added your points on the Belief Survey, you will most likely notice that one column has received more points than the others. The column that you awarded the most points reflects your current view about teaching and learning. The following pages label and more fully describe the four philosophies of education that are prevalent in the field of education today.

Directions: Each box below contains descriptive phrases. Score each group giving yourself a 4 for the most like you, 3 for the next, 2 for the next, and 1 for the least like you. Be sure to put a score in <u>each</u> box. Score across each category. Next, add scores in each column A, B, C, D to obtain column totals. [Adapted from the Instructional Orientation Profile, (Stamm, J., Enz, B., Wactler, C. and Freeman, D. 1996). Stamm, J., & Wactler, C. (1997). *Philosophy of Education Workbook:* New York: McGraw-Hill.]

I believe Classroom Environments should be/should have:

A	B	C	D
• Task-oriented • Organized & Structured • Commercially prepared material	• Student-oriented • Flexible–Spontaneous activity • Student-generated material	• Content-oriented • Goal-directed/Semi-structured • Teacher-prepared material	• Technology-oriented • Production-dominated activity • Materials created on computer

I believe Lesson Plans should be/should have:

A	B	C	D
• Specific objectives are clearly defined • Essential elements of instruction • District guidelines and scope and sequence	• Long-term, loosely structured outcomes • Thematic units and Integrated curriculum • Student choice of what to learn	• Extentions beyond district guidelines • Emphasis on depth of knowledge • Extensive resources (outside speakers, field trips)	• Open-ended and information driven • Multi-level inquiry planning • Emphasize technological skills and information interpreting techniques

I believe Discipline should include:

A	B	C	D
• Positive reinforcement for desired behaviors • Teacher/School-developed rules • Consistent consequences for undesired behaviors	• Classroom community meetings to discuss behavior • Rules established by teacher and students • Serious problems dealt with on individual contract basis	• Teacher modeling of desired behavior • Student responsibility for his or her own conduct • A focus on ethics and moral development	• An emphasis on community responsibility • Teacher and students dialogue to clarify expectations • Procedures to govern student interaction with technology

I believe Classroom Activities should include:

A	B	C	D
• Independent/Seat work • Lecture–Direct instruction • Daily or weekly homework assignments/projects	• Student choices • Cooperative learning • Student-chosen activities and projects	• In-depth research on topics • Lecture/discussion questions • Extensive reading	• Students working on-line • Peer teaching • Student created presentations and projects

I believe Grading and Student Evaluation should include:

A	B	C	D
• Mastery testing • Progress measured objectively and frequently • Tests that assess stated objectives	• Ongoing portfolio assessment • Grades for effort as well as achievement • Self and peer evaluating process as well as product	• Essay and objective tests • Grades on ability to apply knowledge • High standards	• Grading student work on decision making, resources used • Evaluation of students' technical competence • Feedback given via E-mail

I believe Knowledge and Instruction should include:

A	B	C	D
• Logical step-by-step instruction • Drill and practice focused on specific outcome • Focus on mastering the basic/essential skills	• "First-hand" experiences • Manipulation and experimentation • Students construct their own meaning/develop personal understanding	• Intense study and immersion in content • Teacher transmission/model • Depth of knowledge as a goal	• Teaching students how to search for information • Exploration/student interest • An emphasis on meaning of information

I believe the Teacher's Role is:

A	B	C	D
• Manager • Organizer • Planner	• Facilitator • Explorer • Co-learner	• Expert • Mentor • Guide	• Interpreter • Consultant • Connector

Column A total | **Column B total** | **Column C total** | **Column D total**

Figure 2 Instructional beliefs Survey

It is important to remember that one teaching style is not better than another. Each style has terrific advantages and some disadvantages. Often times, you may have two columns that have similar scores. This usually suggests that, as a student, you have had a range of teachers who had divergent teaching practices that deeply influenced your views of teaching and learning.

Our teaching styles usually do not change dramatically **until** we have had a great deal of time developing our own teaching styles through experience in the classroom.

COLUMN A: EXECUTIVE

If you awarded Column A the most points you favor have the **Executive** teaching style. The executive approach is very skills-oriented, and is so labeled because it reflects many of the same values and outcomes that are found in business and industry. This approach utilizes elements of the behaviorist and cognitivist learning theories and more clearly reflect the **Essentialist** philosophy of education.

The executive teacher is a manager. The teacher, as manager, directs students' learning and focuses on end products that can be measured accurately. District guidelines and grade-level scope and sequence determine what will be taught. Such teachers are efficient in lesson planning, devising materials to meet student needs, and in testing of the objective.

The student is seen as the consumer of information. The content to be learned is highly specified and is taught to students in the exact form they will need to know it for a test. The content is usually "delivered" to the awaiting student by a *lecture* method.

High achievement in recalling a great deal of information is the goal. Student learning is considered the goal, and achievement scores the end product.

The classroom environment is highly structured, and it is extremely efficient and is organized around accomplishing tasks.

Positive Factors

- Because both the content to be taught and the outcomes to be achieved are so clearly stated and well defined, new teachers are usually able to find early successes and therefore greater comfort by using this approach.

- Teachers using the executive approach often place a very high value on the use of research-based strategies.

- Administrators, state legislators, and many parents have high praise for teachers who use this approach. It gives comfort to be able to "see clearly" what is expected of each student.

- Teachers who enjoy and excel in being well organized thrive in this environment.

Negative Factors

- Teachers who teach with this approach often suffer from greater "burn-out." Because they incorporate each new research-based strategy into their repertoire, when new research comes along, the executive teacher keeps creating additional demands on his/her teaching, but does NOT give up any past techniques! Eventually, they cannot keep up with their own demands for high performance; they become overwhelmed and often quit teaching.

- Students who need special attention, have cultural or language differences, or have exceptional skills, are often not able to have their needs met in this structured, prescribed environment.

COLUMN B: HUMANIST

If you awarded Column B the most points you favor a **Humanist** teaching style. This approach may be familiar because it shares common elements with current trends in education including student choice of what to study, *cooperative learning*, self-evaluation, and grading for effort. This teaching philosophy is most aligned with the constructivist learning theory and the **Progressivist** philosophy of education.

The humanist teacher is a facilitator of learning. The teacher, as facilitator, is an *empathetic* person who guides the student in the process of self-discovery. The teacher's role is to prepare students to learn how to make good choices both academically and personally. The student is seen as an authentic person with a unique personal history and culture, and individual competencies are valued.

Choice is central to this approach, both in what to learn and how to learn it. In order to help students acquire knowledge, the teacher makes sure the information, resources, and relevant equipment are accessible to students.

The classroom environment is rich with books, tapes, objects, animals, and equipment. Learning through multiple forms of media and materials is considered essential. There is usually a sense of loosely organized clutter.

Positive Factors

- Because meeting a student's individual needs is the focus of this approach, many students thrive in this setting. Each student has a tailored set of expectations for achievement and progress is tracked by the attainment of individual goals.

- Because the environment is rich with a variety of resources, student interest in new topics and ideas is aroused.

- Teachers experienced in this approach often feel that they are connecting deeply with children to teach them personally what they need at a given time. This is often a joyful experience for the teacher.

- Many parents like this approach because they recognize their own child's individual needs are being valued.

Negative Factors

- Teaching from this orientation can be very difficult for the beginning teacher. It often takes several years of teaching experience within a more traditional executive approach before the teacher has the confidence to address the needs of the individual student.

- Administrators, legislators, and some parents are frustrated by this approach because it is more difficult to know exactly what is expected of children at each grade/age level. It is more difficult to track and to develop a standard of comparative progress.

- Teachers who teach from this philosophical orientation sometimes feel they have to "hide" their humanist practices in order to comply with district testing and tracking demands. The feeling of being "subversive" is uncomfortable and frustrating.

COLUMN C: CLASSICIST

If you awarded Column C the most points you favor a **Classicist** teaching philosophy. The roots of the classicist approach date back to ancient Greece. The goal of the teaching philosophy is to develop well-rounded citizens through an intense liberal arts curriculum. A classicist teacher often reflects the cognitive learning theories within their instructional practices and reflects the **Perennial** educational philosophy.

The teacher is a model that inspires passion for a particular content area. The teacher, as model, "lives" his or her subject matter and demonstrates high levels of scholarship for the student to emulate. The classicist prepares extensively for lessons and includes many types of supplemental materials, speakers, field trips, and so on, so the subject "comes alive" for students.

The student is seen as a potential scholar, capable of great contributions if inspired to study hard. Because each content area has a structure of its own, the teacher of a specific content models the manner and principles of procedures appropriate to that field.

The classroom environment reflects the essence of the values of the particular content area. The classicist focuses upon content and arranges for students to confront the subject matter in the way the specialist in the field experiences the content.

Positive Factors

- Teachers who teach from this philosophical orientation are often a favorite "teacher of the year." The teacher's passion for his/her subject is very appealing and inspiring to students. The excitement shared for the subject matter is enjoyable for teacher and student alike.

- Administrators and parents often have high praise for this type of teacher because they get noticed for their excellence and for their ability to inspire students who model their enthusiasm for the subject.

- Students are encouraged to delve deeply into the subject matter and achieve a higher level of understanding.
  - Because there is intrinsic reward for this teacher, there is less "burn out"; they often retire only after a long teaching career.

NEGATIVE FACTORS

- Some students who do not share this teacher's love of the particular subject matter can become "invisible" to the teacher who goes on to focus only on those students who share the teacher's enthusiasm.
- Students who are not talented in the subject area may become easily lost as the level of expected scholarship increases throughout the course. The often rapid pace makes catching-up more difficult.

COLUMN D: INFORMATIONIST

If you awarded Column D the most points, you favor an **Informationist** teaching style. This technological approach is just emerging in classrooms across the country. The information age, which dominates the business world, is manifesting itself in the classroom and is changing not only the role of the teacher, but also of the nature of the pursuit of knowledge itself. This teaching philosophy uses an interesting combination of behaviorism, cognitive information processing, and a constructivist perspective. Since this approach offers the greatest personal freedom and instructional options (the Internet is virtually the world at your fingertips), it most closely reflects the **Existentialist** philosophy of education.

The informationist teacher is an assistant. Since no one person can possibly "know everything" about a topic, the teacher's role is becoming less of an authority and more of a co-learner/explorer.

The student is seen as a "user" of information. Each student is encouraged to search for information relevant or interesting to him or her. Student progress is monitored via e-mail and computer logs.

The environment supports these new forms of communication, rich with online computers and hardware and software to make multiple application of knowledge possible. The focus of the informationist classroom is on worldwide communication. This approach stresses the role of information in everyone's life.

Positive Factors

- As society becomes more technologically dependent, the skills emphasized in this orientation will be more and more valued.
- As our world's knowledge base increases exponentially, it is recognized that no one can stay an expert in an area of knowledge easily. This approach validates the role of every person as a co-learner and explorer of knowledge.
- Teaching and learning is no longer limited to space and time constraints. Therefore, the number of potential learning opportunities for all computer users vastly increases.

Negative Factors

- Some students feel detached, and therefore alone in their learning process. Some may feel a lack of human caring and connection with other students and their instructor.
- If there are technical failures, the learning process is impaired.
- There are risks in relying on information that is "out there" which is inaccurate, misleading, or potentially dangerous to the learner.
- There is a tendency to overload an instructor with too many students, because there is the perception of efficiency and economy of scale that may not be accurate.

Defining Your Own Unique Philosophical Statement

Now that you have read about the four types of teaching philosophies, let's take a few moments to think about how you would begin to write your own philosophy. Rarely is a real-life teacher neatly categorized into completely one or the other philosophy. Generally the strongest teachers are a blend of beliefs and practices. It is the quality of that unique blend that makes teaching an art.

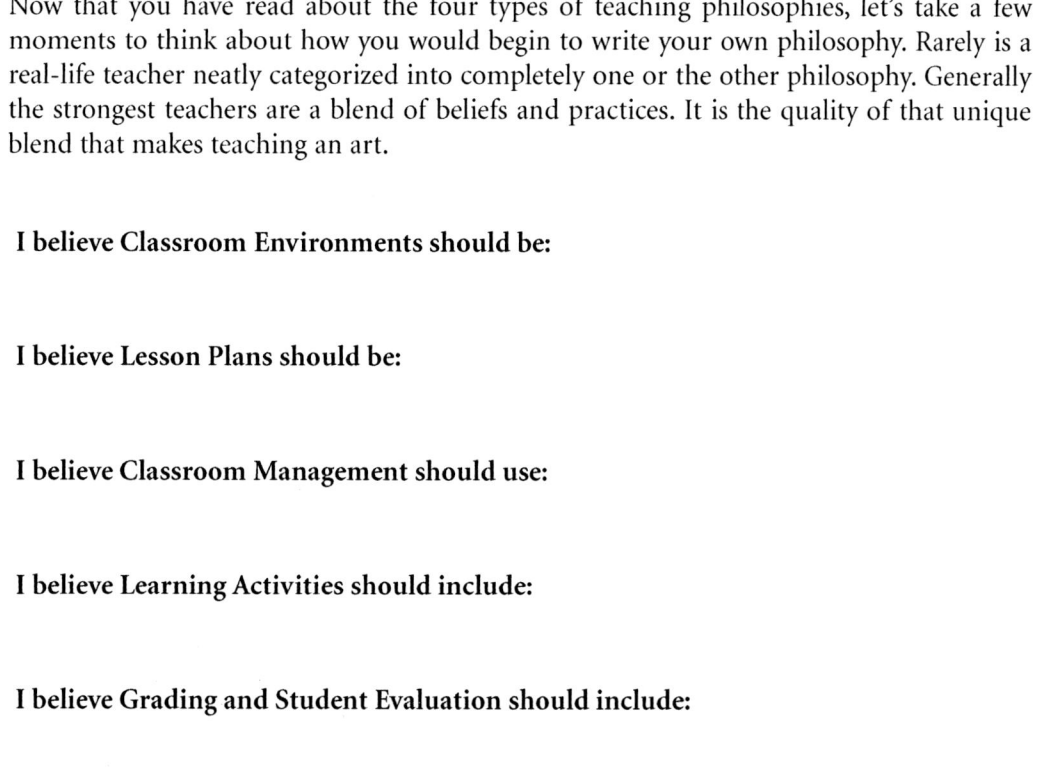

I believe Classroom Environments should be:

I believe Lesson Plans should be:

I believe Classroom Management should use:

I believe Learning Activities should include:

I believe Grading and Student Evaluation should include:

I believe students learn through:

I believe the Teacher's Role is best described as:

GROUP TALK

Identifying Learning Theories in Practice.

Directions: Consider the three major learning theories you read about in Chapter 3: behaviorism, cognitivist, and constructivism. Identify which learning theory(s) is reflected in the following instructional practices, and explain why you chose that theory.

Which instructional approaches do you find the most helpful in your learning? Why?

Approach	Explanation
Drill	This technique is used when students need to learn information at an automatic response level (for instance, math facts). Another time is when students need to practice a skill to perfect a performance, such as a dance routine, or a musical piece.
	Theory:
	Why:
Lecture	The classroom lecture is a special form of communication in which the instructor provides information in a direct manner. Although lecture can certainly be an efficient means of instruction, it often functions as an information delivery system rather than a learning experience.
	Theory:
	Why:
Discussion	Engaging students in a carefully planned classroom discussion stimulates a more active role in the learning process. Learning is rooted in experiencing information, not in the information itself. Discussion encourages the student to respond to the information being presented.
	Theory:
	Why:
Case Study	This approach provides students an opportunity to apply what they learn in the classroom to real-life experiences. This instructional strategy can highlight fundamental dilemmas or critical issues and provides a format for analyzing controversial scenarios.
	Theory:
	Why:
Cooperative Learning	This teaching strategy uses small teams, each with students of different levels of ability, and uses a variety of learning activities to improve their understanding of a subject. Each member of a team is responsible not only for learning what is taught but also for helping teammates learn, thus creating an atmosphere of achievement.
	Theory:
	Why:
Problem-Based Learning (PBL)	This instructional method challenges students to "learn to learn," working cooperatively in groups to seek solutions to real world problems. These problems are used to engage students' curiosity and initiate learning the subject matter. PBL prepares students to think critically and analytically, and to find and use appropriate learning resources.
	Theory:
	Why:

Projected higher enrollment growth for pre-school age children will create many new jobs for preschool teachers.

EXPLORING CAREERS IN EDUCATION

Theories of learning and philosophies of education, combined with your preferences in instructional styles, provide a foundation of knowledge for exploring the range of careers in education. All levels of teaching careers, from preschool, kindergarten, elementary, special education, middle and secondary school teaching, requires a variety of skills and aptitudes, including:

- a talent for working with children
- organizational, administrative, and recordkeeping abilities
- research and communication skills
- the power to influence, motivate, and train others
- patience and creativity (Steffy, Wolfe, Pasche, & Enz, 1999)

In this decade, preschool, kindergarten, elementary, special education, middle, and secondary school teachers will hold about four million jobs in the United States. Through 2015, overall student enrollments in elementary, middle, and secondary schools—a key factor in the demand for teachers—are expected to rise dramatically (Taylor, 1997). Another factor in these job openings will result from the need to replace the large number of baby boomers who are expected to retire from teaching in this period. In addition to enrollment growth and retirement, some states are also instituting programs to improve early childhood education, such as offering full-day kindergarten and universal preschool. These last two programs, along with projected higher enrollment growth for preschool-age children, will create many new jobs for preschool teachers, which are expected to grow much faster than the average for all occupations nationally (Brewer, 2004).

The supply of teachers is expected to increase in response to reports of improved job prospects, better pay, more teacher involvement in school policy, and greater public interest in education. In recent years, the total number of bachelor's and master's degrees granted in education has increased steadily. Because of a shortage of teachers in certain locations, and in anticipation of the loss of a number of teachers to retirement, many states have implemented policies that will encourage more students to become teachers (Taylor, 1997).

What level of teaching do you wish to pursue? We have provided information about the specific talents and skills each major of teaching requires.

What Is Early Childhood Education?

This educational level prepares educators to work with the academic, social, emotional, and physical needs of a child from infancy to age eight. The major focus of the early childhood curriculum encompass a thorough knowledge of child development, including:

- *Physical development*—Concerns the physical growth and control of the body
- *Perception and sensory development*—How a child functions using the senses and the ability to process the information gained
- *Communication and language development*—Using visual and sound stimuli, especially in the acquisition of language and in the exchange of thoughts and feelings
- *Cognitive development*—How the child thinks and processes information
- *Emotional development*—Involves how children manage their feelings
- *Social development*—Concerns the child's identity, his/her relationship with others, and understanding his/her place within a social environment
- *Neurological development*—Recent studies on infant brain development show most of a person's neurons are formed from ages zero through five. If a young child doesn't receive sufficient nurturing, nutrition, parental/caregiver interaction, and stimulus during the crucial ages of zero through five, the child may be left with a developmental deficit that hampers his or her academic success.

A wide array of educational philosophies circulate through the field; however, today most early childhood teacher preparation programs strongly favor a **Constructivist** learning theory. The curriculum is child-centered and there is a focus on the importance of play. Play provides children with the opportunity to actively explore, manipulate, and interact with their environment. It encourages children to investigate, create, discover, and be motivated to take risks and add to their understanding of the world. It challenges children to achieve new levels of understanding of events, people, and the environment by interacting with concrete materials (Seefeldt & Barbour, 1997). Hands-on experiences create authentic experiences in which children begin to feel a sense of mastery over their world. This philosophy follows with Piaget's ideals that children should actively participate in their world and various environments, to ensure they are not "passive" learners but "little scientists" who are actively engaged (Brewer, 2004; Wardle, 2002).

The major national associations for early childhood *professionals* are:

- National Association for the Education of Young Children (NAEYC) *http://www.naeyc.org/*
- National Association of Early Childhood Specialists in State Departments of Education (NAECS/SDE) *http://naecs.crc.uiuc.edu/*
- Association of Childhood Educators International (ACEI) *http://www.acei.org/*

What Is Elementary Education?

Elementary school teachers reflect the broadest range of age certification (typically K through 8). These teachers play a vital role in the development of children. What children learn and experience during their early years can shape their views of themselves and the world, and can affect their later success or failure in school, work, and their personal lives. Elementary school teachers introduce children to mathematics, language, science, and social studies. They use games, music, artwork, films, books, computers, and other tools to teach basic skills.

Elementary school teachers play a vital role in the development of children.

Most elementary school teachers instruct one class of children in several subjects. In some schools, two or more teachers work as a team and are jointly responsible for a group of students in at least one subject. In other schools, a teacher may teach one special subject—usually music, art, reading, science, arithmetic, or physical education—to a number of classes. A small but growing number of teachers instruct multilevel classrooms, with students at several different learning levels. For example, a multilevel class may be comprised of children who are both six and seven, representing first and second grade levels (Cruikshank & Sheffield, 1991).

Elementary teachers use many instructional methods to help children learn. In addition to direct instruction (lecture), teachers use group work, often called cooperative learning, to encourage collaboration in solving problems. As you read in Chapter 1, elementary teachers plan, evaluate, and assign lessons; prepare, administer, and grade tests; listen to oral presentations; and maintain classroom discipline. Elementary teachers, like all teachers, work with students from varied ethnic, racial, and religious backgrounds. With growing minority populations in most parts of the country, it is important for teachers to work effectively with a diverse student population. Likewise, elementary teachers work with students who face a range of learning and physical challenges and emotional problems. Elementary teachers form partnerships with special education teachers to provide appropriate education and support to all students (Walmsley, 1994).

Requirements for regular licenses to teach K through 8 vary by state. However, all states require general education teachers to have a bachelor's degree and to have completed an approved teacher training program with a prescribed number of subject and education credits, as well as supervised practice teaching (i.e., student teaching). Some states also require technology training and the attainment of a minimum grade point average. A number of states require that teachers obtain a master's degree in education within a specified period after they begin teaching (Taylor, 1997).

Professional organizations for elementary teachers include:

- Association for Supervision and Curriculum Development (ASCD) http://www.ascd.org/
- International Reading Association (IRA) *reading.org*
- National Council for the Teaching of Mathematics (NCTM) http://www.nctm.org/
- National Science Teachers Association (NSTA) http://www.nsta.org/index.html

What Is Middle School Education?

As you think back to your schooling during the time you were eleven to thirteen, were you attending an elementary school? If you did, you most likely had one teacher who provided most of the basic curriculum. While you may have had art, music, or physical education teachers, you still spent most of the day with one teacher and one class of students. Or did you attend a middle (sometimes called junior high) school? If you attended a middle school, you most likely had several teachers; one teacher taught math, another science, and still another taught English.

The middle school movement in the United States began in the 1950s. The intent behind the creation of middle schools was to better meet the academic, social, and developmental

Middle school teachers need a strong knowledge of content matter, knowledge of how to teach that content, and experience with young adolescents.

needs of young adolescents in a school setting separate from K through 8 schools, K through 5 elementary schools, and high schools. Adolescents between the ages of ten and fourteen are experiencing a period of dramatic physical and cognitive growth, developing a new and untested ability to think in abstract and complex ways (Hernandez, 2000). Middle school is designed to provide continued work in learning skills while bringing more depth to the curriculum than is the case in elementary schools. It emphasizes guidance and exploration, independence and responsibility.

To prepare someone to teach middle school students requires a strong knowledge of content matter (typically defined as a bachelor's degree or twenty-four hours of content), knowledge of how to teach that content (called pedagogy), and a great deal of experience working with young adolescents (Powell, 2004). An expertly prepared middle school teacher must exhibit:

- *Academic excellence.* Middle-grades teachers must have a deep understanding of the subjects they want to teach (typically a bachelor's degree or twenty-four hours of coursework).
- *Content pedagogy.* Middle-grades teachers need an equally strong knowledge of how to teach the content. This skill helps young adolescents learn the concepts and skills of a demanding curriculum.

Secondary teachers have the opportunity to greatly influence their students' career choices.

- *Developmental responsiveness.* Middle-grades teachers must have a solid understanding of early adolescence, as well as the skills and dispositions to work with young adolescents' unique developmental challenges. These teachers should know how to motivate and engage young adolescents in their own learning.
- *Equity and cultural diversity.* Middle-grades teachers must have a wide repertoire of skills, mixed with a sustained sense of hope, support, and expectations for achievement, to enhance learning and development for the most racially and ethnically diverse school population in our nation's history.

The major national association for middle school professionals is the National Middle School Association, *http://www.nmsa.org*.

What Is Secondary Education?

Secondary schools typically represent grades 9 through 12. Secondary teachers must be content specialists, typically with a bachelor's degree in the content area or a minimum of twenty-four hours of content coursework. In addition, excellent secondary teachers must have the ability to communicate, inspire trust and confidence, and motivate students, as well as understand their young adult students' educational and emotional needs. Secondary teachers have the opportunity to greatly influence their students' career choices (Armstrong & Savage, 2001). Billie vividly remembers two charismatic high school teachers—one a dance teacher and the other a child development teacher. These two women strongly influenced her decision to become both a dance and primary teacher! Did you have a high school teacher with whom you felt you related well?

Basic Curricular Structure At the high school level, students take a broad variety of classes. Typically, American high schools require that courses in the areas of English, science, social science, and mathematics be taken by the students every year. Specifically, most high school students must take:

- Three science courses: biology, chemistry, physics, geology, and forensics
- Three math courses: algebra, geometry, trigonometry, pre-calculus, calculus, and statistics
- English classes, which are usually required all four years of high school
- Two courses in social science content, often including American history, civics, and world history; other courses in law (constitutional, criminal, or international), economics, and *psychology* may be offered
- A year of physical education (usually referred to as gym or PE by students)

High schools offer a wide variety of elective courses, although the availability of such courses depends upon each particular school's financial situation. Most states require students to earn a few credits of classes considered electives, including:

- Visual arts (drawing, sculpture, painting, photography)
- Performing arts (choir, drama, band, orchestra, dance, film)
- Vocational education (woodworking, metalworking, automobile repair)
- Computer science/business education (word processing, programming, graphic design, Web design)
- Physical education (American football, baseball, basketball, track and field, swimming, gymnastics, water polo, soccer)
- Journalism/publishing (school newspaper, yearbook)
- Foreign languages (French, German, and Spanish are common; Chinese, Latin, Greek, Japanese, and Russian are less common, though Latin is gaining increased popularity)
- Family and consumer science/health ("home economics," nutrition, child development)

What Is Special Education?

Special education teachers work with children and youths who have a variety of physical, emotional, or learning challenges. Special education teachers must be patient, able to motivate students, understand their students' special needs, and accept differences in others. Teachers must be creative and apply different types of teaching methods to reach students who are having difficulty learning. Communication and cooperation are essential skills, because special education teachers spend a great deal of time interacting with others, including students, parents, and school faculty and administrators (Deutsch-Smith, 2003).

The majority of special education teachers work with children with mild to moderate disabilities, using and modifying the curriculum to meet the child's individual needs. Most special education teachers instruct students at the elementary, middle, and secondary school level, although some teachers work with infants and toddlers. Some special education majors work with children with severe physical handicaps, autism, or mental retardation (Heward, 2002). The various types of disabilities that qualify individuals for special education programs include:

- specific learning disabilities
- speech or language impairments
- mental retardation
- emotional disturbance
- hearing impairments or visual impairments
- autism
- combined deafness and blindness
- traumatic brain injury

Students are classified under one of the categories, and special education teachers are prepared to work with specific groups. Early identification of a child with special needs is an important part of a special education teacher's job. Special education teachers use various techniques to promote learning. Depending on the disability, teaching methods can include individualized instruction, problem-solving assignments, and small-group work.

Special education teachers help to develop an Individualized Education Program (IEP) for each special education student. The IEP sets personalized goals for each student and is tailored to the student's individual needs and ability. When appropriate, the program includes a transition plan outlining specific steps to prepare students with disabilities for middle school or high school or, in the case of older students, a job or postsecondary study. Teachers review the IEP with the student's parents, school administrators, and the student's general education teacher. Teachers work closely with parents to inform them of their child's progress and suggest techniques to promote learning at home (Heward, 2002).

Special education teachers design and teach appropriate curricula, assign work geared toward each student's needs and abilities, and grade papers and homework assignments. They are involved in the students' behavioral, social, and academic development, helping the students develop emotionally, feel comfortable in social situations, and be aware of socially acceptable behavior. Preparing special education students for daily life after graduation also is an important aspect of the job. Teachers provide students with career counseling or help them learn routine skills, such as balancing a checkbook or manipulating the public transportation system.

As schools become more *inclusive*, special education teachers and general education teachers are increasingly working together in general education classrooms. Special education teachers help general educators adapt curriculum materials and teaching techniques to meet the needs of students with disabilities. They coordinate the work of teachers, teacher assistants, and related personnel, such as therapists and social workers, to meet the individualized needs of the student within inclusive special education programs. A large part of a special education teacher's job involves interacting with others. Special education teachers communicate frequently with parents, social workers, school psychologists, occupational and physical therapists, school administrators, and other teachers (Deutsch-Smith, 2003).

Chapter 14 | *Understanding Educational Philosophy and Your Professional Beliefs* 273

Special education teachers work in a variety of settings. Some have their own classrooms and teach only special education students; others work as special education resource teachers and offer individualized help to students in general education classrooms; still others teach together with general education teachers in classes composed of both general and special education students. Some teachers work with special education students for several hours a day in a resource room, separate from their general education classroom.

Special educators who work with infants usually travel to the child's home to work with the child and his or her parents. Many of these infants have medical problems that slow or preclude normal development. Special education teachers show parents techniques and activities designed to stimulate the infant and encourage the growth and development of the child's skills. Toddlers usually receive their services at a preschool where special education teachers

Think About It
What career path is best for you? Which position best matches your philosophy or theories of education? Use the activities in Figure 3 and 4 to explore your best career goals.

Directions: As you read the descriptions of the different types of teachers, you could see that while all teachers need to have a bachelor's degree, the training and preparation for each level is very specific. When you apply to a teacher preparation program, you will be asked to determine an explicit level or preparation focus. Take a few minutes to consider, from your perspective, the pros and cons of each level.

Level	Pros	Cons
Early Childhood		
Elementary		
Middle		
Secondary		
Special Education		

At this point, what appears to be your top choice? Why?

Figure 3 Thinking about Becoming a Teacher

help them develop social, self-help, motor, language, and cognitive skills, often through the use of play.

Special education teachers enjoy the challenge of working with students with disabilities and the opportunity to establish meaningful relationships with them. Although helping these students can be highly rewarding, the work also can be emotionally and physically draining. The major national associations for special education professionals include:

> The Council for Exceptional Children, 1110 N. Glebe Road, Suite 300, Arlington, VA 22201-5704. Internet: *http://www.cec.sped.org*

> National Center for Special Education Personnel & Related Service Providers, National Association of State Directors of Special Education, 1800 Diagonal Road, Suite 320, Alexandria, VA 22314. Internet: *http://www.personnelcenter.org*

Directions: Interview a teacher (one who represents the level that you are most interested in becoming). The interview will probably take about twenty to thirty minutes to conduct.	
Teacher's name	
Teacher's level	
How long has the teacher been teaching?	How long at this level?
Why did this teacher choose this **profession**?	
Where did they receive their teacher preparation? Do they have an advanced degree or endorsement?	
What do they like best about their teaching position?	
What do they like least?	
What have been some of the greatest challenges they have faced in this position?	
What are some of the rewards of their profession?	

Figure 4 Interview a Teacher

TALKING TO TEACHERS—THE MOTIVATION TO TEACH

Why do individuals choose to become a teacher? Perhaps because the challenges of teaching are outnumbered by the rewards that come from helping students realize their dreams. The following teacher shares her reasons for becoming an educator. Review her story and see if you understand and relate to her feelings and experiences.

Sarah Wolfe has been a classroom teacher for ten years and is currently an Organizational Staff Development Coordinator in Prince William County Schools.

I have had several memorable teachers in my life, but my parents modeled teaching best. They were teachers in their real lives but vastly different in their approaches. From my mother, I learned the love of reading. Each day she made time to read to herself, or us, and taught us how to live through the pages of a book. From my father, I learned dedication to the craft. Preparation is what makes it look easy; expectation is what makes learning hard. Many nights there were piles of books, articles, and papers on our dining room table and Dad would heave through it, take in information, then write out page after page in long hand on dusty yellow legal pads. Writing was one of his gifts, speaking and engaging audiences were his others. I build on these memories each day I walk to the front of the classroom.

I am a teacher and a student of children. I thrive on the enlightened looks and confident strides children make when they learn something new. Teaching is problem solving and problem making. I always felt like a conductor—an engineer of learning. I know what the coordinates (standards) of the curriculum are, but the journey always takes different paths and forks depending on how the children decide to get there. I supply the tools, the compass, and the travel brochures. They learn how to use them to set their own courses.

One of my most memorable days at school came when I had an instructional brainstorm around ten pm on a Thursday; the night before I was to teach a science lesson about the scientific process and extinction of living things. I decided my second graders would connect more to the objective if they became members of several dinosaur digs. Each student was given a "real" job on the dig site. I had researchers, engineers, draftsmen, paleontologists, photographers, editors, and reporters. Each played an essential role in the discovery of the dinosaur. It took most of the day and each child, regardless of his/her disability, talent or instructional need, was completely enthralled with the process. I knew I had truly accomplished my objectives when I was walking the class out to the buses and my most challenging child hugged my waist and said, "I really want to come back tomorrow and do it again!"

What philosophy of education is most consistent in Sarah's actions?

What teaching style is the most reflective of her practices?

What continues to inspire her career efforts?

Who initially inspired you to consider teaching as a profession?

Looking Forward

What motivates us to become teachers? Is it our theories, our philosophies, our past experiences—or a unique combination of both? Read the special vignette on page 275 to learn what motivated one Nationally Board Certified teacher to become a professional educator.

While everyone has participated in schooling, very few individuals become teachers. Through education, training, and experience, teachers develop a specialized knowledge base that enables them to analyze the content to be learned, comprehend their students' needs and interests, and determine the best methods and strategies to teach the students who will be learning it. All this mental processing is usually done in seconds, as the needs of students change within minutes in an average learning situation. How do teachers become so proficient?

RESEARCH CITATIONS

Armstrong, D. G. & Savage, T. V. (2001). *Teaching in the Secondary School: An Introduction,* 5th Ed. Upper Saddle River, NJ: Prentice Hall.

Ashmore, H. S. (1989). *Unseasonable Truths: The Life of Robert Maynard Hutchins.* Boston, MA: Little Brown & Co.

Bagley, W. C. (1909). *Classroom Management: Its Principles and Technique.* London, UK: Macmillan.

Brewer, J. A. (2004). *Introduction to Early Childhood Education: Preschool Through Primary Grades,* 5th Ed. New York, NY: Allyn & Bacon.

Cruikshank, D. E. & Sheffield, L. J. (1991). *Teaching and Learning Elementary and Middle School Mathematics.* London, UK: Macmillan.

Damrosch, L. (2005). *Jean-Jacques Rousseau: Restless Genius.* Boston, MA: Houghton Mifflin.

Deutsch-Smith, D. (2003). *Introduction to Special Education: Teaching in an Age of Opportunity,* 5th Ed. New York, NY: Allyn & Bacon.

Garff, J. & Kirmmse, B. H. (2004). *Soren Kierkegaard: A Biography.* Boston, MA: Princeton University Press.

Hernandez, M. A. (2000). *Middle school years: Achieving the Best Education for Your Child:* Grades 5–8. Clayton, UK: Warner Books.

Heward, W. L. (2002). *Exceptional Children: An Introduction to Special Education,* 7th ed. Upper Saddle River, NJ: Prentice Hall.

Hook, S. (1995). *John Dewey: An Intellectual Portrait.* Amherst, NY: Prometheus Books.

Martin, J. (2003). *The Education of John Dewey.* New York, NY: Columbia University Press.

Mayer, M. S. & Hicks, J. H. (1992). *Robert Maynard Hutchins: A Memoir.* Berkeley, CA: University of California Press.

Murphy, M. (2005). *The History and Philosophy of Education: Voices of Educational Pioneers.* Upper Saddle River, NJ: Prentice Hall.

Noddings, N. (1995). *Philosophy of Education.* Boulder, CO: Westview Press.

Powell, S. D. (2004). *Introduction to Middle School.* Upper Saddle River, NJ: Prentice Hall.

Pring, R. (2005). *Philosophy of Education.* London, UK: Continuum International Publishing Group.

Seefeldt, C. & Barbour, N. H. (1997). *Early childhood education: An introduction,* 4th Ed. Upper Saddle River, NJ: Prentice Hall.

Starobinki, J. (1988). *Jean-Jacques Rousseau: Transparency and Obstruction.* Chicago, IL: University of Chicago Press.

Steffy, B., Wolfe, M., Pasche, S., & Enz, B. (1999). *Life Cycle of the Career Teacher.* Thousand Oaks, CA: Corwin Press.

Taylor, F. (1997). *Careers in teaching,* 7th Ed. London, UK: Kogan Page Ltd.

Walmsley, S. A. (1994). *Children Exploring Their World: Theme Teaching in Elementary School.* Portsmouth, NH: Heinemann.

Wardle, F. (2002). *Introduction to Early Childhood Education: A Multidimensional Approach to Child-Centered Care and Learning.* New York, NY: Allyn & Bacon.

Wesley-Null, J. (2003). *A Disciplined Progressive Educator: The Life and Career of William Chandler Bagley.* History of Schools and Schooling, V. 43: Peter Lang Publishing.

READING ON THE HUMAN BRAIN AND NEUROSCIENCE

Bransford, J., Brown, A. & Cocking, R. (2000). *How People Learn: Brain, Mind, Experience and School.* Washington, DC: National Academy Press.

Butterworth, B. (1999). *What counts: How Every Brain is Hardwired for Math.* New York, NY: Free Press.

Byrnes, J. (2001). *Minds, Brains, and Learning: Understanding the Psychological and Educational Relevance of Neuroscientific Research.* New York, NY: The Guilford Press.

Calvin, W. (2002). *A Brain for all Seasons: Human Evolution and Abrupt Climate Change.* Chicago, IL: University of Chicago Press.

Damasio, A. (1999). *The Feeling of What Happens: Body and Emotion in the Making of Consciousness.* New York, NY: Harcourt.

Diamond, M. & Hopson, J. (1998). *Magic Trees of the Mind: How to Nurture Your Child's Intelligence, Creativity, and Healthy Emotions.* New York, NY: Dutton Press.

Fauconnier, G. & Turner, M. (2002). *The Way We Think: Conceptual Blending and the Mind's Hidden Complexities.* New York: Basic Books.

Freeman, W. (2000). *How Brains Make up Their Minds.* New York, NY: Columbia University Press.

Goldblum, N. (2001). *The Brain-Shaped Mind: What the Brain Can Tell us About the Mind.* Cambridge, UK: Cambridge University Press.

Greenspan, S. & Shanker, S. (2004). *The First Idea: How Symbols, Language, and Intelligence Evolved From our Primate Ancestors to Modern Humans.* Cambridge, MA: Da Capo Press.

Johnson, S. (2004). *Mind Wide Open: Your Brain and the Neuroscience of Everyday Life.* New York, NY: Scribner.

LeDoux, J. (2002). *Synaptic Self: How Our Brains Become Who We Are.* New York, NY: Viking Press.

Klein, S. (2000). Biological Psychology. Upper Saddle River, NJ: Prentice Hall.

Kotulak, R. (1996). *Inside the Brain: Revolutionary Discoveries of How the Mind Works.* Kansas City, MO: Andrews McMeeley Publishing.

Pinker, S. (2002). *The Blank Slate: The Modern Denial of Human Nature.* New York, NY: Penguin Books.

Ratey, J. (2001). A User's Guide to the Brain. New York, NY: Pantheon Books.

Chapter 15

Understanding Learning Theories

Theories are propositions that help explain complex *phenomena*. The question that has long mystified scholars is whether a single theory can describe, in all situations, how humans learn. Such a comprehensive theory must account for all the facts of how children learn language, math, social interactions, solve problems, etc. Theories are also dynamic and fluid—they must continue to evolve as our understanding of human development, science, and the impact of social and cultural influences expand (Cromer, 1997; Schunk, 2003).

The study of learning is primarily the product of philosophical writings regarding the nature of knowledge, which can be traced as far back as Plato. Early philosophers and scientists attempted to answer the question: "How do we think, reason, learn or know?" but it was not until the nineteenth century that attempts were made to study these topics experimentally (Driscoll, 1994). Though there are many learning theories in current literature that attempt to explain these phenomena, most of these theories can be organized into three broad categories:

- Behaviorism
- Cognitivism
- Constructivism

In Chapter 15 we will discuss these theories and provide a brief biography of the major theorists that have influenced educational theory and practices over the last 150 years.

BEHAVIORIST LEARNING THEORIES

Beginning in the late nineteenth century, theorists began to formalize the study of learning. Theorists such as Ivan Pavlov (see Box 1) studied the process of learning and how humans can be taught to remember. Pavlov found an association between a *stimulus* and a response that is called classical conditioning. Classic conditioning occurs when a natural reflex responds to a stimulus. The most popular example is Pavlov's observation that dogs salivate when they eat or even see food. Essentially, animals and people are biologically "wired" so that a certain stimulus will produce a specific response (Cromer, 1997).

Pavlov's work was extended by John Watson (see Box 2) and and B. F. Skinner (see Box 3). **The behaviorists believe environment shapes behavior. They are concerned with the changes in a student's behavior that occur as a result of learning. Behaviorist theory emerges in the form of operant conditioning, using *reinforcement*—or rewards for the desired behavior.** Behavioral or operant conditioning occurs when a response to a stimulus is reinforced. Basically, operant conditioning is a simple feedback system: If a reward or reinforcement follows the response to a stimulus, then the response becomes more probable in the future (Sherwood & Sherwood, 1970). This practice is reflected in the classroom by the use of gold stars, time at the computer, choice time on Friday afternoons, and so on.

For most of the twentieth century, behavioral theory provided the foundation of most of the learning theory that was applied to child-rearing and in classrooms. Parents and teachers still find that, in many instances, individuals do learn when provided with the appropriate blend of stimuli, rewards, and negative reinforcement (Kohn, 1993). Behavioral principles are often most effective with young children and simpler tasks. For instance, how many of us were rewarded with dessert when we ate all of our vegetables at dinner? However, there have been many criticisms of behaviorism, including the following:

1. Behaviorism does not account for all kinds of learning, since it disregards the independent activities of the mind. There are many activities children engage in that are not reinforced with rewards or praise.
2. Behaviorism alone can't fully explain how children learn language. While children may imitate adult use of language, imitation and reinforcement does not account for the development of new language patterns (grammar). For instance, when a child uses the phrase "*We goed to the zoo,*" he is not imitating what an adult has spoken, rather the child is over-applying the grammar feature, language pattern, for past-tense "ed." (Chomsky, 1969).

BOX 1 MORE ABOUT IVAN PAVLOV

Ivan Pavlov (1849-1936) was born in a small village in central Russia. His family hoped he would become a priest and he attended a theological seminary. After reading Charles Darwin, he became more interested in science and began attending the University of St. Petersburg where he studied chemistry and physiology. Pavlov received his doctorate in 1879 and continued his studies and doing his own research in topics that interested him: digestion and blood circulation. His work became well known and he was appointed professor of physiology at the Imperial Medical Academy.

Pavlov studied the digestion system. He was especially interested in the interaction between salivation and the action of the stomach. Without salivation, the stomach wasn't able to initiate digestion. Pavlov wanted to see if external stimuli could affect this process, so he rang a metronome at the same time he gave the experimental dogs their food. After a while, the dogs—which before only salivated when they saw and ate their food—would begin to salivate when the metronome sounded, even if no food was present. In 1903 Pavlov published his results calling this a "conditioned reflex." This is different from an innate reflex, such as yanking a hand back from a flame, in that it had to be learned. Pavlov called this learning process "conditioning" (in which the dog's nervous system comes to associate the sound of the metronome with the food, for example). He also found the conditioned reflex will be repressed if the stimulus proves "wrong" too often. If the metronome sounds repeatedly and no food appears, eventually the dog stops salivating at the sound (Todes, 2000).

BOX 2 MORE ABOUT JOHN WATSON

John Watson (1878-1958), often called the founder of the science of Behaviorism, was born in South Carolina and grew up on a farm. John entered Furman University at age sixteen. He received a master's degree after five years and went on to the University of Chicago to pursue a doctorate in psychology, which he received in 1903. Five years later, Johns Hopkins University appointed him professor of experimental and comparative psychology.

In 1913 he published an article outlining his ideas and essentially establishing a new school of psychology, in which Watson described the goal of psychology as the prediction and control of animal/human response and behavior (Brewer, 1991).

Inspired by the work of Ivan Pavlov, Watson studied the biology, physiology, and behavior of animals. At that time he also began studying the behavior of children, concluding that humans were simply more complicated than animals, but operated on the same principles. All animals, he believed, were extremely complex machines that responded to situations according to their "wiring," or nerve pathways, conditioned by experience. He also dismissed heredity as a significant factor in shaping human behavior (Todd & Morris, 1994). Watson strongly sided with nurture in the nature-nurture discussion, and is perhaps most well-known for the following quote:

> Give me a dozen healthy infants, well-formed, and my own specified world to bring them up in and I'll guarantee to take any one at random and train him to become any type of specialist I might select—doctor, lawyer, artist, merchant-chief and, yes, even beggar-man and thief, regardless of his talents, penchants, tendencies, abilities, vocations, and race of his ancestors (Watson, 1930).

BOX 3 MORE ABOUT B.F. SKINNER

Burrhus Frederic Skinner (1904–1990), often called the father of applied behaviorism, dedicated his life's work to studying the relationship between reinforcement and observable behavior. He is considered by many to be one of the most important figures in twentieth-century psychology. The principles of reinforcement he outlined were built upon by clinical psychologists and applied to the treatment of mental disorders. The application of behaviorism to clinical psychology still appears today in treatments for anxiety disorders and reflects many approaches to classroom management (Bjork, 1997).

Skinner's work in education began in the early 1950s during a visit to his daughter's fourth grade math class. This experience provided insight into current teaching practices to shape the remainder of his career. His observations revealed that the instructional process was violating the basic principals of learning. He saw that the teacher's instruction was not supporting the current level of learning for all individuals in the classroom. In behaviorist terms, instruction (shaping) should adapt to each child's current performance level. However, in the math class, he clearly observed that some of the students had no idea how to solve the problems, while others knew the material and learned nothing new. In shaping, each best response is immediately reinforced. Skinner had researched delay of reinforcement and knew how it hampered performance. But, in the math class, children did not find out if one problem was correct before doing the next; they had to answer a whole page before getting any feedback, and then probably not receiving any until the next day. But how could one teacher with twenty or thirty students possibly shape mathematical behavior for each one simultaneously? Clearly teachers needed help. That afternoon, Skinner constructed his first teaching machine (O'Donohue & Ferguson, 2001).

Skinner's first teaching machine simply presented problems, in random order, for students to do with feedback after each one. This machine did not teach new behavior; all it did was give more practice on skills already learned. Within three years, however, Skinner developed *programmed instruction*. Through careful sequencing, students responded to material broken into small steps. The steps were similar to what a skilled tutor would ask of a student with whom they were working one on one. The first response of each sequence was prompted, but as performance improved, less and less help was given. By the end, a student was doing something he or she could not have done at the beginning (Skinner, 1987).

Some of the better programs from the 1960s are still used, and with the coming of the computer and internet, the sophisticated perfect machine Skinner lacked is now available (Hergenhahn & Olson, 2004).

Behaviorism in the Classroom

A typical behaviorist approach in the classroom often occurs as the teacher models the correct response to new information. As the children practice the correct response she provides positive reinforcement for the correct response. If an incorrect response is made, the teacher quickly re-teaches and models the correct response before the lesson can proceed. Usually the information is very logically presented in a highly sequenced series of steps. (See the following Classroom Glimpse.)

Chapter 15 | *Understanding Learning Theories*

CLASSROOM GLIMPSE

> Mrs. Barr is presenting a lesson on the sound of the letter Bb. She asks her kindergarten students to listen to the sound and say it with her. She points to the letter symbol and says bah-bah-bah. The children listen and then repeat what she says. She praises the children and gives them a positive reinforcement by putting a marble in a small glass jar. The children are pleased to hear the clinking sound—they know if they earn ten marbles in the jar by the end of the day they will earn a sticker!
>
> Next, Mrs. Barr tells the children to listen as she says three words. Baby, Button, Bottle. She asks them to repeat the words with her. As she says the words she emphasizes the b sound. She asks the children what sound starts each of the words. The children excitedly reply Bah! Once again a smiling Mrs. Barr rewards their efforts with another bright colored marble clinking in the jar.
>
> Now Mrs. Barr tells the children to listen carefully. She says three words: Cat, Bunny, Dog. She asks the children which one begins with the b sound. The children reply BUNNY! She smiles and repeats their correct answer. For the third time the marble clinks in the jar.
>
> Finally, Mrs. Barr gives the children a worksheet that has ten rows of pictures. Each row has three pictures. The children are told that they need to circle all the pictures that start with the letter sound of Bb. The children quickly return to their desks, grab a crayon and wait until Mrs. Barr does the first practice row with them as a whole group.

This very brief vignette illustrates the modeling, reinforcement and step-by-step instructional sequence. While effective, can you imagine how tedious the day might become if all lessons were taught in this one instructional approach?

Eventually, educators began to feel that, while although stimulus-response does explain many human behaviors and has a legitimate place in instruction (for instance, behaviorist theories still provide the foundation for programmed learning and all computer-assisted instruction used in classroom today), behaviorism alone was not sufficient to explain all the phenomena observed in more complex learning situations. These realizations brought more prominence to the cognitive theories of learning (Hergenhahn & Olson, 2004).

COGNITIVE LEARNING THEORIES

Cognitive theories (sometimes called information processing) first appeared in the 1920s, but were usurped by behavioral theories for a number of years, only to re-emerge as a dominant force again in the mid-1950s. **This theory views learning as an active mental process of acquiring, remembering, and using knowledge. Learning is evidenced by a change in knowledge that makes a potential change in behavior possible, but not necessary** (Schunk, 2003).

Cognitive theorists, like R.M. Gagne, are concerned with the operations that happen inside the brain as we learn (see Box 4). Other cognitive theorists, like Jean Piaget and Albert Bandura, take the perspective that students actively process information. These individuals believe learning takes place through the efforts of the individual as they organize, store, and then find relationships between information, linking new to old knowledge. Piaget also viewed learning as a changing process and children as individuals that developed over time (see Box 5). Albert Bandura, also believed that the environment and the individual influenced each other and learning occurs within that interaction (see Box 6).

BOX 4 MORE ABOUT ROBERT GAGNE

Robert Gagne (1916–2002) is often credited for helping turn the art of instruction into science. The beginning of Gagne's unique contributions were developed during World War II when he was asked to find a way to instruct non-teachers to make airplane mechanics out of farmers in thirty days, instead of two years of trial and error. Through this experience, Gagne identified the five kinds of performance that require unique types of instruction.

A leader in the field of instructional design since the 1940s, Gagne identified five major categories of learning. The significance of these classifications is that each type requires different instruction. The five major categories of learning are: verbal information, intellectual skills, cognitive strategies, motor skills, and attitudes. Different internal and external conditions are necessary for each type of learning. This work led to the publication of *The Conditions of Learning* (Gagne & Medsber, 1965), which outlined the relation of learning objectives to appropriate instructional designs.

Gagne further suggests that learning tasks for intellectual skills can be organized in a hierarchy according to complexity: stimulus recognition, response generation, procedure following, use of terminology, discriminations, concept formation, rule application, and problem solving. The primary significance of the hierarchy is to identify prerequisites that should be completed to facilitate learning at each level. Prerequisites are identified by doing a task analysis of a learning/training task. Gagne believes that learning hierarchies provide a basis for the sequencing of instruction (Gagne, Wager, Golas, & Keller, 2004).

As a professor of psychology at Princeton University, his interest in research shifted toward the learning of school subjects. The Information Processing Model, described later, helps teachers to deliberately arrange the learning conditions to promote the achievement of an intended goal (Driscoll, 1994). Cognitivists see instruction as a way of supporting the various internal processes by activating mental sets that:

- affect attention and selective perception
- enhance encoding
- provide an organization of the new data

Cognitivists, like Gagne, view the teacher's role as coordinating the learning environment so that learning remains focused on the goal of instruction.

BOX 5 MORE ABOUT JEAN PIAGET

Special Feature by Nancy Perry, Ph.D.

Jean Piaget 1896–1980 was born in Neuchâtel, Switzerland on August 9, 1896. As a child he had a strong interest in nature and biology; in fact, he published his first paper on albino sparrows at age eleven! Graduating with a Doctorate in Zoology from the University of Neuchâtel in 1918, Piaget took a position teaching psychology and philosophy at Sorbonne University in Paris. While at Sorbonne, Piaget worked on the development of intelligence tests with Alfred Binet. During this time, Piaget became intrigued by children's erroneous responses to various test items. When Piaget began to ask the children about how they arrived at their answers to the questions, he came to realize there was a pattern in the logic children used to solve the problems. Younger children were using one set of strategies and logical thought processes to arrive at their answers, and older children another. Based on this discovery, Piaget came to believe the answers to our questions about cognitive development might be discovered by studying how children's ability to logically reason grows over time (Piaget, 2000; Piaget, 2001 reissue of earlier work).

To study how knowledge develops, Piaget and his students interviewed, observed, and conducted simple experiments with thousands of elementary school children. Piaget also conducted in-depth observations on each of his three children. Through these clinical investigations, Piaget discovered that we progress through four stages of cognitive development: **sensorimotor, preoperational, operational, and formal operations.**

During the *sensorimotor stage* of cognitive development, infants use their senses to gather knowledge. They learn by manipulating objects and creating *schemas,* or categories of thought, about how the objects feel, taste, smell, move, and act.

At the *preoperational stage,* roughly between the ages of two and seven, children combine their sensory abilities with their newly acquired symbolic abilities (e.g., language and imagination) to gather information. The combination of these abilities helps young children connect their past experiences with new experiences more quickly, which deepens their understanding of the world. However, children of this age still experience difficulties with cause and effect because they cannot fully focus on all of the possible variables that cause an object to act in the way it does. Children of this age also experience difficulty understanding that others may think differently about an object or event, or have a different opinion about how these objects and events actually work. Piaget calls this **egocentrism**—the inability to view objects and situations from another person's perspective.

During the *concrete operational stage,* between the ages of seven and nine, children gain more flexibility in their thinking. They are able to coordinate information more precisely and consider several possible outcomes to problems based on the information they have collected. However, children in this stage of development still need concrete manipulatives to understand unfamiliar concepts and principles such as mathematical ideas not easily visualized.

Finally, during the *formal operational stage,* from about age eleven or twelve to adulthood, children master the ability to use abstract reasoning to solve problems. They can imagine all of the variables that might influence the outcome of their actions and systematically analyze each part of a problem without the use of concrete examples.

BOX 5 MORE ABOUT JEAN PIAGET (continued)

Although many people contend that Piaget's stages of development are static, they are not. Piaget believed the development of knowledge is a process of continual construction and reorganization. Knowledge constructed at each stage of development is reorganized in the following stage, leading toward progressively refined reasoning abilities and ideas about any given subject. This construction and reorganization is made possible by the dynamic and continuous processes of *adaptation, reflective abstraction, and equilibration.* These three processes are evident in all stages of cognitive development, including infancy, but our use of them becomes more flexible over time.

Adaptation consists of the dual processes of *assimilation* and *accommodation.* According to Piaget, assimilation and accommodation are how our minds make sense of objects and situations in our environment and how they work. For example, when we are faced with an unfamiliar stimulus, such as a platypus, we attempt to *assimilate,* or take in, and categorize all of the characteristics of the platypus, to our existing knowledge base. Now, if we have experience with platypus-like creatures, we fit the platypus into our understanding of these creatures—perhaps we connect it to our existing understanding of ducks or seals. In this case, not much changes in our thinking. But, if we are totally perplexed by this platypus, and are not satisfied that its characteristics relate to our current understanding of ducks or seals, we have to *accommodate* the structures of our thinking to add the platypus into our existing knowledge base. In this case, our thinking changes—we create a new schema; either by adapting our thinking about ducks and/or seals, or by creating an entirely new category of thought for large creatures with a bill like a duck and a body like a seal.

Reflective abstraction is the process of drawing out, interpreting, and coordinating information from the things we observe. It is our search for relationships, such as similarities and differences, between what we currently know and what we are learning about. This process enters into the knowledge construction process during assimilation. As we **abstract** or gather information about objects, we assimilate the observable properties of the object, as we did with our platypus. We then investigate the actions of the object or the object's responses to our actions. Finally, we seek information about unobservable properties of the platypus such as purpose or intent. Once we have done all of this, we **reflect** upon the information we have acquired and begin searching our existing schema to determine how it applies to what we already know. In essence, we put the new information into a relationship with our old body of knowledge to determine if we need to accommodate our thinking. If we determine our old thought patterns are sufficient enough to aid in our understanding of the new stimuli, nothing changes. If not, we create a new schema, or category of thought, to account for the platypus.

It is our desire to achieve *equilibrium,* a sense of comfort our current line of thinking sufficiently explains that way the world works, which fuels the construction of knowledge. Each time we assimilate something that does not fit within our view of the world we experience *disequilibrium,* or cognitive conflict. It is this sense of uneasiness or internal contradiction that pushes us to reflect upon and adapt our own thinking. This, in turn, begins the continuous process of adaptation, reflective abstraction, and equilibration that leads to our ever-growing knowledge of the world and how it works (Piaget, 2000, Piaget, 2001).

BOX 6 MORE ABOUT ALBERT BANDURA

Albert Bandura (1925–) received his Ph.D. in 1952 from the University of Iowa where he was initially influenced by behaviorist theory. In 1953, he started teaching at Stanford University. However, Bandura felt behaviorism, with its limited emphasis on observable variables, avoided understanding mental processes. Bandura found this a bit too simplistic for the phenomena he was observing—aggression in adolescents—and so decided to add a little something to the formula. He suggested that, while environment did cause behavior, behavior causes environment as well. He labeled this concept **reciprocal determinism**: The world and a person's behavior cause each other.

Later, he went a step further. He began to look at personality as an interaction among three dynamic variables—the environment, behavior, and the person's psychological processes. These psychological processes consist of the ability to entertain images in the mind and language. At the point where he introduces imagery, in particular, he ceases to be a strict behaviorist, and begins to join the ranks of the cognitivists. Adding imagery and language to the mix allows Bandura to theorize much more effectively about learning through observation and self-regulation (Evan, 1989; Bandura, 1997).

Attention—You learn through observation of a model (something to learn); you need to pay attention. Extreme emotions like fear or anger can impede your ability to pay attention, as can physical states like sleepiness or hunger.

Retention—Once you have observed the model, you must be able to remember what you have paid attention to. You store what you have seen in the form of mental images or verbal descriptions. When information is stored, you can later "bring up" the image or description, so you can reproduce it with your own behavior.

Reproduction—The ability to translate the images or descriptions of the model into actual behavior; for example, completing long division, doing back flips, or writing an essay. Your ability to imitate improves with practice—and your ability improves even when you just imagine yourself performing! Many athletes, for example, visualize their performance prior to competing.

Motivation—Even considering all of the factors above, you're still not going to learn or do anything unless you are motivated to. You must have some reason, or motivation, for doing it. Bandura mentions a number of motives:

- **past reinforcement**—traditional behaviorism.
- **promised reinforcements**—(incentives) we can imagine.
- **vicarious reinforcement**—seeing and recalling the model being reinforced.

Notice that reinforcement is traditionally considered to be the cause of learning. Bandura differs by saying that reinforcement doesn't cause learning, but gives us a reason to demonstrate what we have learned (Bandura, 1986).

Sequence	Description of Learning Function	Example of Learning Experience
Sensory reception	One or more of the body's senses (e.g., sight, smell, touch, sound, and taste) perceive the information.	While shopping at the mall, Mary sees, hears, and smells hundreds of pieces of information.
Sensory memory	Acts as a buffer for information received by the senses. Filters the vast array of information to only those of interest at a given time.	Amid all the sights and sounds, Mary hears a few notes coming through the clutter.
Paying attention	Immediately, after sensing information, the act of selective perception.	Mary begins to recognize the notes.
Short-term memory	Serves as a temporary note pad for new information. Short-term memory is usually forgotten quickly. However, some information (based on the individual's level of interest) is processed.	Mary recognizes the song as one of her favorites, but it is a different version than the one she has sung to dozens of times before.
Semantic encoding	Information meaningful to the individual is encoded for emotional content, personal relevance and is reviewed in terms of prior experiences.	Mary remembers the last time she heard this song played was when she met her new boyfriend.
Long-term memory	Intended for long-term storage of interpreted information. Information from the long-term memory can be retrieved and brought to consciousness.	Mary continues to remember other times she has heard this song. She decides she likes the "old" version better.
Response generator	If warranted, the response generator causes muscles to take action and the response may or may not be emitted back to the environment.	Mary decides to buy the old version of the song to give to her new boyfriend.

Figure 1 Cognitive Theory Processing

Cognitivism in the Classroom

Cognitive learning theories emphasize how information is processed. Cognitive theorists believe a teacher can encourage learning by providing information to students and helping them organize the information in such a way they are able to recall it later (Hergenhahn & Olson, 2004). Figure 1 offers the sequence of learning from a cognitive theorist perspective.

This learning sequence is called the Information Processing Model. It provides a blueprint of how the mind senses, processes, stores, and recalls information. Cognitivists believe this information can help teachers design instruction with particular concern to content, sequence, and structure.

What does this sequence look like instructionally? Consider the egg lesson outlined below.

Sequence	Example of Learning Experience
Sensory reception	Students come into the class. They see the teacher has put an egg, in a plastic cup, paper, and a magnifying glass at each student's desk. Each groups of four desks also has a jug of water.
Sensory memory	Teacher has written question on the board. *What do you know about eggs?* She asks her class this question. The students begin to answer and as they do the teacher writes their responses on the board. *Eggs are smooth, can be eaten, can grow into little chicks. Have yolks, whites.*
Paying attention	The teacher now draws the student's attention to the materials on the student's desk. The teacher asks the students to take the magnifying glass to examine the shell of the egg.

These first three steps help to focus student attention, stimulate their interest and prior knowledge about the topic the teacher intends to introduce.

Short-term memory	The teacher asks the students to draw what they see and share that information with a partner. The students quickly discover that the egg is not smooth as they initially predicted, rather it has tiny little holes. The teacher asks, "*Why do you think the egg has holes?* The students suggest that the eggs have holes to let light in the shell, or to let air in the shell.
Semantic encoding	The teacher tells the students to fill their cups half full with water and to place their eggs into the cup. Then asks them to observe what happens. As they watch the teacher continues to guide their observations with questions. Does the egg float or sink to the bottom of the glass? What does the egg look like in the water? Do you see little bubbles? Which part of the egg is giving off bubbles? What are the bubbles telling us?

> **Think About It**
>
> Contrast this lesson with the behaviorist lesson plan (the sound of the letter Bb). What differences do you notice in the:
>
> Teacher role:
>
> Student's role:

Long-term memory	The students are beginning to change their perceptions and knowledge about eggs and their structures. The many questions the teacher is posing is helping the students to reshape and refine their prior knowledge of eggs. The discussion between the students and the writing down and sharing their information with the group is also helping this new knowledge go from short-term memory to long-term memory.
Response Generator	The talking and writing and exploring serves as a part of the physical actions as they continue to motivate new learning and encourage the students' retention of this information.

In the 1980s several lesson plan formats were developed to help teachers create lessons that would help children move from simple memorization of facts—the egg shell has holes that allows for air exchange—to a deeper understanding of that fact which then allows for better retention of information.

CONSTRUCTIVIST LEARNING THEORIES

Constructivism also began in the 1920s. Its leading theorist, Lev Vygotsky, believed culture to be the prime factor of individual development. (See Box 7). Humans create culture, and every child is raised in the context of that particular culture. Therefore, culture affects a child's learning development. Cultural factors include:

- language
- morality
- belief systems
- religion
- socialization

Culture teaches children what to think and how to think. Cognitive development results from an interactive process, whereby a child learns through problem-solving experiences shared with someone else, usually a parent or teacher, but sometimes a sibling or peer (Hergenhahn & Olson, 2004). Initially, the person interacting with the child assumes most of the responsibility for guiding the problem solving, but gradually this responsibility transfers to the child.

Constructivism is founded on the premise that, by reflecting on our experiences, we construct our own understanding of the world we live in. Each of us generates our own "rules" and "mental models" which we use to make sense of our experiences (Schunk, 2003).

Cultural factors that may affect a child's learning development include language, morality, belief systems, religion, and socialization.

Learning, therefore, is simply the process of adjusting our mental models to accommodate new experiences. There are several guiding principles of constructivism:

- Learning is a search for meaning. Therefore, learning must start with the issues around which students are actively trying to construct meaning.
- Meaning requires understanding **wholes** as well as parts. And parts must be understood in the context of wholes. Therefore, the learning process focuses on main concepts, not isolated facts.
- In order to teach well, we must understand the mental models students use to perceive the world and the assumptions they make to support those models.
- The purpose of learning is for an individual to construct his or her own meaning, not just memorize the "right" answers and regurgitate someone else's label or meaning (see Case 1: Annie's Construction).
- Since education is inherently interdisciplinary, the only valuable way to measure learning is to make the assessment part of the learning process, ensuring it provides students with information on the quality of their learning.

BOX 7 MORE ABOUT LEV VYGOTSKY

Lev Vygotsky (1896–1934) graduated with degrees in law, history, and philosophy earned concurrently at two different Moscow universities in 1917, at the ripe old age of twenty-one. Though Vygotsky never had formal training in psychology, his pioneering work in developmental psychology has had a profound influence on education since the 1930s. Though Vygotsky produced most of this work in the 1920s, the Russian Revolution and Stalinist suppression prevented most of Vygotsky's theories from being available in the West until the 1980s.

Vygotsky argued that a child's development cannot be understood by a study of just the individual. Instead, to understand development and learning, we must also examine the child's social and cultural world (home, school, community). The major theme of Vygotsky's theoretical framework is that social interaction plays a fundamental role in the development of cognition. Vygotsky described learning as being embedded within the social events and occurrences as a child interacts with the people, objects, and events in his/her environment.

A second aspect of Vygotsky's theory is the idea that the potential for cognitive development is limited to a certain time span that he calls the *"zone of proximal development"* (ZPD). This is the distance between the child's actual developmental level (as determined by independent problem solving) and the level of potential development as determined through problem solving under adult guidance or in collaboration with more capable peers. The zone of proximal development represents the amount of learning possible by a student given the proper instructional conditions (Newman, 1993).

The theory of social constructivism translates into current classroom practice in the use of **curriculum** that is based on solving real-world concerns and problems in small groups that emphasize interaction between learners and learning tasks. **Instruction** should occur with appropriate adult help, as students are often able to perform tasks they are incapable of completing on their own. This support is called scaffolding—where the adult continually adjusts the level of his or her help in response to the child's level of performance—and is an effective form of teaching. Scaffolding not only produces immediate results, but also instills the skills necessary for independent problem solving in the future. **Assessment** methods must take into account the zone of proximal development. What children can do on their own is their level of *actual development,* and what they can do with help is their level of *potential development.* Two children might have the same level of actual development, but given the appropriate help from an adult, one might be able to solve many more problems than the other. Assessment methods must target both the level of actual development and the level of potential development (Wertsch, 1988).

Constructivism in the Classroom

Constructivist theory is seen in the classroom in the form of cooperative learning and learning investigations initiated by the students' own interests. With appropriate adult help, students can often perform tasks they are incapable of completing on their own. With this in mind, scaffolding—where the teacher continually adjusts the level of his or her help in response to the student's level of performance—is an effective form of teaching. Scaf-

CASE STUDY 1

Annie's Construction When Annie was ten months old she began to call her Daddy "Dada" and her Mommy "Mama." Annie also imitated what her family called her Grandma, "Gi-Gi." Though her family called her Grandpa "Papa," Annie refused to call him by that name, instead she called him "Da-Gi." Annie's personal construction of "DaGi" for Grandpa is an example of a personal mental model based on rules Annie determined.

- What "rules" might Annie have developed?

folding not only produces immediate results, but also instills the skills necessary for independent problem solving in the future. Constructivism in middle and high school classrooms also takes on another dimension—the expertise of the young adults and the context of solving real problems and doing real work. The following vignette illustrates this process.

In the fall of 2005, hurricane Katrina slammed the gulf coast of Louisiana, Mississippi, and Alabama. The electronic media featured the horrors of the natural disaster for hours on end. Many of the students in a lower socioeconomic middle school in urban Phoenix had relatives who lost everything in this event. One story that especially touched the hearts and minds of the students in this poor Arizona middle school was the complete loss of a New Orleans middle school library. The students began to share their concerns with their teachers. After a few days of discussion in their social studies class, the students decided to take action. They determined that they wanted to raise funds to purchase books for the New Orleans middle school. Working with their own school library-media specialist, and their English, social studies, and math teachers, they began to research the costs of the literature books and contacted the New Orleans school district to determine the titles in the destroyed library's inventory. With the help of the school principal and the English teacher, the students contacted local community leaders (including some of their own parents) to determine the best way to raise the money. For nearly four weeks, part of their work at school consisted of interacting in cooperative groups, with each group charged with researching part of the solutions to this larger problem. They wrote letters to book clubs, local businesses, local philanthropists, and local media. They figured the costs for the books (they soon realized they couldn't replace all the books but they could replace the fiction section in the library) so they took a class vote and decided the students would prefer to have books like Harry Potter, than reference texts. The students coordinated three fundraising drives:

- A donated dinner by a local restaurant where parents and community members bought tickets
- A silent auction at the donated dinner (goods were donated by local businesses)
- A community dance where a local radio personality donated his time to be the DJ

> **Think About It**
>
> Though no test will record these students' learning, what do you think they learned through this effort?

By the end of November, one hundred determined twelve-year-olds had raised nearly 7,000 dollars to help replenish the library in New Orleans.

Who drove the curriculum and efforts of this event?

What math did the students need to do to determine how much money to raise?

What English skills did the students need to use to contact local community leaders?

Teachers today have the opportunity to choose from a diverse set of learning theories when designing their lessons. However, it must be noted that no single theory currently offers an adequate explanation for the remarkably complex phenomena of human intelligence. As a result, perhaps the best approach is for future teachers to consider an eclectic approach that draws on the idea of a learning theory continuum (see Figure 2).

GROUP TALK

What learning theories do you see reflected most often in the K through 12 classrooms where you are observing?

What theory does your professor most often use in this class?

Which theory do you feel most comfortable with in terms of your own future instruction?

Understanding learning theories not only helps us understand others' instructional practices, but this knowledge also helps us make good decisions in our instruction so that our students' learning experiences can be optimized.

Major Theory	Key Principles	Types of Learning
Behaviorism	• Behavior is repeated until it becomes automatic. • The behavior of the learner indicates learning has occurred. • The influence of the external environment contributes to the shaping of the individual's behavior. • The environment presents a stimulus that prompts a behavior. • Whether the behavior occurs again is dependent on the consequence that follows it.	• New physical skills • Recall of basic facts • Performing well defined procedures or skills
Cognitivism	• Learning is influenced by existing knowledge. • Learning is based on the thought process behind the behavior. • Learning is governed by internal processes rather than by external circumstance (behaviorism). • Defines the process of selecting information (attention), translating information (encoding), and recalling information when appropriate (retrieval).	• Problem solving • Reasoning • Information processing • Classifications
Constructivism	• Learning occurs when the learner applies current knowledge to solving new problems. • Learning occurs through interaction with others. • Individuals construct knowledge by working to solve realistic problems, usually in collaboration with others. • Learning is seen as a change in meaning constructed from new experience. • Suggests that individual interpretation of experience vs. objective representation (information processing perspective).	• Need for creativity • Complex problem solving • Need to apply knowledge to changing situations

Figure 2 Comparing and Contrasting Learning Theories

BIOLOGICAL FOUNDATIONS FOR LEARNING

The behaviorists, cognitivists, and constructivists who developed the three preceding theories of learning had to infer the process of learning from careful, long-term observations of external behavior. Since the 1980s, technological innovations have enabled neuroscientists to study the living brain. Brain imaging techniques such as functional magnetic resonance imaging (fMRI) are non-invasive procedures that allow researchers to graphically record and simultaneously display three-dimensional, color-enhanced images of a living brain as it processes information (Sochurek, 1987). These data provide researchers with a new way to understand the organization and functional operations of the brain as it relates to human learning (see Box 8).

BOX 8 MORE ABOUT fMRI

Magnetic resonance imaging (MRI) is an technique used primarily in medical settings to produce high quality images of the organs and systems inside of the human body. MRI provides an unparalleled view inside the human body (Schwartz, 2002).

Functional Magnetic Resonance Imaging (fMRI) is a relatively new imaging technology most often utilized to study the brain. Investigations in the fields of vision, language, motor function, memory, emotion, and pain have been greatly assisted by fMRI technology.

fMRI can be used to map changes in the blood-oxygen flow, which allows for functional mapping of the human brain. Consequently, an fMRI can provide high resolution, noninvasive reports of neural activity. For instance, fMRI allows us to see how speech is processed and when and how we receive visual information. This new ability to directly observe brain function opens an array of new opportunities to advance our understanding of brain organization, as well as a potential new technique for assessing neurological health and cognitive development (Smilkstein, 2003).

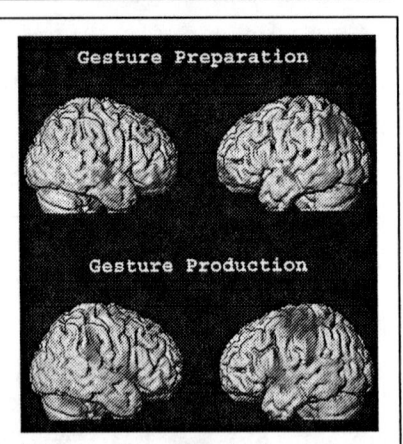

fMRI has been the single most useful innovation for brain research to date.

© Visuals Unlimited/CORBIS

Though this science is relatively new, it is producing important new information about how children learn to read and do arithmetic. Scientists now have a fair idea of where in the brain these skills reside and which skills are acquired quickly and slowly. For example, it seems that turning groups of letters into words is, initially, a relatively slow process, while making sense and meaning of these words is extremely rapid (Wolfe, 2001). Likewise, mental arithmetic once learned seems to work in the same way in children as adults. These scanning techniques may one day also help tell teachers objectively what methods are best to help children learn. It may also help to support specific types of learning strategies for children who have learning difficulties (Posner, 2003).

This emerging learning theory is based on the biological structures and functions of the brain, and reinforces various aspects of the propositions put forth by behaviorists, cognitivists, and constructivists. However, this theory also focuses heavily on the role of emotion, personal interest, and motivation in the learning process. Humans do not simply learn things devoid of feeling (Wolfe, 2001). What we learn is influenced by prior personal experience and interests, biases, and prejudices. All of these elicit emotion, which can inhibit or encourage subsequent learning. Emotions and thoughts literally shape each other and cannot be separated (see Figure 3).

The premise of the biological view of learning suggests that, as long as the brain is not prohibited from fulfilling its normal processes (due to medical or physical conditions), learning will occur. Every person is born with a brain which functions as an immensely powerful processor (Sylwester, 2000; Caine & Caine, 1991). The core principles of a biological view of learning state:

1. The brain is a parallel processor, meaning it can perform several activities simultaneously, like seeing, tasting, and smelling.
2. Learning engages the whole physiology.
3. The search for meaning—making sense of what is happening—is inborn.
4. The search for meaning comes through organization and categorization of information (called patterning; cause and effect).
5. Emotions are critical to the ability to detect patterns.
6. The brain processes wholes and parts simultaneously.

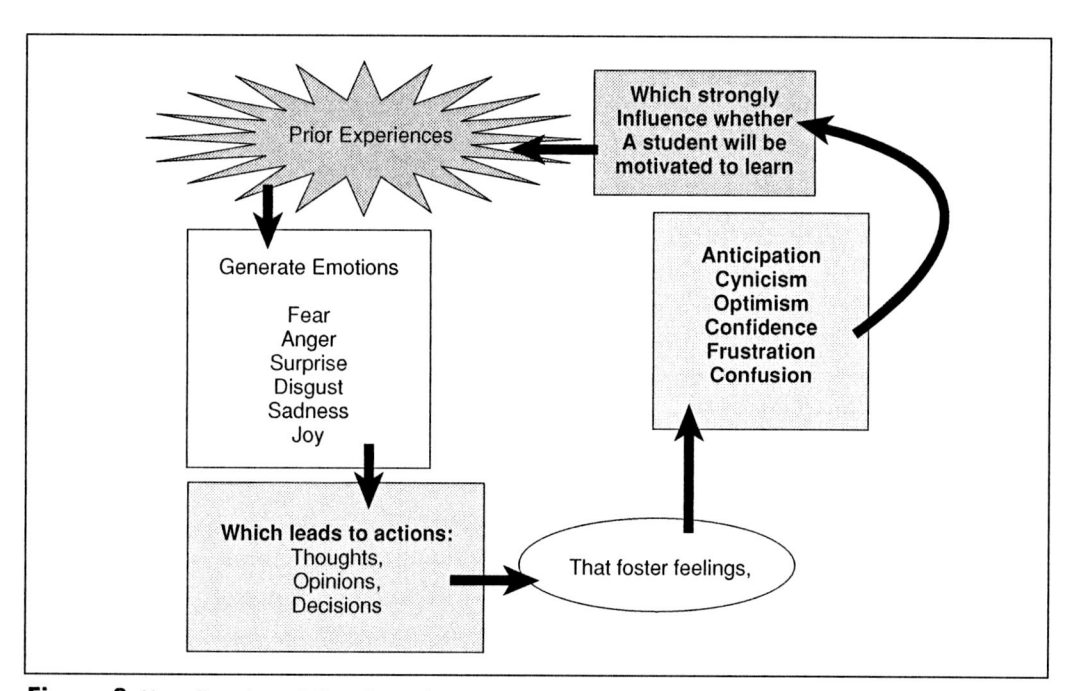

Figure 3 How Emotions Affect Learning

7. Learning involves both focused attention and peripheral **perception**.
8. Learning involves both conscious and unconscious processes.
9. Learning is enhanced by challenge/curiosity and inhibited by threat.
10. Each brain is unique.

The three instructional techniques associated with biological learning theory are:

- *Orchestrated immersion*   Teachers create learning environments that fully immerse students in an educational experience—engaging as many senses as possible.
- *Relaxed alertness*   Teachers eliminate fear in learners while maintaining a highly active and challenging environment.
- *Active processing*   Teachers allow learners to strengthen and internalize information by actively processing it with peers and through hands-on learning activities.

The "Classroom Glimpse" offers an illustration of how emotions influence learning.

The following Group Talk activity offers an opportunity for you to process this new information about the emotional learning cycle. Take a few minutes to read this information. After you have read the information, consider the questions. Share your thoughts with a peer.

CLASSROOM GLIMPSE

Tara loves to sing (**prior experiences**). Every time she sings her teachers, family and friends praise her beautiful voice (**generates emotions** such as happiness, joy, pride). Subsequently, these positive feelings encourage Tara to make the decision to practice and work even harder on her singing (**actions**). She takes vocal lessons and tries out for the school choir. Her decision to practice and take lessons continues to deepen her love of music and her improve her vocal skills. This new knowledge further inspires confidence (**feelings**). Tara's motivation to learn more about music and singing creates a continuous self-propelling cycle of **motivation and learning**.

Chapter 15 | *Understanding Learning Theories*

GROUP TALK

Examining the Connections Between Emotions and Learning

As you read the following vignette about Ms. Nora's fourth grade class, consider your own experiences in school and what you have just learned about the biological foundation of learning. Then, consider what might have influenced the academic outcomes for James, Jose, and Derrick.

Ms. Nora calls her fourth grade students in from lunch recess. It is hot outside and the children are sweating. Ms. Nora can feel the temperature rising as they enter the room. James, Jose, and Derrick are not only physically hot, their tempers are flaring from a contested game of playground soccer. As they come into the classroom the boys are shouting, calling each other names, and shoving each other.

Ms. Nora brusquely reminds them to put their playground disputes behind them and immediately starts to distribute "Mad Math Minutes" worksheets. The goal of this exercise is to do as many single-digit multiplication problems—correctly—in one minute. This drill is to help the students practice for the state-mandated accountability test at the end of month.

At the end of the one-minute activity Ms. Nora asks the children to exchange papers to do the grading. Most of the children score fairly well—ranging from twenty-five to thirty correct responses out of fifty. However, James, Jose, and Derrick have only answered ten to fifteen problems and all three of them have made several computational mistakes. Ms. Nora is frustrated with the boys and chastises them loudly in front of their peers.

At the end of the day, as Ms. Nora records their daily grades, she notices that these three normally well-behaved boys continued to have difficulty on the spelling test and their comprehension counts worksheet.

1. What factor(s) do you think contributed to the boys' academic difficulty in class today?

2. What might you (as teacher) have done when the boys entered the classroom?

3. Though the vignette describes an elementary school experience with young boys, are adults' ability to learn affected by their emotions in similar ways? Provide a personal example.

APPLYING LEARNING THEORIES TO CLASSROOM PRACTICE

In the previous sections, we have explored a variety of learning theories: behaviorism, cognitivism, constructivism, and biological foundations. While it is important to understand these theories in terms of human development, how do these theories help explain and/or enhance classroom instruction?

The following vignette examines one high school dance teacher's class. As you read about her lesson, consider what learning theory(s) underlies each particular part of the lesson. Use Group Talk 2 to identify the theories.

CLASSROOM GLIMPSE

9:00—Warm up. Ms. Denay always begins her fifty-minute high school dance class with a ten-minute ballet warm-up. While the students practice the warm-up skills she has taught them, she moves among them, refining the placement of arms, legs, and torso. As she observes their movements she verbally praises their efforts.

9:10—Group Directions. The next part of the lesson involves the students practicing a rather complex jazz dance. The three-minute dance has multiple sections where three different groups of dancers enter and leave the stage at various times; but there are also times when all groups of dancers are all on the stage performing all movements, hopefully, in perfect synchronization. To rehearse the various components of the dance, Ms. Denay asks groups A, B, C to practice each of their parts separately.

9:15—Group Practice. The three groups move to three corners in the gym. During the first part of the practice, Ms. Denay instructs the students to perform using only counts. In other words, all of the students count, in sets of four, as they rehearse the choreography. Counting enables the students to slowly practice the series of movements and encourages their efforts to move in unison. Next, Ms. Denay plays the music and once again the students—this time more rapidly—practice dancing their parts.

9:25—Whole Class Practice. After the class has practiced the dance twice as separate groups, Ms. Denay brings the class together to perform the entire dance. She has set up the video camera to record their effort in order for the students to critique and improve their piece.

9:30—Whole Group Observation. Before they watch the video, Ms. Denay asks the students to consider what they should look for. As a group they decide they need to watch the performance twice. First, they will watch for their own group effort, then they will watch the video as a whole performance. They decide to focus their observation on moving in unison (this has been somewhat problematic in the past and they have been working on this aspect of their performance in their practice) and entering the stage on time.

9:35—Discussion/Feedback/Problem Solving. The dancers reassemble quickly to discuss what they saw in their group performance and then to discuss what they saw in the routine as a whole. Groups A and C were pleased—they felt they had done an excellent job at moving in unison and were right on time with their on-stage entry. Group B had hesitated with one of its entries on the stage, and they felt the hesitation created the secondary problem of causing them to be out-of-step with each other. Ms. Denay asked the class to offer Group B suggestions on how to solve this problem. Group A offered that they had a lead dancer who the others followed to be sure they entered exactly on time. Group B accepts the suggestion and appoints Sherre to be lead.

9:40—Whole Group Performance. The class performs the entire dance once again. Ms. Denay videotapes the dance.

9:45—Observation. The class observes the second performance. Clearly, Group B's decision to have a lead dancer helped them significantly. Mrs. Denay dismisses the class to start dressing for their next course.

GROUP TALK

Identifying Learning Theories in Practice

Using Figure 2 (page 295) Comparing Learning Theories, consider what Ms. Denay did at each part of her lesson to ensure her students learned. What learning theory was reflected in her actions?

9:00—Warm-up
9:10—Group Directions
9:15—Group Practice
9:25—Whole Class Performance
9:30—Whole Class Observation
9:35—Group Discussion—Feedback—Problem solving
9:40—Whole Class Performance
9:45—Whole Class Observation and Feedback

As you consider this lesson as a whole, did one instructional theory dominate or did Ms. Denay use a range of approaches? How do you believe this influenced the effectiveness of the lesson?

If you were Ms. Denay, describe how you might build on this lesson tomorrow.

What learning theory would be reflected in this strategy?

LOOKING FORWARD

In this chapter we reviewed the three major learning theories and their proponents. In addition we briefly discussed the emerging neurological perspective of how learning occurs. Interesting, it reflects the views of all three learning theories, depending on the type of learning the student is trying to accomplish.

A philosophy, reflects a system of thought. In this case the philosophies reveal distinct perspectives of the purpose and approaches to education. Similarly, we will discuss teaching styles, which are more contemporary. You will find yourself relating to these beliefs and subsequent approaches to education. Finally, we will look at the different levels of teaching, from early childhood to secondary education and the newest field of study, special education.

RESEARCH CITATIONS

Bandura, A. (1986). *Social Foundations of Thought and Action.* Englewood Cliffs, NJ: Prentice Hall.

Bandura, A. (1997). *Self-Efficacy: The Exercise of Control.* New York, NY: Freeman.

Bjork, D. W. (1997). *B.F. Skinner: A Life.* Washington, DC: American Psychological Association.

Brewer, C. L. (1991). Perspectives on John B. Watson. In G. A. Kimble, M. Wertheimer, & C. L. White (Eds.), *Portraits of pioneers in psychology.* Washington, DC: American Psychological Association.

Buckley, K. W. (1989). *Mechanical Man: John B. Watson and the Beginnings of Behaviorism.* New York, NY: Guilford Press.

Caine, R. & Caine, G. (1991). *Making Connections: Teaching and the Human Brain.* Alexandria, VA: Association Supervision and Curriculum Development.

Chomsky, C. (1969). *The acquisition of syntax in children from 5 to 10.* Cambridge, MA: M.I.T. Press.

Cromer, A. H. (1997). *Connected Knowledge : Science, Philosophy, and Education.* New York, NY: Oxford University Press.

DeNicolas, A. T. (1989). *Habits of Mind: An Introduction to the Philosophy of Education.* St. Paul, MN: Paragon House Publishers.

Driscoll, M. P. (1994). *Psychology of learning for instruction.* Needham Heights, MA: Allyn & Bacon.

Evan, R. I. (1989). *Albert Bandura.* Westport, CN: Praeger Publishers.

Gagne, R. M. & Medsker, K. L. (1995). *The conditions of learning: Training applications.* Belmont, CA: Wadsworth Publishing.

Gagne, R. M., Wager, W. W., Golas, K. & Keller, J. M. (2004). *Principles of instructional design,* 5th Ed. Belmont: CA. Wadsworth Publishing.

Hergenhahn, B. R. & Olson, M. H. (2004). *Introduction to the theories of learning,* 7th Ed. Upper Saddle River, NJ: Prentice Hall.

Kohn, A. (1993). *Punished by rewards: The trouble with gold stars, incentive plans, A's, praise, and other bribes.* Boston, MA: Houghton Mifflin.

Newman, F. (1993). Lev Vygotsky; revolutionary scientist *Critical Psychology.* Bath, UK: Routledge.

O'Donohue, W. T. & Ferguson, K. E. (2001). *The Psychology of B F Skinner.* London, UK: Sage Publications.

Piaget, J. (2000). *The Psychology of the Child.* New York, NY: Basic Books.

Piaget, J. (2001). *Psychology of Intelligence.* Bath, UK: Routledge.

Posner, M. I. (2004). *Cognitive neuroscience of attention.* New York, NY: Guilford Press.

Schunk, D. H. (2003). *Learning Theories: An Educational Perspective,* 4th Ed. Upper Saddle River, NJ: Prentice Hall.

Sherwood, E. & Sherwood, M. (1970). *Ivan Pavlov.* Heron Books, London, Eng.

Skinner, B. F. (1987). *Upon further reflection.* Upper Saddle River, NJ: Prentice-Hall, Inc.

Sylwester, R. (2000). *A biological brain in a cultural classroom: Applying biological research to classroom management.* Thousand Oaks, CA: Corwin Press.

Todd, J. T., & Morris, E. K.(1994). *Modern perspectives on John B. Watson and classical behaviorism.* Westport, CT: Greenwood Press.

Todes, D. P. (2000). *Ivan Pavlov: Exploring the animal machine.* New York, NY: Oxford University Press.

Watson, J. B.(1930). *Behaviorism.* Chicago, IL: University of Chicago Press.

Wertsch, J. V. (1988). *Vygotsky and the Social Formation of Mind.* Boston, MA: Harvard University Press.

Wolfe, P. (2001). *Brain matters: Translating research into classroom practice.* Alexandria, VA: ASCD.

READING ON THE HUMAN BRAIN AND NEUROSCIENCE

Bransford, J., Brown, A. & Cocking, R. (2000). *How people learn: Brain, mind, experience and school.* Washington, D.C: National Academy Press.

Butterworth, B. (1999). *What counts: How every brain is hardwired for math.* New York, NY: Free Press.

Byrnes, J. (2001). *Minds, brains, and learning: Understanding the psychological and educational relevance of neuroscientific research.* New York, NY: The Guilford Press.

Calvin, W. (2002). *A brain for all seasons: Human evolution and abrupt climate change.* Chicago, IL: University of Chicago Press.

Damasio, A. (1999). *The feeling of what happens: Body and emotion in the making of consciousness.* New York, NY: Harcourt.

Diamond, M. & Hopson, J. (1998). *Magic trees of the mind: How to nurture your child's intelligence, creativity, and healthy emotions.* New York, NY: Dutton Press.

Fauconnier, G. & Turner, M. (2002). *The way we think: Conceptual blending and the mind's hidden complexities.* New York, NY: Basic Books.

Freeman, W. (2000). *How brains make up their minds.* New York, NY: Columbia University Press.

Goldblum, N. (2001). *The brain-shaped mind: What the brain can tell us about the mind.* Cambridge, UK: Cambridge University Press.

Greenspan, S. & Shanker, S. (2004). *The first idea: How symbols, language, and intelligence evolved from our primate ancestors to modern humans.* Cambridge, MA: Da Capo Press.

Johnson, S. (2004). *Mind wide open: Your brain and the neuroscience of everyday life.* New York, NY: Scribner.

LeDoux, J. (2002). *Synaptic self: How our brains become who we are.* New York, NY: Viking Press.

Klein, S. (2000). *Biological psychology.* Upper Saddle River, NJ: Prentice Hall.

Kotulak, R. (1996). *Inside the brain: Revolutionary discoveries of how the mind works.* Kansas City, MO: Andrews McMeeley Publishing.

Pinker, S. (2002). *The blank slate: The modern denial of human nature.* New York, NY: Penguin Books.

Ratey, J. (2001). *A user's guide to the brain.* New York, NY: Pantheon Books.

Smilkstein, R. (2003). *We're born to learn: Using the brain's natural learning process to create today's curriculum.* Thousand Oaks, CA: Corwin Press.

Schwartz, J. (2002). *The mind and the brain: Neuroplasticity and the power of mental force.* New York, NY: Harper Collins Publishers.

Chapter 16

What Makes a Teacher Effective?

CHARACTERISTICS OF EFFECTIVE TEACHERS

Effective teachers, from preschool through the university level, are somehow able to connect with all the students in the class. They are also able to motivate their students and create an interest in learning, whether the ABCs or calculus (Cruickshank, Jenkins, & Metcalf, 2003). Research in teacher effectiveness has consistently demonstrated that when students are interested in a subject they usually perform better. In addition, effective teachers enjoy and are enthusiastic about the teaching and learning process, as enthusiasm appears to promote student interest, motivation, and inspiration (Bettencourt, Gillett, Gail, & Hull, 1983; Borich, 2004). Effective teachers are deeply committed to helping students learn, and work tirelessly to develop effective lessons and learning experiences.

Take a few moments to assess your favorite teacher's professional *characteristics*. Use Figure 1, **The Professional Characteristics Checklist.** Place a check by the attributes you felt your favorite teacher(s) possessed (Enz, Honaker, & Kortman, 2002).

From Learning to Teach by Billie J. Enz, Bette S. Bergeron, and Michael Wolfe. Copyright © 2007 by Kendall/Hunt Publishing Company. Reprinted by permission.

> **The Professional Characteristics Checklist**
>
> **Directions:** Picture one of your favorite teachers in your mind. Make a check next to the following attributes that accurately describe that teacher.
>
> _____ **Commitment**—Teacher had a genuine concern for students and was dedicated to helping them become successful learners.
>
> _____ **Creativity**—Teacher sought opportunities to provide unique learning experiences and developed imaginative lessons.
>
> _____ **Enthusiasm**—Teacher showed delight in teaching students and content. High levels of energy and effort were observable.
>
> _____ **Flexibility**—Teacher responded to unforeseen circumstances in an appropriate manner and modified actions or plans when necessary.
>
> _____ **Integrity**—Teacher maintained high ethical and professional standards and responded to student needs appropriately.
>
> _____ **Organization**—Teacher was efficient and successfully managed multiple tasks simultaneously and established/maintained effective classroom routines/procedures.
>
> _____ **Perseverance**—Teacher gave best effort, strove to complete tasks and improve teaching skills and management strategies.
>
> _____ **Positive Disposition**—Teacher possessed pleasant interpersonal skills and was patient, resilient, optimistic, and approachable.
>
> _____ **Professional Appearance**—Teacher dressed in a manner that inspired confidence and public trust.
>
> _____ **Reliability/Dependability**—Teacher took responsibility for students' academic, emotional, and physical well-being.
>
> _____ **Self-Confidence**—Teacher gave students a sense of assurance and inspired confidence.
>
> _____ **Self-Initiative/Independence**—Teacher was a creative problem-solver.
>
> _____ **Tact/Judgment**—Teacher was diplomatic and courteous when handling difficult situations.

Figure 1 More about Essentialism

As you assessed your favorite teacher's personal and professional characteristics, did you think about your own? Do you possess these *attributes?* The following list includes many of the attributes mentioned, and a few more. The additional characteristics include oral and written expression and collegiality. These qualities are also essential to be an effective teacher. Take a few moments to reflect upon these professional characteristics by using Figure 2, **The Professional Characteristics Self-Assessment Checklist.**

Chapter 16 | *What Makes a Teacher Effective?* 307

This checklist is designed to help potential teachers appraise their personal and professional attitudes and actions. Scale Guide: **S**=Sometimes, **U**=Usually, **A**=Always. Provide a concrete example of how you demonstrate this attribute.

Think About It

Look through your responses on the checklist.
- Where do you excel?
- Where are there potential areas of difficulty?
- If you have marked "sometimes" how could you strengthen this quality?

S	U	A	Professional Characteristics
			Oral Expression—I am articulate and communicate concisely. I model fluent and grammatically correct language. *Example:*
			Written Expression—I communicate clearly and concisely and use grammatically correct language and appropriate mechanics. *Example:*
			Tact/judgment—I am diplomatic and courteous when handling difficult situations that may arise with family, friends, and colleagues. *Example:*
			Self-Initiative/Independence—I am an active and creative problem solver. I take responsibility to solve problems that arise. *Example:*
			Self-Confidence—I am a thoughtful, independent problem-solver and make decisions based on multiple sources of information. *Example:*
			Collegiality—I take advantage of working with, and learning from others. I enjoy sharing my ideas. *Example:*
			Commitment—I am able to commit to projects and sustain my interests over time. *Example:*
			Creativity—I actively seek opportunities to learn new information. I am imaginative and like to try new things. *Example:*
			Flexibility—I respond to unforeseen circumstances in an appropriate manner and modify my actions or plans when necessary. *Example:*
			Integrity—I maintain high ethical and personal standards. *Example:*
			Organization—I am efficient and successfully manage multiple tasks simultaneously. *Example:*
			Perseverance—I give my best efforts consistently and strive to complete tasks in my daily life. *Example:*
			Positive Disposition—I possess pleasant interpersonal skills and am patient, resilient, optimistic, and approachable. *Example:*
			Reliability/Dependability—I take responsibility for my actions, thoughts, and behaviors. *Example:*

Adapted from Enz, B. J., Hurwitz, S. & Carlile, B.J. (2005). *Coaching the Student Teacher: A Developmental Approach.* Dubuque, IA: Kendall/Hunt Publishers.

Figure 2 The Professional Characteristics Self-Assessment Checklist

What Is a New Teacher Expected to Do?

In the mid-1990s a committee of teachers, teacher educators, and state agency officials created the Interstate New Teacher Assessment and Support Continuum (INTASC). The standards developed by INTASC outlined the knowledge, **dispositions,** and performances deemed essential for all new teachers regardless of subject or grade level (Darling-Hammond, 2000). These standards represent a shared view among states and within the profession of what constitutes competent beginning teaching. These standards are often used in teacher education programs to guide the planning of courses or how pre-service teachers are assessed (see Box 1. **More About INTASC Standards**). The INTASC Standards include:

1. *Content Pedagogy*—The teacher understands the central concepts, tools of inquiry, and structures of the discipline he or she teaches and can create learning experiences that make these aspects of subject matter meaningful for students.
2. *Student Development*—The teacher understands how children learn and develop and can provide learning opportunities that support a child's intellectual, social, and personal development.
3. *Diverse Learners*—The teacher understands how students differ in their approaches to learning and creates instructional opportunities adapted to diverse learners.
4. *Multiple Instructional Strategies*—The teacher understands and uses a variety of instructional strategies to encourage student development of critical thinking, problem solving, and performance skills.
5. *Motivation and Management*—The teacher uses an understanding of individual and group motivation and behavior to create a learning environment that encourages positive social interaction, active engagement in learning, and self motivation.
6. *Communication and Technology*—The teacher uses knowledge of effective verbal, nonverbal, and media communication techniques to foster active inquiry, collaboration, and supportive interaction in the classroom and with professional peers.
7. *Planning*—The teacher plans instruction based upon knowledge of subject matter, students, the community, and curriculum goals.
8. *Assessment*—The teacher understands and uses formal and informal assessment strategies to evaluate and ensure the continuous intellectual, social, and physical development of the learner.
9. *Reflective Practice: Professional Growth*—The teacher is a reflective practitioner who continually evaluates the effects of his or her choices and actions on others (students, parents, and other professionals in the learning community) and who actively seeks out opportunities to grow professionally.
10. *School and Community Involvement*—The teacher fosters relationships with school **colleagues,** parents, and agencies in the larger community to support students' learning and well-being.

BOX 1 MORE ABOUT INTASC

The **Interstate New Teacher Assessment and Support Consortium** (INTASC) is a consortium of state education agencies and national educational organizations dedicated to the reform of the preparation, licensing, and ongoing professional development of teachers. Created in 1987, INTASC's primary constituency is state education agencies responsible for teacher licensing, program approval, and professional development. Its work is guided by one basic premise: An effective teacher must be able to integrate content knowledge with the specific strengths and needs of students to assure that *all* students learn and perform at high levels.

The mission of INTASC is to provide its member states a forum to learn about and collaborate in the development of

- compatible educational policy on teaching among the states
- new accountability requirements for teacher preparation programs
- new techniques to assess the performance of teachers for licensing and evaluation
- new programs to enhance the professional development of teachers

INTASC believes that all education policy should be driven by what we want our P–12 students to know and be able to do. Thus, all aspects of a state's education system should be aligned with and organized to achieve the state's policy as embodied in its P–12 student standards. This includes its teacher licensing system. Teacher licensing standards are the state's policy for what all teachers must know and be able to do in order to effectively help all students achieve the P–12 student standards. The teacher licensing standards become the driving force behind how a state's teacher licensing system (program approval, licensing assessments, professional development) is organized and implemented. Thus, a state's process for approving teacher preparation programs should be designed to verify that a program is aligned with the teacher licensing standards and provides opportunities for candidates to meet the standards. The state licensing assessments should verify that an individual teacher candidate has the knowledge and skills outlined in the licensing standards.

INTASC has been working to develop model policy that states can use as a resource as they work to align their own teacher licensing systems. To date, INTASC has accomplished the following:

- Developed model "core" standards for what all beginning teachers should know, be like, and be able to do in order to practice responsibly, regardless of the subject matter or grade level being taught.
- Translated the core standards into model licensing standards in mathematics, English language arts, science, special education, foreign languages, and arts; and are developing standards for elementary education and social studies/civics.
- Initiated development of a new licensing examination, the Test for Teaching Knowledge, which will measure a beginning teacher's knowledge and skill in the core standards.
- Developed and validated a model *performance assessment* in the form of a candidate portfolio in math, English/language arts, and science that is linked to INTASC's standards.
- Developed principles for quality teacher preparation programs to guide teacher preparation programs on how to incorporate INTASC's performance-based standards.

Adapted from tahttp://www.ccsso.org/projects/Interstate_New_Teacher_Assessment_and_Support_Consortium/

SKILLS OF EFFECTIVE TEACHERS

We introduced you to the concept of effective teachers and effective schools. You quickly learned that effective schools take a great deal of thought, knowledge, skill, and effort on the part of many dedicated educators. But the most important components in an effective school are the teachers. We will examine the deliberate actions teachers engage in that help them be more effective in helping students achieve and develop positive attitudes toward school and learning. Like the research about effective schools, research on effective teachers has been conducted by comparing high-achieving classrooms to low-achieving classrooms. Extensive classroom observations of virtually hundreds of teachers over the past two decades, have examined the differences between these two groups (Borich, 2004; Brophy & Good, 1986). Qualitative analysis found that highly effective teachers share many common features and tend to behave and teach in similar ways, regardless of school, subject, or the ability level of their students. Effective teachers engage students in discussions more than lectures. But while lecturing, effective teachers combine a variety of visual aids in their teaching. Effective teachers require students to be active learners by engaging students in a wide range of activities (Marzano, Pickering, Polack, 2001; Daniels & Bizar, 1998). They have students work in small groups and have students answer each other's questions. Though there have been whole texts devoted to this topic, we will briefly synthesize this information into three intertwined layers:

1. The overall tone of the classroom
2. The thoughtfulness and clarity of the lessons
3. Variety of instructional strategies

Overall Tone
- Classroom community
- Classroom management
- Task orientation
- Student success
- Student outcomes

Thoughtful Clear Lessons
- Students
- Content
- Materials
- Lesson presentation
- Student assessment

Instructional Strategies
- Drill—practice
- Lecture
- Discussion
- Case study
- Cooperative learning
- Problem-based learning

This chapter will now explore the craft of teaching by magnifying critical competencies in the standards that have the most direct daily impact on students: instructional planning, instructional strategies, management, and assessment.

OVERALL TONE—BUILDING CLASSROOM COMMUNITY

As you reviewed your favorite and worst teacher in Chapter 14, you may have remembered a sense of classroom environment these teachers created. In most cases, we remember our favorite teacher as having a predictable and orderly classroom, where the teacher treated students with respect and kindness. These teachers had the ability to create a class community—a learning environment where all students supported one another. Interestingly, research suggests most students (regardless of age) do better academically in classrooms where they feel safe and respected (Nodding, 1984). Conversely, less effective teachers usually appear to have classes that are unpredictable and chaotic, or extremely rigid and strict (Irvine, 2001). Less effective teachers often appear disorganized and are frequently inconsistent in teaching methods and classroom management (e.g., one day the teacher is overly strict, the next day he/she is lax with discipline).

A strong classroom community is extremely conducive to learning. Classrooms that have a positive classroom community contain an aura of tolerance where no one student or group of students is ridiculed or excluded based on any educational, social, or emotional concerns. In classrooms where teachers have established a positive classroom community, stu-

Feature	Descriptions
Climate	• Establishes a class in which students can respectfully express feelings/opinions • Uses students' interests to build and extend curriculum • Is interested in the students as individuals • Encourages a "safe" place for students to learn
Classroom Management	• Uses classroom rules established with students • Uses instructional routines • Recognizes students' positive efforts
Student Success	• Believes all students are capable of learning • Understands students learn differently • Uses a variety of different approaches to accommodate students • Understands the role of family/community in the schooling process • Invites students to offer feedback and support to each other's work and efforts

Figure 3 Building Classroom Community

dents learn how to participate in class meetings, work flexibly *and* collaboratively in small groups, and resolve conflicts peacefully. A successful classroom community promotes social competence and academic success and a sense of safety and belonging. Effective teachers take deliberate actions that establish and continually build a positive classroom community (Cabello & Terrell, 1994). Figure 3 **Building Classroom Community** offers a few of the beliefs effective teachers hold and the deliberate actions these teachers take in order to develop a positive classroom climate.

Theory Into Practice Creating a sense of community in the classroom enables teachers to address students' social, emotional, and cognitive development. Abraham Maslow's "*Hierarchy* of *Needs*" (1957) (Figure 4) illustrates that having one's basic needs met is the foundation for building "higher levels" of knowing and understanding (see Box 2 for more information about Maslow). Only after the first three basic needs are met can human beings begin to focus energy and effort and learn efficiently.

When basic needs have not been met, children may have great difficulty learning and relating positively to others. Creating a caring community in the classroom is one of the most effective strategies for addressing children's basic needs for physical and emotional comfort so that they can be open to learning, feel hopeful about the future, and reach their full potential.

Thoughtful, Clear Lessons—Planning for Student Success

Effective teachers are also incredibly good planners. They think ahead and deliberately plan for student success. Writing lesson plans is like planning a journey. If you expect to get where you want to go, you need to map your route carefully to make the most efficient use of time and resources (Hunter, 1994; Enz, Hurwtiz, & Carlile, 2005). Likewise, teachers need to plan carefully to help students learn what is being taught, and how to make full use of opportunities to connect curriculum content and involve students in the learning process. Basically, a lesson plan is a simple document that answers three questions:

1. What do you want students to be able to know or do?
2. How will you teach the lesson?
3. How will you assess what students have learned?

During the process of answering these three basic questions, effective teachers also make highly creative decisions. In fact, effective teachers consider all of the following variables as they plan instruction (Borich, 2004; National Board Certified Teachers, 1987):

1. *Knowledge of Students*—Effective teachers know their students and what their students need to be successful. Effective teachers consider and design instruction that will meet the needs/interests of their students. Specifically, effective teachers know their students':
   - ability levels
   - backgrounds
   - interest levels
   - ability to work together in groups
   - prior knowledge and learning experiences

Chapter 16 | What Makes a Teacher Effective?

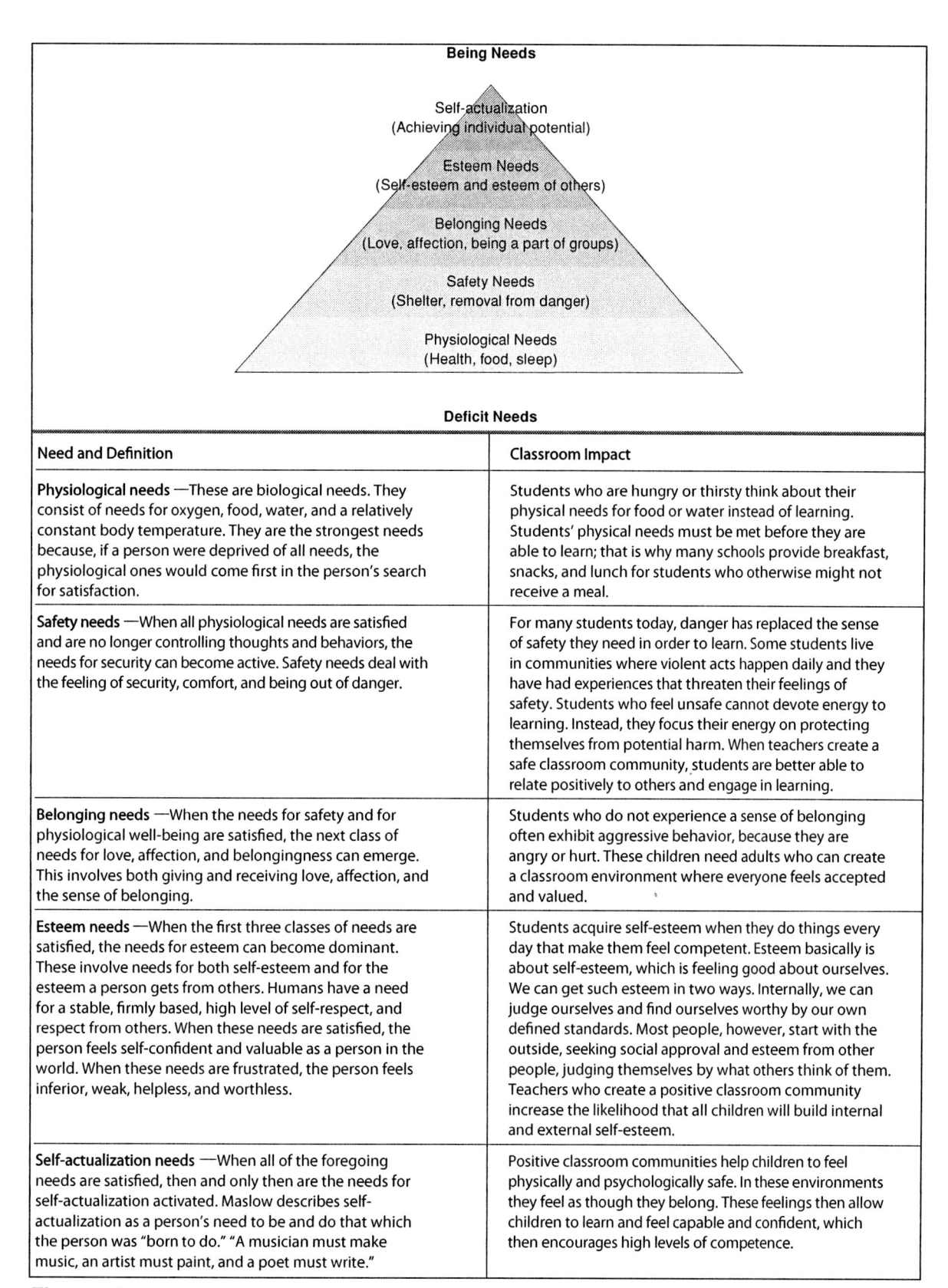

Being Needs

- Self-actualization (Achieving individual potential)
- Esteem Needs (Self-esteem and esteem of others)
- Belonging Needs (Love, affection, being a part of groups)
- Safety Needs (Shelter, removal from danger)
- Physiological Needs (Health, food, sleep)

Deficit Needs

Need and Definition	Classroom Impact
Physiological needs —These are biological needs. They consist of needs for oxygen, food, water, and a relatively constant body temperature. They are the strongest needs because, if a person were deprived of all needs, the physiological ones would come first in the person's search for satisfaction.	Students who are hungry or thirsty think about their physical needs for food or water instead of learning. Students' physical needs must be met before they are able to learn; that is why many schools provide breakfast, snacks, and lunch for students who otherwise might not receive a meal.
Safety needs —When all physiological needs are satisfied and are no longer controlling thoughts and behaviors, the needs for security can become active. Safety needs deal with the feeling of security, comfort, and being out of danger.	For many students today, danger has replaced the sense of safety they need in order to learn. Some students live in communities where violent acts happen daily and they have had experiences that threaten their feelings of safety. Students who feel unsafe cannot devote energy to learning. Instead, they focus their energy on protecting themselves from potential harm. When teachers create a safe classroom community, students are better able to relate positively to others and engage in learning.
Belonging needs —When the needs for safety and for physiological well-being are satisfied, the next class of needs for love, affection, and belongingness can emerge. This involves both giving and receiving love, affection, and the sense of belonging.	Students who do not experience a sense of belonging often exhibit aggressive behavior, because they are angry or hurt. These children need adults who can create a classroom environment where everyone feels accepted and valued.
Esteem needs —When the first three classes of needs are satisfied, the needs for esteem can become dominant. These involve needs for both self-esteem and for the esteem a person gets from others. Humans have a need for a stable, firmly based, high level of self-respect, and respect from others. When these needs are satisfied, the person feels self-confident and valuable as a person in the world. When these needs are frustrated, the person feels inferior, weak, helpless, and worthless.	Students acquire self-esteem when they do things every day that make them feel competent. Esteem basically is about self-esteem, which is feeling good about ourselves. We can get such esteem in two ways. Internally, we can judge ourselves and find ourselves worthy by our own defined standards. Most people, however, start with the outside, seeking social approval and esteem from other people, judging themselves by what others think of them. Teachers who create a positive classroom community increase the likelihood that all children will build internal and external self-esteem.
Self-actualization needs —When all of the foregoing needs are satisfied, then and only then are the needs for self-actualization activated. Maslow describes self-actualization as a person's need to be and do that which the person was "born to do." "A musician must make music, an artist must paint, and a poet must write."	Positive classroom communities help children to feel physically and psychologically safe. In these environments they feel as though they belong. These feelings then allow children to learn and feel capable and confident, which then encourages high levels of competence.

Figure 4 Maslow's Hierarchy

BOX 2 MORE ABOUT ABRAHAM MASLOW

Abraham Maslow (1908–1970) was an American psychologist. He received his BA in 1930, his MA in 1931, and his PhD in 1934, all in psychology and all from the University of Wisconsin.

He is mostly noted today for his proposal of a hierarchy of human needs, which he often represented as a pyramid. The base of the pyramid consists of the *physiological* needs, which are necessary for survival (1954). Once these basic needs are taken care of (resolved), an individual can concentrate on the second layer, the need for *safety and security.* The third layer is the need for *love and belonging,* followed by the need for *esteem.* Finally, *self-actualization* forms the apex of the pyramid.

In this scheme, the first four layers are what Maslow called *deficiency needs* or D-needs. If they are not filled, you feel anxiety and attempt to fill them. If they are filled, you feel nothing; you feel only that something is lacking. Each layer also takes precedence over the layer above it; you do not feel the lack of safety and security until your physiological needs are taken care of, for example. In Maslow's terminology, a need does not become salient until the needs below it are met.

Needs beyond the D-needs are "growth needs" or "*being values,*" which Maslow called B-needs. When fulfilled, B-needs do not go away. Rather, B-needs motivate us further. He outlines about fourteen of these values or B-needs, including beauty, meaning, truth, wholeness, justice, order, simplicity, richness, and so on.

Maslow also proposed that people who have reached self-actualization will sometimes experience a state he referred to as "transcendence," in which they become aware of not only their own fullest potential, but the fullest potential of human beings at large (Maslow, 1971).

- special needs or accommodations
- learning preferences

2. *Knowledge of Content*—Effective teachers know the content they teach. They use local school district curriculum guides but also utilize national and state curriculum standards in designing instruction. Likewise, they determine ways to connect student interests to the new content to be taught.

3. *Knowledge of Materials*—Effective teachers use a wide variety of materials to teach their students the content to be learned. They know that nearly all students do better if they can be exposed to content in a variety of ways. For example: technology, software, audiovisuals, community resources, equipment, manipulatives, library resources, local guest speakers, and volunteers, can assist in teaching and will help students learn new content.

4. *Knowledge of Lesson Presentation*—Effective teachers use variety in lesson planning and structure based on attributes of the content to be taught and the needs of their learners. There are different types of lesson structures. Some examples of lesson formats are provided at the end of this chapter.

5. *Knowledge of Instructional Strategies*—Effective teachers have a wide range of teaching strategies, and know that determining which method is "right" for a particular lesson depends on many things. Among them are age and developmental level of their students; what the students already know; what they need to know to succeed with the lesson; the subject-matter content; the objective of the lesson; the available people, time, space and material resources; and the physical setting.

6. *Knowledge of Student Assessment*—Effective teachers use student assessment to guide their understanding of student learning and their own classroom teaching. Effective teachers know that how a student performs is a good reflection of the instruction they received, therefore effective teachers develop many strategies to informally assess students' progress throughout the lesson.

Now let's return to our three questions that describe the components of an effective lesson plan.

Planning Question 1: What do you want the students to know and be able to do? To answer this question, an effective teacher must first determine the learner outcome(s) (sometimes called lesson objective)—this is the term educators use to describe what the students need to know and be able to do by the end of the lesson.

Learner outcomes usually contain an **observable** verb such as *recall, solve, measure,* or *construct,* which allows the teacher to be able to determine the students' comprehension and level of involvement at given points in the lesson (Hunter, 1994). For example:

The student will be able to:

- *Define* the term photosynthesis
- *Label* the parts of an insect
- *Calculate* the diameter of a circle

Learner outcomes are clearly stated and help make student progress easier to determine. In addition learner outcomes should be clear that students can "know" about a topic or subject at different levels. The major idea of the *taxonomy* is that educational objectives can be arranged in a hierarchy from less to more complex. (See Box 3 and Figure 5, **More about Benjamin Bloom,** and **Bloom Cognitive Taxonomy.**) Bloom's Taxonomy (1957) provides a range of educational objectives, verbs that reflect students' knowledge level, questions that would typically illicit the level of response, and possible outcomes that would reflect that particular level of learning.

In addition, when teachers develop instructional outcomes, it is important for these learning goals to be:

- **Logically Sequenced**—When students are asked to complete tasks in an order that is logical and builds naturally from one step to another, the teacher will spend more time teaching and less time keeping students on task.
- **Appropriate to Student Achievement Level(s)**—Students are more likely to stay with a task, and subsequently learn more of the material taught, *if* the material presented is already part of the students' prior experience. In addition, students must be present-

BOX 3 MORE ABOUT BENJAMIN BLOOM

Benjamin Bloom (1913–1999) was an American educational psychologist at the University of Chicago in the 1960s. Dr. Bloom's two most significant contributions to the field included his classification of educational objectives (mid-1950s) and the theory of mastery learning.

Bloom's Taxonomy (classification system) was a way to categorize performance objectives that commonly occur in educational settings. Dr. Bloom and his colleagues identified three broad categories of performance: affective, psychomotor, and cognitive learning.

Affective learning is demonstrated by behaviors indicating attitudes of awareness, interest, attention, concern, and responsibility; ability to listen and respond in interactions with others; and the ability to demonstrate those attitudinal characteristics or values that are appropriate to the test situation and the field of study. This domain relates to emotions, attitudes, appreciations, and values such as enjoying, conserving, respecting, and supporting. Verbs applicable to the affective domain include accepts, attempts, challenges, defends, disputes, joins, judges, praises, questions, shares, supports, and volunteers.

Psychomotor learning is demonstrated by physical skills such as coordination, dexterity, manipulation, grace, strength, speed; actions that demonstrate the fine motor skills such as use of precision instruments or tools; or actions that evidence gross motor skills such as the use of the body in dance or athletic performance. Verbs applicable to the psychomotor domain include bend, grasp, handle, operate, reach, relax, shorten, stretch, write, differentiate (by touch), express (facially), perform (skillfully).

Cognitive learning is the ability "to learn new information." Cognitive objectives revolve around knowledge, comprehension, and application of any given topic. (See Figure 5. Bloom's Cognitive Taxonomy).

Another important contribution made by Bloom was his theory on **mastery learning.** Mastery learning is an instructional method that presumes all children can learn if they are provided with the appropriate learning conditions. Specifically, mastery learning is a method whereby students are not advanced to a subsequent learning objective until they demonstrate proficiency with the current one.

Mastery learning curricula generally consist of content that all students begin together. Students who do not satisfactorily complete a topic are given additional instruction until they succeed. Students who master the topic early engage in enrichment activities until the entire class can progress together. In a mastery learning environment, the teacher directs a variety of group-based instructional techniques, with frequent and specific feedback by using *diagnostic assessment*, as well as regularly correcting mistakes students make along their learning path. Mastery learning requires well-defined learning objectives organized into smaller, sequentially organized units. Mastery learning includes:

- Activities emphasizing problem solving and other "higher-order" thinking skills.
- Students actively engaging in the learning process with frequent interaction and feedback with the instructor and other students.

Successful interactions with the curriculum and positive relationships with the instructor should result in increased student self-concept and lead to happier, more productive individuals (Bloom, 1956; 1980).

Research into Practice: Bloom Cognitive Taxonomy		
LEVEL	DEFINITION	VERBS
Knowledge	Student recalls or recognizes information, ideas, and principles in the approximate form in which they were learned.	Write List Label Name State Define
Comprehension	Student translates, comprehends, or interprets information based on prior learning.	Explain Summarize Paraphrase Describe Illustrate
Application	Student selects, transfers, and uses data and principles to complete a problem or task with minimal direction.	Use Compute Solve Demonstrate Apply Construct
Analysis	Student distinguishes, classifies, and relates the assumptions, hypotheses, evidence, or structure of a statement or question.	Analyze Categorize Compare Contrast Separate
Synthesis	Student originates, integrates, and combines ideas into a product, plan, or proposal new to him or her.	Create Design Hypothesize Invent Develop
Evaluation	Student appraises, assesses, or critiques on a basis of specific standards and criteria.	Judge Recommend Critique Justify

Eby, J. (1984). *Taxonomy of Educational Objectives: Handbook I: Cognitive Domain,* New York: NY: Longman Publishing Group.

Figure 5 Bloom Cognitive Taxonomy

ed materials with which they will experience a high rate of success. Students in fourth grade and higher should experience a success/accuracy rate of at least eighty percent. Students in kindergarten through third grade should experience a success rate of at least ninety percent.

- **Directly Linked to Unit Goals and to State/District/School Standards**—Students will learn best when the information builds upon and reinforces knowledge presented in previous days/weeks. This does not mean learning always develops in a "lock-step," linear pro-

Many studies show that learning is enhanced when students become actively involved in the process.

gression. Integrated instruction brings ideas together and forms connections in the learner's mind. Teacher's who integrate curricula and relate the information to be learned to their students' lives, increase the likelihood that the new information will be meaningful and relevant.

Planning Question 2: How will you teach the lesson? Knowing what needs to be taught/learned is only the first step in lesson planning. Just as critical is determining *how* to effectively deliver instruction (Cruickshank, Jenkins, & Metcalf, 2003). The opportunity for creativity starts when a teacher considers the procedures for the lesson.

One goal all teachers should strive for is **active learning**. Active learning is instruction that allows students to talk, listen, read, write, and reflect as they approach course content through problem-solving exercises, informal small groups, *simulations,* case studies, role-playing, and other activities—all of which require students to apply what they are learning. Many studies show that learning is enhanced when students become actively involved in the process. Instructional strategies that engage students in the learning process stimulate critical thinking and a greater awareness of other perspectives (Brophy & Good, 1986). Although there are times when lecture is the most appropriate method for disseminating information, research in learning and retention suggests that the use of a variety of instructional strategies can positively enhance student learning (Cotton, 1995; Marzano, Pickering, & Pollock, 2001). Obviously, teaching strategies should be carefully

> ## GROUP TALK
>
> Take a few minutes to determine if the following statements are well-written, observable objectives:
>
> **Students will be able to:**
>
> | Yes | No | Objective |
> |-----|-----|-----------|
> | | | Appreciate the story |
> | | | Analyze a story |
> | | | Summarize the story |
> | | | Invent a story |
> | | | Critique a story |
> | | | Illustrate a story |
>
> Share your responses with your group.
>
> 1. Can you come to consensus on all of the sample objectives, above?
>
> 2. Which objectives were harder to determine? Why?

matched to the teaching objectives of a particular lesson. In Chapter 14, we provided a description of a variety of effective **instructional strategies**, including:

- Drill
- Lecture
- Discussion
- Case Study
- Cooperative Learning
- Problem-Based Learning (PBL)

Planning Question 3: How will you assess what the students have learned?

While there are many types of "tests" available to teachers, we will discuss *ongoing assessment*, which relies heavily on teacher observation of students' performance or the collection of student products, often called artifacts. When students are assessed as part of the teaching-learning process, then assessment information tells teachers what each student knows and can do, and what he or she is ready to learn next (Daniels & Bizar, 1998). Teachers also use their assessment of students' learning to reflect on their own teaching practices so they can adjust and modify curricula, instructional activities, and classroom routines that are ineffective (Danielson, 1996). Other questions teachers need to consider when determining how and when they will assess students' progress, include:

- **When should the teacher assess student progress?** Students' understanding should be assessed at significant points throughout the entire lesson. This includes constant monitoring of students' performance or occasionally pausing the lesson to ask all students to demonstrate their understanding of the information being taught.
- **How can the teacher determine if all students can perform correctly?** Beyond observation, the teacher may ask students to write the answer, tell a neighbor, respond in unison, indicate the answer on individual slates, signal the answer, demonstrate the skill, and so on.
- **Why should teachers assess students frequently?** Before the teacher proceeds from one goal to the next, all students need to demonstrate an understanding of the content presented. If all students do not understand the lesson, the teacher will need to adjust teaching strategies, try again, and then re-assess the students' progress to determine understanding before moving on to the next objective.
- **How do teachers collect information about students' progress?** In addition to instructional strategies, effective teachers use a variety of tools to gather information about their students. Teachers then use the information when planning future lessons, and/or for making accommodations for students who are struggling. These tools can include: observations, interviews, student self-assessment, student artifacts, and portfolios.

Think About It

Which information-gathering tools have you seen teachers use? Which tools do your college instructors use?

While teachers do not use all of these tools in every lesson, each tool does provide unique and important information about what the students are learning and how effective the instruction has been (Newman, 1996; Schmoker, 1999). Therefore, it is important to incorporate each of these tools systematically as a lesson unit is planned. Figure 6 **Information-Gathering Tools Checklist**, provides an overview of each of these information-gathering tools.

Lesson Plans in Review We now know that effective teachers use effective plans, which include *clear objectives,* a variety of *instructional strategies,* and *appropriate assessments.* What do these components look like in action?

Let's observe Mr. Flynn as he develops his lesson plan. Mr. Flynn has planned a lesson for his sophomore English class. The students are learning about factual writing, and part of their culminating project will be to publish a class newspaper. Today they will learn about the parts of a lead paragraph, in preparation for writing a lead paragraph for a topic they have selected. The lesson outcomes/objectives are:

- Explain that the lead paragraph of a news story usually answers who, what, when, where, why, and how.
- Determine, from selected newspaper articles, the information that answers who, what, when, where, why, and how.

Mr. Flynn is establishing foundational background, so the level of objective he is writing reflects the knowledge and comprehension levels of Bloom's Cognitive Taxonomy. The objectives he has written also define the outcome he expects his students to demonstrate at the end of the lesson.

Mr. Flynn has decided the best way to share this foundational information with his students is through a brief lecture and modeling the expected outcome. The students work together to discuss their answers and reinforce the information their teacher has presented.

Mr. Flynn also knows that when he asks the students to work together to determine the components of a lead paragraph, it will enable him to circulate about the room to gather information to confirm the students' comprehension of the lesson. These observations enable him to check student understanding and provides a feedback loop to himself— a way to reflect upon his own teaching.

> **Think About It**
>
> Take a few moments and use Figure 7. Lesson Planning Checklist, and review Mr. Flynn's lesson plan. What are the strengths of his lesson plan? How might it be improved?

There are many types of lesson plan formats that teachers use. How a teacher selects a format often depends on his/her philosophy of education, theories of learning, or personal past experiences. We will share two formats with you:

- Direct Instruction
- Five E's (Inquiry)

As you are reading, think about your own philosophies and theories, and which plans—or combinations—might best suit your own style of teaching.

DIRECT INSTRUCTION LESSON PLAN

The *direct instruction* (or *direct presentation*) lesson plan is usually a reflection of the behaviorist and cognitive processing perspectives of learning (Hunter, 1995; Enz, Hurwitz, & Carlile, 2005). This type of lesson is best used when introducing new information and when covering a great deal of information. Figure 8. **Direct Lesson Outline** provides a structure for this direct lesson plan format, and Figure 9 **Direct Lesson in Action** provides you with a sample format for using this approach.

FIVE E'S LESSON FORMAT

The Five E's (Engagement, Exploration, Explanation, Extension, and Evaluation) (Figure 10) is designed for the inquiry nature of guiding and science lessons (Gagne, Briggs & Wager, 1992). It more closely aligns with a combination of the cognitive information processing and constructivist perspectives of learning. Figure 11 provides a sample lesson using this inquiry approach to teaching and learning.

Directions: Interview a teacher about the information-gathering tools he or she typically uses to collect information about children's development and their progress. Place a check by the tools/techniques used; write any comments, suggestions, or additions he/she describes; then summarize what you learned about assessment from this interview.

I. Teacher Observations—The most sensitive student assessment is teacher observation. In all cases, the teacher labels, dates, and organizes the observation records to document development over time.

- ☐ Checklists—sometimes called structured observation. The teacher uses predetermined observation guides to document students' development and progress on specific skills or concepts.
- ☐ Anecdotal records—sometimes called unstructured observation. The teacher records student interactions with peers, print, literature, writing process, in-class discussion, center activities, etc.
- ☐ Vignettes—sometimes called teacher reflections. The teacher recalls student interactions and records them after the event has occurred.

II. Interviews/Questions Techniques—Interviews may be conducted with the student, parents, and special area teachers. Interviews may occur informally during the school day or may be formalized when the teacher needs to narrow the focus of the questions to reflect a previously identified concern. Teachers may consider four types of interview questions:

- ☐ Descriptive—What did you do during _____?
- ☐ Structured—Can you tell me when _____?
- ☐ Contrast—How are these stories alike/different?
- ☐ Process—How did you decide to _____?

III. Student Self-Assessment Techniques—Students should be actively involved in assessing their own work, reflecting upon their progress, and establishing new learning goals.

- ☐ Teacher-made questionnaires/surveys.
- ☐ Teacher-student conferences.

IV. Products, work samples, and artifacts—Teacher collects multiple examples of student-created products to assess each child's development. For example, in the area of literacy, these items could include:

Reading

- ☐ List of books "read"
- ☐ List of questions about books
- ☐ List of favorite stories

Writing

- ☐ Journal entries
- ☐ Learning Logs
- ☐ Formal Written Assignments

V. Portfolio Management System—Teacher devises a management system to collect and analyze samples of students' work, teacher's anecdotal notes, and formal and informal assessment measures. A portfolio allows the teacher to document a student's progress over time and share that information with the student, the student's parents, and other teachers and administrators.

Figure 6 Information-Gathering Tools Checklist

1. **What do you want the students to be able to know or do?**
   - Desired learner outcome(s) are described in clear observable terms.
   - The outcomes are logically sequenced.
   - The outcomes are measurable.
2. **How will you teach the lesson?**
   - The activities selected will accomplish the objective(s)/outcomes.
   - Procedures engage students in active learning.
   - Transitions are planned from one activity to another.
3. **How will you assess what the students have learned?**
   - Assessment focused directly on instructional outcomes.
   - Assessment technique provided options for immediate feedback (teacher/student).
   - Written lesson plans include informal assessments of student learning.

Figure 7 Lesson Planning Checklist

Objectives:
- What do you want the students to learn?
- What do you want the students to demonstrate?

State Standard: District Curriculum Goal:

Introduction:
- How will you gain the students' attention?
- How will you connect students' prior knowledge to new learning?
- How will you motivate students?

Instructional Content:
- What strategies will you use to teach the content?
- How will you sequence the delivery and learning of the content?
- How will students be actively engaged?

Assessment:
- How will you determine the students' level of understanding?
- How will you document the students' learning?
- How will you differentiate to accommodate all learners?

Closure:
- How will you help students retain information learned?
- How will you help students apply knowledge learned?

Resources/Materials:
- What resources/materials/equipment will you use to teach the content?
- What preparations are necessary?

Figure 8 Direct Lesson Outline

Learner Outcomes: Lesson objective and sub-objectives **Unit of Study:** Newspaper   **Daily Lesson Plan:** Lead Paragraph **Lesson Outcomes: Students will be able to:** • Explain that the lead paragraph of a news story usually answers who, what, when, where, why, and how. • Determine from selected newspaper articles the information that answers who, what, when, where, why, and how.
Introduction—Focus, anticipatory set, motivation In yesterday's class we learned that the headlines of newspapers are designed to help you read the paper. You all were very good at reading headlines and predicting what the article would be about. Now we're going to learn another way to get the news quickly and easily. The first paragraph of an article is called the lead paragraph; it is designed to help you read the paper and quickly learn all about the outcome of the state basketball tournaments or the latest on state or national events.
Instructional Input (Content)—Teaching procedures and student activities • Write who, what, when, where, why, and how in a vertical column on the board (**modeling**). Ask students to write these words in their notes (**active participation**). Tell them they will need to use these words in the activity they are about to begin. Tell students that with the help of their partner they will be asked to find information in a newspaper article and write it in a column to the right of their "who, what, when, where, why, how" column. Demonstrate on the board where information is to be written. • Walk around room. Ensure students list the information in their notes (**check for understanding**). Students are more likely to stay on task if teacher is in close proximity. • Ask students to listen carefully as the teacher reads a lead paragraph from a selected article. Ask the class to listen for who the article is about, what happened, when it happened, where it happened, why it happened, and how it happened. As students hear the answer to each question, they should write the answer in the designated column of their notes (**guided practice**). • When the class is finished writing their answers, ask them to share the answers to the following questions: who, what, when, where, why, and how. If all/most students appear to say the correct answers, move on to the next activity.
Assessment: Checking for understanding and lesson assessment • Have students work in pairs. Hand out selected news stories, one per student. • Explain that students are to take turns reading the first paragraph out loud to their partners. Then, with the partner's help, each student is to identify the who, what, when, where, why, and how information from the article. • Ask students, "In which paragraph did you find this information"? • Tell students to write the information in the appropriate column in their notes. • Partners are to check for accuracy of the information recorded.
Closure: Lesson summation of learner's new knowledge • Observe students' responses. Ensure the tasks are being completed correctly (**check for understanding**). When each pair has finished, challenge students to pull information together by asking them to remember, without looking at their notes, all six questions usually answered in the lead paragraph of an article. • Ask students to remember in which paragraph they found the information. • After a brief wait ask students to share with their partner those six questions and the name of the paragraph where the answers were found.
Resources: Equipment, materials, teaching aids Sample article with appropriate lead paragraph—for guided practice. Sample articles with appropriate lead paragraphs—one per student.

Figure 9 Direct Instruction in Action

Engagement: The activities in this section capture the students' attention, stimulate their thinking, and help them access prior knowledge.	• Demonstration
	  • teacher and/or student
	• Reading from a
	  • current media release
	  • science journal or book
	  • piece of literature (biography, essay, poem, etc)
	• Free write
	• Analyze a graphic organizer

Exploration: In this section students are given time to think, plan, investigate, and organize collected information.	• Reading authentic resources to collect information
	  • to answer open-ended questions
	  • to make a decision
	• Solve a problem
	• Construct a model
	• Experiment design and/or perform

Explanation: Students are now involved in an analysis of their exploration. Their understanding is clarified and modified because of reflective activities.	• Student analysis and explanation • Supporting ideas with evidence • Reading and discussion
Extension: This section gives students the opportunity to expand and solidify their understanding of the concept and/or apply it to a real-world situation.	• Problem solving • Experimental inquiry • Thinking Skills Activities • Classifying, abstracting, error analysis • Decision-making
Evaluation: By the end of the lesson there should be a means of determining how well students have learned and can apply the new concepts and the related vocabulary. Such evaluation does not have to be at the end of the lesson. It can be embedded in other phases.	• Teacher- and/or student-generated scoring tools or rubrics

Figure 10 Five E's Science Lesson Plan

> **Lesson Title:** Camouflage: Eating All the Little Fishes
>
> **Lesson Outcome:** The first graders will learn how camouflage helps animals survive.
>
> **Engagement:** Teacher reads the story "How to Hide a Butterfly and Other Insects" by Ruth Heller. This simple text has color pictures that demonstrate how insects use camouflage to hide from their enemies and prey. The first graders have fun looking for the hidden insects.
>
> **Exploration:** The teacher breaks the children into six groups of four students each.
> - Each group has a different colored, patterned cloth that is placed on the table, and each table had a tiny cup containing many different colored paper "fishes."
> - The "fishes" are sprinkled on the cloth.
> - The teacher turns out the lights.
> - The children are asked to find as many of the fishes as they can and remove them from the cloth.
> - The children have 20 seconds to find all the fish they can.
> - The teacher turns the light back on and the children freeze.
> - The fish left are sorted and counted by color.
>
> **Explanation:** The teacher asks the children if they notice anything about the fish that are left on the cloth. The children in each group should realize that the fish left are the same color as the cloth.
>
> **Extension:** The teacher asks the children to think about, then write, their explanation of how the fishes in their experiment are like the butterflies and insects in the story, "How to Hide a Butterfly and Other Insects." The teacher gives each group chart paper and markers to record their thoughts.
>
> **Evaluation:** The teacher gives each child drawing paper and crayons. The teacher asks the children to draw a habitat (a concept previously learned), and to draw pictures of camouflaged animals that might live in this habitat. As the children complete this task, the teacher circulates and asks children about their unique creations.

Figure 11 Five E Lesson Plan

LOOKING FORWARD

In this chapter, we have explored a variety of concepts related to effective teachers—including their characteristics and how they plan their lessons. We also explored how effective lessons incorporate three interrelated elements: objectives, instructional strategies, and assessments. These elements may be implemented differently, depending upon which lesson plan format that the teacher implements.

Is any one lesson plan design better than the other? No, each design has its pros and cons depending on the audience. The important thing is to know what you want your students to learn and then map it out so you know the direction that is best for your students. It might be the long and winding road that takes you where they need to go, but the destination is the same.

RESEARCH CITATIONS

Bettencourt, E., Gillett, M., Gall, M., & Hull, R. (1983). Effects of teacher enthusiasm training on student on-task behavior and achievement. *American Educational Research Journal, 20,* 435–450.

Bloom, B. S. (1956). Taxonomy of educational objectives: Classification of educational goals. *Handbook 1: Cognitive domain* (pp. 201–207). New York, NY: Longman.

Bloom, B. S. (1980). *All our children learning.* New York, NY: McGraw-Hill.

Borich, G. (2004). *Effective teaching methods.* Upper Saddle River, NJ: Merrill/Princeton Hall.

Brophy J. & Good, T. (1986). Teacher behavior and student achievement. In M. C. Wittrock (Ed.), *Handbook of research on teaching* (3rd ed., pp. 328–375). Upper Saddle River, NJ: Merrill/Prentice Hall.

Cabello, B., & Terrell, R. (1994). Making students feel like family: How teachers create warm and caring classroom climates. *Journal of Classroom Interaction, 29,* 17–24.

Cotton, K. (1995). *Research you can use to improve results.* Alexandria, VA: Association for Supervision and Curriculum Development.

Cruickshank, D. R., Jenkins, D. B., & Metcalf, K. K. (2003). *The act of teaching.* New York, NY: McGraw-Hill.

Daniels, H. & Bizar, M. (1998). *Methods that matter.* Portland, ME: Stenhouse.

Danielson, C. (1996). *Enhancing professional practice: A framework for teaching.* Alexandria, VA: Association for Supervision and Curriculum Development.

Darling-Hammond, L. (2000). Reforming teacher preparation and licensing: Debating the evidence. *Teachers College Record, 102,* (1): 28–56.

Enz, B. J., Honaker, C. & Kortman, S. (2002). Trade secrets: Tips, tools and timesavers for middle/secondary teacher 2nd Ed. Dubuque, IA: Kendall/Hunt.

Enz, B. J., Hurwitz, S. & Carlile, B. J. (2005). *Coaching the student teacher: A developmental approach,* 3rd Ed. Dubuque, IA: Kendall/Hunt.

Eby, J. (1984). *Taxonomy of educational objectives: Handbook I: Cognitive domain.* New York: Longman.

Gagne, R., Briggs, L. & Wager, W. (1992). *Principles of instructional design* 4th Ed. Fort Worth, TX: HBJ College.

Hunter, M. (1994). *Mastery teaching.* Thousand Oaks, CA: Corwin.

Irvine, J. J. (2001). *Caring, competent teachers in complex classrooms.* Washington, DC: American Association of Colleges of Teacher Education.

Marzano, R. J., Pickering, D. J., & Pollock, J. E. (2001). *Classroom Instruction that works: Research-based strategies for increasing student achievement.* Alexandria, VA: Association for Supervision and Curriculum Development.

Maslow, A. (1954). *Motivation and personality* (2nd ed). New York, NY: Harper.

Maslow, A. (1957). *The search for understanding.* New York, NY: West.

Maslow, A. (1971). *The farther reaches of human nature.* New York, NY: Viking.

National Board Certified Teachers (1987). Last accessed date, from *http://www.nbpts.org/about/coreprops.cfm*

Newmann, F. M. (1996). *Authentic achievement: restructuring schools for intellectual quality.* San Francisco, CA: Jossey-Bass.

Noddings, N. (1984). *Caring: A feminine approach to ethics and moral education.* Berkeley, CA: University of California.

Schmoker, M. (1999). *Results: The key to continuous school improvement.* (2nd ed.). Alexandria, VA: Association for Supervision and Curriculum Development.